THE
BOLT
SUPREMACY

INSIDE JAMAICA'S
SPRINT FACTORY

RICHARD MOORE

PEGASUS BOOKS
NEW YORK LONDON

For Virginie

————

THE BOLT SUPREMACY

Pegasus Books Ltd.
148 W. 37th Street, 13th Floor
New York, NY 10018

First Pegasus Books cloth edition May 2017

Interior design by Maria Fernandez

Library of Congress Cataloging-in-Publication Data is available.

ISBN: 978-1-68177-407-7

10 9 8 7 6 5 4 3 2 1

Printed in the United States of America
Distributed by W. W. Norton & Company

In Jamaica little is done without a touch of embellishment or some panache. Jamaicans walk with style, drive cars with style, and play with style. It is not so much scoring a goal or hitting a boundary that is important, but the way that it is done. People leaving church will admit openly that they did not understand what the preacher said, 'but he sound good'.

Mervyn C. Alleyne, *Roots of Jamaican Culture*

LIST OF ILLUSTRATIONS

Page

ix Men's 100m final, London Olympics 2012 (Getty Images)

14 Bolt with lightning at the 2013 IAAF World Championships, Moscow (Getty Images)

23 UTech Classic, 2014 (Robin Moore)

38 Usain Bolt's first running track

58 UTech Classic, 2014 (Robin Moore)

78 Javon Francis, UTech Classic, 2014 (Robin Moore)

86 Dennis Johnson, 2014 (Robin Moore)

108 Statue of Herb McKenley, Jamaica (Robin Moore)

119 Stephen Francis with Asafa Powell (Getty Images)

143 Usain Bolt practises starting while coach Glen Mills watches on (Rex Features)

155 Dr Hans-Wilhelm Müller-Wohlfahrt (Offside)

168 Shelly-Ann Fraser-Pryce in front of her family home, 2008 (Getty Images)

183 Usain Bolt winning the men's 100m Olympic final, Beijing, 2008 (Getty Images)

205 Yohan Blake, 2014 (Getty Images)

216 Victor Conte (PA Images)

236 Paul Wright, 2014 (Robin Moore)

257 UTech Classic, 2014 (Robin Moore)

263 Usain Bolt is disqualified from men's 100m final for a false start at the 2011 IAAF World Championship, Daegu (Rex Features)

267 Shelly-Ann Fraser-Pryce with her mother in front of her family home, 2008 (Getty Images)

297 UTech Classic, 2014 (Robin Moore)

308 Zharnel Hughes, 2014 (Robin Moore)

CONTENTS

Prologue   1

1. A Force Five Hurricane   7
2. The Wellspring   18
3. Bolt's Own Country   35
4. The Brotherhood   57
5. Donkey Man   72
6. The Architect   85
7. Cuban Swimming Pool Crisis   106
8. Shifting the Paradigm   117
9. Jets and Sharks   133
10. Healing Hans   153
11. Real As It Gets   167
12. Shock and Awe   178
13. The Beast   200
14. Threads   210
15. The Tester   233
16. Genes and Yams   245
17. The G of the Bang   260
18. After the Hurricane   284
19. The In-Between   302

Afterword: The Weeble   317
Acknowledgements   322

INTRODUCTION

London, November 2016

On a dark and bitterly cold evening in late November 2016 large black boards surround Leicester Square in London. The only colour is a red-carpeted corridor leading to the entrance of the Odean Cinema. Security staff throng the area and, in a tightly controlled public pen, a small crowd presses against the barriers. When he steps out of an SUV and on to the red carpet, there's a cheer for Usain Bolt. Then a louder one for Liam Payne of boys' band One Direction.

The fastest man in history, in smart suit and polished shoes, makes his way slowly along the carpet, stopping for interviews and blowing on his hands to try and stop them from freezing. By the time he reaches the entrance to the cinema there's a rattling in his skull—he's shivering. But inside, there's a warm welcome from friends including Mo Farah, the British distance runner,

Linford Christie, the 1992 Olympic 100m champion, and Bolt's
fellow Jamaican, the DJ Sean Paul. 'We need our mood lifted
sometimes and Usain does that,' Paul said on his way in. 'He's a
national hero, a leader.'

Bolt greets them all but reserves his most effusive welcome for
a diffident figure with dark eyes and greying, shoulder-length hair.
This is Hans-Wilhelm Müller-Wohlfahrt and he looks about as comfortable on the red carpet as Bolt would be in an operating theatre.
'Healing Hans,' as Müller-Wohlfahrt is sometimes known, is Bolt's
Munich-based doctor. A not uncontroversial figure, he has worked
with many world class athletes—including Christie, who hugs him—
but in a career that has spanned five decades he has never had a
bond with an athlete as strong as the one he has forged with Bolt.

In *I Am Bolt*, the documentary film we are in London to see,
Müller-Wohlfahrt makes a couple of appearances, coming to the
rescue in the build-up to the Rio Olympics, Bolt's swansong on this
stage, when it seemed that the sprinter's body was broken beyond
repair. He was injured in an incident in a nightclub in Kingston,
the Jamaican capital, in January, eight months before the Games.
'I was stepping over a barrier, I stepped on the edge of the ledge
and rolled my ankle,' Bolt said. Next day, the ankle was badly
swollen. There were three weeks off training, then another three.
'He doesn't sound worried,' said his laconic coach, Glen Mills.
'That doesn't necessarily mean he's not.'

At the London premiere Bolt was joined by most of the people
who have been with him on his 15-year journey. It remained a
small, tightly-knit group, as though Bolt was a cottage industry
rather than a global brand. As well as Müller-Wohlfahrt there was
the school friend who is now his manager, Nugent 'NJ' Walker, his
parents, Wellesley and Jennifer, and his agent, Ricky Simms. The
only significant absentee was the reclusive Mills.

The film showed how close Bolt came to not making it to Rio,
or not making it there in the shape he needed to be in to win.
The injury was only part of it. The mental struggle was tougher.

Bolt suffered from a lack of motivation. He wondered what the point was. 'It's not as fun as it used to be,' admitted. 'The older I get the less fun it is. More sacrifices, less partying, less drinking. I hate doing something that I don't really enjoy.' He wanted, he said, 'to be a human again.' There was footage of Bolt in Beijing at the 2008 Olympics and the contrast was striking. Back then he was an overgrown, excitable child, permanently smiling. Like his hairline ('Bad genes,' he tells his father, 'that I got from you'), his smile had receded in the intervening eight years. 'It's hard to be as hungry as a person who has never won a championship, a gold medal,' he reflected. With surprising candour, he hinted that money had been his original motivation: '[When] I started out, I wanted to clear mum and dad's debts, then it was to buy nice stuff, cars and clothes, then it was to secure my future. Now I've done that stuff I just want to give up. It's hard at this stage. I find motivation difficult.' All that was left was to repeat—to try and win a third Olympic triple of 100m, 200m and 4x100m. At a certain point, said Michael Johnson, 'the battle isn't with your rivals, it's with yourself. It's a lonely place.'

Then, on 12 February 2016, Bolt's motivation returned, and with a vengeance. His great rival, Justin Gatlin, gave an interview to TMZ Sports. Gatlin, who has famously served two doping bans, ran Bolt close in 2015. At 33, he seemed to be getting quicker. On TMZ, Gatlin looked ahead to Rio. 'I'm going to win,' he said, 'then we're going to go on a tour of the USA, a tour all around the country with [the Olympic gold medal] on a chain.'

As Bolt watched the Gatlin interview his temples appeared to throb with rage. 'As soon as I watched that video, as *soon* as I watched that video, everything changed,' he said. 'I'm not saying I got back my full motivation, or I was cured or saved, or it was an epiphany, but I got back that feeling in my stomach.' It wasn't just Gatlin who got under Bolt's skin, it was the brash, trash-talking American sprinters: 'They don't understand that what makes me strive is the fact that they talk all the time . . . when you talk and tell me what you're going to do, it just makes me want to work harder. So big up to you, Justin.'

This was a different Bolt to the sprinter who appears so relaxed and playful: A competitive edge that he has, largely, successfully managed to conceal. There is much else that doesn't fit with his image as laid-back and easy going. We see him with Mills on the track at the University of the West Indies where he trains every day: a secluded and peaceful place on the outskirts of Kingston, with its spectacular views of the Blue Mountains. With all that money in the bank, all that seemed to drive Bolt in the build-up to Rio was the idea of beating the Americans. 'Who is Justin Gatlin, I've beaten him many times, he's nobody.' He said his rivals' comments showed a lack of respect: 'I've never said these things 'cause I give every athlete respect, especially the little one, even [Mike] Rodgers—you've never won any medal! And you're going to have that conversation with me? I've built this sport, [and] you guys have been through so many drugs charges . . .'

This outburst followed another interview with Gatlin after the Jamaican trials, where Bolt suffered a hamstring injury. It meant he missed the 100 metres final and the chance to qualify automatically for the Olympics. It seemed that the defense of his Olympic 100m title was in jeopardy. But the doctor at the trials confirmed that Bolt was indeed injured—'a medical pass,' is how Gatlin described it. Bolt recovered (thanks again to Müller-Wohlfahrt) and was not only fit but fired up when he arrived in Rio. He stayed in the athletes' village, as he always does, sharing a room with a teammate and travelling on the athletes' bus to the stadium, going through the same security checks as every other athlete.

When he got to the track, the races seemed just as routine. Rio was his coronation. It wasn't as spectacular as Beijing or as thrillingly close as London. Instead, Bolt's rivals melted away, as though out of respect. He won the 100 metres in 9.81, by some margin the slowest of his three titles, but still a relatively comfortable 0.08 seconds quicker than Gatlin. Rio was, paradoxically, the toughest and easiest of Bolt's Olympic triumphs: Toughest on paper, easiest on the track. It seemed a Games too far for the old guard (Gatlin, Tyson Gay, Asafa Powell) and a Games too soon for the new generation, led by Andre de Grasse of Canada who was third in 9.91. In adding gold medals in the 200m and 4x100m, Bolt closed his Olympic account with an historic third consecutive treble. (The only cloud scudding across the horizon was that one of his teammates in Beijing and London, Nesta Carter, tested positive for a stimulant when his 2008 sample was re-tested. The case remains unresolved at the time of writing but it could see the Jamaicans, including Bolt, having to hand back their relay gold from Beijing. Bolt would thus cease to be a triple-triple Olympic champion.)

As in Beijing and London, Rio was not, from a Jamaican perspective, all about Bolt. A new kid on the block: Elaine Thompson, who deposed another Jamaican, Shelly-Ann Fraser-Pryce, as 100m champion, then added gold in the 200m, the first time a Jamaican woman had done the sprint double. A quietly-spoken 24-year-old with a sweet smile and yellow flowers in her hair, Thompson seemed to come from nowhere, but she had rolled off the production line at the Jamaican sprint factory, coming through the schools system, then the schools' championship ('Champs'), and one of the two main Kingston clubs, one of which (Racers) is run by Glen Mills, the other (MVP) by Stephen Francis. Like Fraser-Pryce, Thompson is a Francis protégée.

I had only a passing knowledge of these things when I set out to write this book, the aim of which was to try and understand how a small Caribbean island had become the global sprinting superpower. It was Bolt's story that initially attracted me but the wider story of Jamaica and its track and field culture that captivated me. And the deeper I went, the more I came to appreciate that Jamaica is as important to Bolt as he is to Jamaica. There is something fundamentally Jamaican about one of Bolt's greatest off-the-track achievements, as articulated by Ziggy Marley, whose late father remains, arguably, the only Jamaican more famous than

Bolt. Bolt and Bob Marley both demonstrated, said Ziggy Marley, that 'You can be yourself and achieve what you need to achieve without losing your identity, without losing who you are.'

But amid the plaudits and praise there was the elephant in the room: Could we—should we—believe in Bolt and his fellow Jamaicans' remarkable success? Over the last few years the integrity and credibility of Olympic sport and those who run it has been dealt blow after blow after blow: A state-sponsored program of doping and corruption uncovered in Russia; the World Anti-Doping Agency's athletes' confidential medical files hacked (reportedly by Russian hackers); the re-testing of samples from the Beijing and London Games producing 101 fresh positives, with, according to the IOC's medical director, 'many more to come' from the 2012 Games (and, it seems safe to assume, from the Rio Games, with samples stored for up to ten years as new testing methods are developed).

All of which makes it increasingly difficult to know what we should and should not celebrate. The sporting public are victims of this, but so too are clean athletes. After all, a Russian conspiracy is one thing but until evidence emerges of more regimes intent on corrupting sport, or indeed a global conspiracy, we have to believe that clean athletes are among those who set world records and win gold medals—to believe otherwise would be to give in to cynicism.

Some of the most damaging revelations have come out since this book was originally published in the UK in June 2015. But none of them have prompted me to reassess or revise what I wrote. If I was embarking on the story now and leaving for Jamaica tomorrow I would take the same approach. It was with an open mind that I set out to find out more about the Caribbean island with the rich track and field tradition that began to dominate sprinting in the early 2000s and, in Bolt, Blake, Powell, Campbell-Brown, Fraser-Pryce and Thompson, to name only a few, has produced some of the fastest athletes in history.

Richard Moore,
London, December 2016

PROLOGUE

Even the simplest assessment of the circumstances surrounding the explosive success of Jamaican sprinting sets off alarms . . . What are the odds that a tiny island country suddenly dominates global competition . . . just because?
Dan Bernstein, CBS Chicago

London, 5 August 2012, 9.45 p.m.

The eight men are called to the blocks. Each goes down slowly and methodically. They dig their feet in and delicately place their hands in the corners of the lane. A plastic bottle lands behind them, thrown by a man in the crowd, but it goes unheard. They wait and 80,000 people in London's Olympic stadium hush. An echoey, tense kind of silence.

They are called to 'set'. They hold this position for two seconds. The gun goes and an electric charge runs through the crowd.

I am sitting thirty rows from the front, level with the finish line, experiencing the paradox of the 100 metres: simultaneously the quickest and the longest nine-point-something seconds. Trying not to blink, aware that it will all be over quickly, but concentrating so hard that the seconds seem to stretch. The dots gradually enlarge and emerge as a line of sprinters, one of them, when he is unfurled, a full head taller than the others: Usain Bolt.

1

Justin Gatlin is quickest out of the blocks, Yohan Blake, Bolt's clubmate and the world champion, a fraction slower, then Tyson Gay in the next lane along. Asafa Powell, the third Jamaican, reacts almost as quickly as Gatlin, and Ryan Bailey is also up. Bolt is sixth, though he is 'still with the crowd', as he puts it later; still in contact with the five in front.

They are approaching now, growing larger. Bolt draws level with Gatlin at fifty metres. Gay is still marginally ahead; Powell is fading, so is Bailey. Now Bolt and Blake lead, but it's still close. They reach seventy metres, and Bolt surges, as though engaging a new gear. It is an extraordinary spectacle, Bolt in full flight, and it makes the outcome inevitable. Blake dips for second, Gatlin takes bronze.

It is different to Beijing, four years earlier, when the twenty-one-year-old Bolt produced a performance seared into the imagination, one that left an imprint like only a few other moments in sport, when incredible talent combined with soaring ambition and absolute fearlessness. How many compare? Having galloped into an outrageous lead against the fastest men in the world, Bolt was able to look left, look right, thump his chest, spread his arms, then visibly relax and spend the final ten metres coasting and celebrating. It was as decisive and seemingly effortless as Diego Maradona's mazy run against England in 1986, Mike Tyson's ninety-second demolition of Michael Spinks in 1988, or, in the same year, Ben Johnson's 9.79-second destruction of Carl Lewis in the Olympic 100 metres final.

In an event measured by fractions of fractions of seconds, Bolt did something in Beijing that should not have been possible. It looked like he was playing a different game, or that he belonged to a different species. And it was all so graceful. 'He's beautiful to watch,' said Renaldo Nehemiah, the former 110 metres hurdles world record holder. 'His stride, I mean, it's poetry in motion. He's not like a beast running. He's like a gazelle.'

In London four years later there is no showboating, apart from a small gesture by Bolt's standards: a finger to his lips, 'Sssshhhh.' 'I almost did what I did in Beijing, I almost did it,' he chuckles later. 'But I thought, Nah, I'll just run through the finish.' He wins in 9.63 seconds, a new Olympic record.

In a low-ceilinged, brightly lit room deep in the bowels of London's Olympic stadium, somewhere below the main stand, Usain Bolt shuffles into the press conference, this one after the 200 metres, which he has also won. First he requests a drum roll. 'I'm now a legend,' he says. 'I am the greatest athlete to live. To all the people who doubted me, who thought I would lose here, you can stop talking now. I am a living legend.' Then he explodes with laughter.

Who, now, does he regard as his peers in the sporting world: Muhammad Ali, Michael Jordan, Pele? Beyond sport, has he superseded Bob Marley as the greatest Jamaican in history?

'Ali was the greatest in his sport, Jordan the greatest in his, and I am the greatest in mine, so I guess I am at that level,' Bolt replies. 'I am in the same category as Michael Johnson too. Bob Marley? I'm just carrying on his duty. We have the same goal, to make Jamaica a country that is loved around the world.'

Twenty minutes later, about to leave, he asks once again for the reporters' attention. There is a glint in his eye and a smile on his face. 'I have one more thing to say. I am now a living legend. Bask in my glory. If I don't see that in the paper and on TV in all your countries I will never give an interview again. Tell everyone to follow me on Twitter.'

It wasn't just Bolt. It was Shelly-Ann Fraser-Pryce, Yohan Blake, Warren Weir. It was Asafa Powell, Veronica Campbell-Brown, Nesta Carter, Sherone Simpson. Seven gold medals from the eight sprint events in London: Jamaica, a tiny island, had come close to complete domination for a second Olympic Games in succession. Twenty of the fastest twenty-five men's 100 metres in history had now been run by Jamaicans. It was, depending on where you stood, incredibly impressive, or deeply suspicious.

Like many – such as Carl Lewis, the nine-time Olympic gold medallist, or Dan Bernstein, the CBS columnist, who wrote 'Anyone wasting words extolling the greatness of Usain Bolt should know better' – I was, if not suspicious, then certainly sceptical. Bernstein was right: if we didn't know better than to assume that the Olympic 100 metres champion was clean, then we hadn't learned anything from Ben Johnson, Marion Jones, Justin Gatlin and countless others, nor from the asterisks, denoting drugs cheats, that rain down like confetti on the all-time fastest list.

I had another reason for being preoccupied by this question during the London Games. I had gone there straight from the Tour de France – there were only four days in between. A toxic atmosphere engulfed the Tour. It had been noxious for years as the full extent of institutional doping became apparent, but in 2012 it was especially bad. Bradley Wiggins led for most of the race and was asked daily whether he was-cheating. The questions were fuelled by justified, historical suspicion (not necessarily of Wiggins, but of the event) and sustained by the simmering rage of social media. One day Wiggins exploded when asked about his cyber critics: 'I say they're just fucking wankers, I cannot be doing with people like that. It's easy for them to sit under a pseudonym on Twitter and write that sort of shit, rather than get off their arses in their own lives and apply themselves and work hard at something and achieve something.'

The questions were legitimate, but they led us all – journalists, fans, athletes – into an endless downward spiral. This was not journalism: it was journalists responding to and genuflecting before the echo chamber of social media. It made no distinction between facts and conjecture, opinion and evidence.

Going from the Tour de France to the London Olympic Games was like stepping from a sewer into a golden meadow. The sun shone, a sweet scent filled the air, and the tweets emanated from birds rather than trolls. London itself was transformed. People smiled. Conversations were started on the Tube. Policemen posed for pictures mimicking Bolt's victory pose, which some call 'the Lightning Bolt' but Bolt himself calls 'To Di World', inspired by a Jamaican dancehall move.

There was no cynicism, no angst, no hand-wringing. Only innocence and joy. In Bolt's press conference, he was not asked if he was a cheat. He was asked: 'Are you a legend now, Usain?'

It was intoxicating, almost impossible not to be swept along on this tide of goodwill. It was also unsettling: superficial and fake. I loved it, and hated it. Which is also how I feel about the doping question. Conflicted. Because for all that the atmosphere at the Tour was poisonous and corrosive, the question itself fascinates me. It encompasses lying, cheating, subterfuge, deceit, mystery – all the things that make crime fiction so compelling. It goes to the very heart of elite sport: to what lengths will people go? It also goes to the heart of the experience of watching and enjoying sport: should we – can we – believe what we are seeing?

It is *the* question. Yet at the Tour I became weary of it, partly because journalism should be about trying to find things out, not asking the same thing every day; but also because I believed Bradley Wiggins was clean. I had followed him closely for over a decade. I knew the people around him. I was convinced he was no Lance Armstrong, against whom there had been strong evidence from the start, whereas really the only 'evidence' against Wiggins was the fact that he was winning an event with a dubious history.

When I heard the cynical view that Olympic gold medals and Tour de France victories were impossible without drugs, I passionately disagreed. As an objective journalist I shouldn't have cared, but as a human being I felt the treatment of Wiggins – the things asserted by people who I knew had no idea – was unfair. Yet I didn't know, and my only 'evidence' was anecdotal. I couldn't know unless I lived with him. I couldn't know unless I *was* him. And this was what was so unsettling.

With Bolt, I knew less. But because I knew less, I seemed more inclined to agree with the Lewises and the Bernsteins and assume the worst. Ironically, the greater the distance, the easier it seems to be to form a strong opinion. The closer you get, the more aware you become of contradiction and nuance; the more your certainty begins to crumble while ambiguity flourishes. Which seems a good reason not to remain at a distance, with your hazy view and lazy opinions, but to at least try and get up close to find out what you can.

That is what I resolved to do in the days after the London Games. The broader question that inspired this book was not: is Bolt clean? That is too loaded. Rather, I wanted to find out why he is so good. The two questions might be related. But equally, they might not be. In a way, my question was: how can we be certain of our heroes? Can we dare to hope?

In trying to find out, I found myself drawn more to the culture that produced Bolt than to Bolt himself. Because he is not a one-off; far from it.

1

A FORCE FIVE HURRICANE

I ain't doing no interviews.
Glen Mills

Moscow, August 2013

It's the eve of the world athletics championships in Moscow, and the Jamaican team is holding an open training session. They are gathered in clumps on a warm-up track that is semi-hidden amid trees and statues in the grounds of the Luzhniki Stadium, a grey, hulking Communist-era structure about to stage its final international event before it is rebuilt for the 2018 football World Cup – only the outer walls and the Lenin statue will remain.

No doubt this feels a very long way from home for the Jamaicans warming up in front of us, working in little groups, practising starts, stretching in the warm Moscow sunshine or having their muscles kneaded on massage tables.

The post-Olympic year can feel low-key: a bit after-the-Lord-Mayor's-Show. Few athletes are at their best. When he appeared at the Golden Gala in Rome in June – and suffered a rare defeat to Justin Gatlin – Usain Bolt admitted that it is a struggle for the mind and also the body, 'because Olympic year is when most athletes push themselves to the limit'.

But the difficulties faced by the Jamaican athletes in 2013 have gone well beyond the usual post-Games hangover. It's an Olympic hangover all right – a hangover of Olympic proportions. It began days after the Golden Gala with the news that Veronica Campbell-Brown, the three-times Olympic gold medallist, had tested positive for a diuretic. A month later, the news was even more shocking: five failed drugs tests at the Jamaican national championships, including two more of the country's biggest stars, Asafa Powell and Sherone Simpson.

It appeared to be nothing less than a cull. And confirmation of the doubts that had swirled around the Jamaicans. In response, some prominent Jamaican athletes seemed to adopt a siege mentality. In Monaco, before the Diamond League meeting in late July, Shelly-Ann Fraser-Pryce, the double Olympic 100 metres champion, took part in a bizarre press conference.

Fraser-Pryce had travelled there straight from Lignano, the northern Italian town where she had been training with Powell and Simpson, both clubmates. Their hotel had been raided by Italian police and products seized from Powell and Simpson's rooms. It wasn't clear yet whether they contained any banned substances – nor, indeed, whether Powell and Simpson were guilty of a doping offence. But as she sat down beside Carmelita Jeter, the American who had finished second to her at the London Olympics, the usually exuberant Fraser-Pryce displayed the body language of a crime suspect.

'No questions will be answered on the doping cases,' said the translator, opening the conference. 'This was a remark they asked us. Questions only on the competition tomorrow and the world championships.'

The second question came from Simon Hart of the *Telegraph*. 'If we're not allowed to ask about doping, can I ask Shelly-Ann what the atmosphere is like among the athletes at Lignano who haven't tested positive?'

'There will be no answers on that,' the translator cut in. 'They don't want to answer on that. Not today. Sorry.'

'Why?' chorused the journalists. Jeter picked up the microphone, said, 'Thank you,' and walked out. Fraser-Pryce looked unsure what to do, then followed. The press conference had lasted two minutes thirty-one seconds.

Even stranger was an incident I witnessed weeks later at the Diamond League meeting in Brussels, after Fraser-Pryce won the 100 metres. 'Shelly-Ann, have you been drug-tested in Brussels?' asked John Leicester of the Associated Press.

'No, I haven't been drug-tested here in Belgium,' Fraser-Pryce said testily. 'Do you want to drug-test me?'

'No, I don't want to drug-test you,' said Leicester, 'that's not my job. How many times have you been drug-tested this year, do you know?'

'Well, I'll count all those pink papers that I have, and I'll definitely try and send them to you, but many times, more than eighteen times for the year.'

'More than eighteen, or eight?' Leicester persisted.

'More than eighteen, OK?'

'Well I'll take you up on your offer,' said Leicester.

'Certainly, you can leave your email address and fax number with my manager at the back.'

Afterwards, in the corridor outside the room, Leicester spoke to Fraser-Pryce's manager, Adrian Laidlaw. 'The good thing about this conversation is I'll now make sure that she never makes a statement like that again,' he told Leicester.

In Moscow three weeks later, I am watching Fraser-Pryce, the five-foot-zero 'Pocket Rocket', practise her starts, exploding out of the blocks, sprinting thirty metres, then slowing and walking languidly back to the start, hands on hips, the sun reflecting off the pink streaks in her hair.

Bolt is here too. With his workout finished, his sluggish movement suits the muggy, oppressive heat of Moscow in August. He heads to the massage table, set up between the track and the small rickety stand, and lies down, propping himself up on his elbows so he can talk (which makes him unusual: most athletes don headphones the second they stop training). Bolt's masseur, serious and stern-faced, tackles his legs with vigour: first calves, then hamstrings, stopping regularly to apply more baby oil to his hands. He rolls up Bolt's knee-length shorts until he is kneading his buttocks. Gradually Bolt surrenders to it, resting his head on the table while the masseur goes on kneading, thumbs probing.

Nearby is Bolt's walrus-like coach, Glen Mills, who achieves the near impossible by showing even less urgency than Bolt. He plays a game with the dozen or so journalists clustered at the front of the small stand, sitting close enough to be able to hear them calling his name, far enough away that he can pretend he doesn't. The Jamaican assistant team manager, Dave Myrie, is dispatched to ask Mills for an interview. He wanders towards him, then returns shaking his head. 'You know Glen by now.'

Muzak wafts across the track from tinny speakers on top of the single-storey pavilion on the back straight: 'She Loves You' and 'My Way' are staples. Now, over the strains of Queen's 'I Want to Break Free', the seated Mills half turns, and says, 'I ain't doing no interviews.'

Bolt eases himself off the massage table and puts on his oversized headphones, then his rucksack, which hangs low and loose on his back. He ambles towards the track centre, stumbling theatrically over a parking cone on the way. Mills, sitting nearby, doesn't flinch. He doesn't seem to notice.

Only when Bolt is gone do you begin to take in the other Jamaican athletes going through their warm-up drills. 'No talent, all guts' reads the slogan on one T-shirt, but the talent here would grace any national team. Yet it is deprived of three of its biggest stars: Powell, Campbell-Brown and Simpson (a fourth, Yohan Blake, is missing through injury). 'They will be well missed,' lamented the veteran coach, Fitz Coleman, when the team gathered in Kingston before flying to Moscow. 'As far I'm concerned, they are still a part of our team.'

In light of Mills's reticence, Michael Clarke, the head coach in Moscow, steps forward. Clarke wears a black Puma cap, dark Ray-Bans, a yellow Puma T-shirt, and a thick gold chain around his neck. The interview gets off to an awkward start when a Russian reporter, clutching black-and-white photocopied pictures of Bolt and Fraser-Pryce (to help her identify the athletes, she explains), asks, 'Who's that man in blue?' Clarke turns to look. 'That's Coach Mills.'

Clarke says that the team is aiming for more medals than the nine they won last time. 'Any black horses?' asks the same Russian reporter. Some of us stare in embarrassment at the ground, but Clarke is unruffled. 'Well, I think this year's going to be a change of the guard,' he says. 'We have a very young team; I think the average age is around twenty-one, twenty-two. And we should have some young persons vying for some medals. As for specifics, I can't tell you right now who they are.'

'Has morale been affected by the recent controversies?' Clarke is asked.

'From what I have seen thus far, coming from a cross section of athletes, there doesn't seem to be any negative impact on the present situation as it concerns the drugs situation,' says Clarke.

Has he spoken to the squad as a whole? 'Not on that issue.'

What about the recent claims that the Jamaicans are years behind in drug-testing? 'I don't think we are behind. I think we are slowly keeping pace with what's expected.'

As he's speaking, Dennis Gordon, the team's media liaison officer, appears at Clarke's shoulder and leans in. 'Answer no questions about doping,' says Gordon.

'What?' says Clarke.

'Answer no questions about doping.'

'Ah,' says Clarke, looking back up, 'I've just been instructed by our media liaison person not to take any questions about doping.'

A change of tack. Bolt – how is he? 'Usain is one of those unique individuals with a very capable personality – very affable, very genial, very funny. I think everyone gravitates towards his charisma. He's fine.'

Back to the main point, in a roundabout way. Why are the Jamaicans so fast? Clarke gives it some thought. 'In recent years, academic research has been done to explain somewhat, or to give some understanding as to why we are as good as we have been. I think part of it is genes and some have postulated about yam and some are saying it's because of the system we have in place.

'We have various competitions from the infant level to the primary school to the secondary school to the clubs, tertiary, even community track and field. And most organisations have what you call sports day and primarily the sports day consists of running events – or egg-and-spoon races. That basically comes from our English background. It's the system that's in place and it's highly competitive. The athletes at the 1948 and 1952 Olympics have given us a platform to build on.'

It is Clarke's first time as head coach to the senior national team, but he feels no pressure. 'Expectations, yes, but there is no pressure.' The spirit in the squad, he adds, is 'very high, very good. And calm. It's like a volcano waiting to erupt.'

Warren Weir saunters over to speak to some journalists. The baby-faced Olympic bronze medallist, a clubmate of Bolt, says he wants to put a smile back on people's faces. 'Yeah, it's always good to give people good news after the bashing our sport has gotten. People want to see people running clean, people running fast and clean, and it's always good to let them know there are clean ones out there.'

So when we see so many Jamaicans run so fast, we can believe in them? 'Yes!' Weir splutters. 'Yes, you can still believe that there are good athletes out there: I myself can testify to that. I'm one of the clean ones. So there are actually good ones out there. We can't bash all for some.'

Team morale is unaffected, he says. 'It hasn't shifted us. We are rallying together; whether bad news or good news we always look on the positive side of life. We don't let the bad news hold us down or make us underperform.'

That much appears to be true. In Moscow, the Jamaicans simply pick up where they left off in London. On day two, Bolt reaches the 100 metres final along with three of his countrymen: Nesta Carter, Kemar Bailey-Cole and Nickel Ashmeade. It's a dark Moscow night and the rain is lashing down as the runners are introduced, Bolt with his hands on his hips, his head tilted back as though meditating. When the TV camera pans from Justin Gatlin to him, he begins an elaborate routine of pretending to open and put up an umbrella. The rain falls harder than ever and Bolt stands under his imaginary umbrella wearing a fake-bemused expression.

Gatlin gets away quickly, bull-like, head down, low. 'The rain made it slick under the fingers,' he says later, 'but I got out the blocks. Reacted well. Drove about forty-five metres, then felt Bolt next to me.' As he feels Bolt's presence, Gatlin makes the fatal mistake of reacting. 'You know, I gotta remember in my head that I'm not six-five. I'm only six-one. When you get someone who's six-five, you try to match the stride length; I shoulda just kept attacking the ground.'

Although Gatlin beat Bolt in Rome, the script at a major championship is by now familiar, and when Bolt draws level, there can be only one outcome. He pulls clear, wins in 9.77 seconds, while Gatlin hangs on, dipping too early ('We call it the phantom finish line – you see the person in front of you dip and you dip as well') for second. Carter wins what seems like a separate race for bronze. Lightning illuminates the sky as Bolt crosses the line, and Bob Marley's 'Three Little Birds' fills the Moscow air:

> *Don't worry 'bout a thing,*
> *'Cause every little thing gonna be alright . . .*

In the mixed zone, inside the stadium, where athletes are shepherded through pens and reporters hang over barriers catching their words

on recorders, there is a stir when Bolt finally appears after his lap of honour. There is always a stir when Bolt appears. He shuffles through the pen in his socks, while Ricky Simms, the Irishman who is his agent, follows holding his Puma spikes in one hand.

Bolt starts to speak in his deep baritone. He explains that he would have liked to go faster, closer to his world record of 9.58, but a niggle after the semi-final put paid to that. Still, it looked quite easy. 'I never look at it as easy,' he says. 'I work hard. I push myself through a lot of pain.'

According to some, Bolt came to Moscow to 'save' the sport after a year of terrible headlines, most of them about athletes from his country. His face crumples into a smile, and he giggles, as though the question is ridiculous: he is only one man. 'For me, I think I go out there . . . I'm just doing my part by running fast, letting the world know you can do it clean.'

*

Twenty-four hours after the men's 100 metres, Fraser-Pryce, despite 'pain in my left butt-cheek', appears for the women's final. Apart from the pink ponytail ('Fuchsia,' she clarifies later. 'It makes me pretty . . . prettier'), she doesn't go out of her way to attract attention, not like Bolt. She quietly and intensely focuses on what she has to do, oblivious to the crowd and the other runners, narrowing her eyes, squinting down the track.

Her start is explosive – much better than it was in London twelve months earlier – and she surges in the second 50 metres for a convincing win, over two-tenths of a second clear of Murielle Ahouré of the Ivory Coast, with Jeter third. Her time, 10.71 seconds, is just one-hundredth outside the championship record. Afterwards, Fraser-Pryce says that she'll celebrate 'with some ice on my gluteus maximus'. She has been working hard all year on her 200 metres, and has her eyes on a first sprint double in a major championship.

She reaches the final of the longer event and starts in lane four, with Allyson Felix of the US, the reigning world and Olympic 200 metres champion, in lane three. There's the explosive start again, and Felix is straining to stay in contact on the bend – straining too hard – when she pulls up and collapses to the track clutching her hamstring. It's a second gold for Fraser-Pryce. Twenty-four hours later, Bolt does the same, winning ahead of Weir.

The Jamaican men and women win the 4x100 metres too. And after the men's relay there's an exchange with Bolt inside the stadium that reveals another side of his personality. As he waited for the baton, with Gatlin in the lane inside but moving to the outside of his lane, the two almost collided. In the confusion, the US, slightly ahead on the final bend, messed up the transition. They handed the advantage to Jamaica – to Bolt – for the final leg. Gatlin was furious, claiming afterwards that without the mistake, the US would have won.

'They couldn't have said that,' says Bolt when told what Gatlin said. Shaking his head, affecting a casual pose as he leans against the fence in the mixed zone, he continues: 'They couldn't have said that, they couldn't have said that.' He tries to make a joke of it, but the sparkle is missing from his eyes, which have turned dark. He is angry – affronted. 'They were like two metres in front of me. I've been in a worse position running from my blocks and won. I wasn't worried at all about the US beating us. We had a great team.'

If not two metres, then how much would the Americans have needed to beat the Jamaicans? 'Probably they would have had to have ten metres to win that race,' says Bolt. We laugh. He isn't smiling.

Beijing, Berlin, Daegu, London and Moscow merely continue Jamaica's extraordinary domination of the sprint events at the major championships. Yet the mood in Moscow is very different to London. I can feel it, it's in the air. There's the scepticism of the outside world, the defensiveness of the Jamaicans. It's all very reminiscent of the Tour de France. The Olympics feel a long time ago.

On the day after the world championships comes another bombshell. 'An inside look at Jamaican track's drug-testing woes' reads the headline in *Sports Illustrated*. The article is by Renée Anne Shirley, the former executive director of the Jamaica Anti-Doping Commission (JADCO), and in it she describes the positive tests for Powell, Simpson and Campbell-Brown as equivalent to 'a force five hurricane crossing directly over the island'. A table accompanying the article shows how little drug-testing JADCO did in the six months before the London Games.

On the eve of my first visit to Jamaica, I met Shirley at an anti-doping conference in London, where she was speaking. Her participation in the conference had been in doubt – she had problems getting a visa, which she believed was connected to her article. She explained that if the positive tests unleashed a 'force five hurricane', her revelations unleashed another one. 'I've been called a Judas, a traitor, that I've committed treason, that my passport should be taken away,' she said. Then she described 'the lonely road of the whistleblower': 'I expected a lot of it, I have weathered a lot of it, but it amazes me the things said about me . . . pressure has been put on my family. I have been blacklisted. I don't get invitations to anything, I don't get Christmas cards. The other issue is personal safety. I've relocated, I've taken precautions. I have to be careful.'

This all sounded ominous. Then Shirley, who lasted eight months at JADCO before leaving, said something else that interested me. 'As a proud Jamaican, all I wanted to do was be able to defend the Jamaicans as best I could.' Instead, when people like Carl Lewis asked questions, or when Shirley herself raised her concerns about the effectiveness of anti-doping, they were attacked.

'Every time something comes up, it's "This person is against Jamaica,"' said Shirley. 'But to come out and say, "The rest of the world is against us," it does not answer the question.'

There were lots of questions. And only really one place to try and find the answers.

2

THE WELLSPRING

Jamaican youth continue to excel in track and field because the poorest
child from the deepest rural hinterland of Jamaica and the most depressed
urban ghetto can get a chance to compete.
Betty Ann Blaine, *Jamaica Observer*

Kingston, March 2014

Outside the stadium it is like a large music festival or major sports
event. Stalls and street vendors line Arthur Wint Drive, selling food
and drink, flags and memorabilia in team colours.

In the stifling heat, women sit beneath umbrellas and beside large
coolboxes filled with drinks, and men materialise alongside me as I
walk from the car park to the arena, hustling and hassling – 'higgling',
they call it. 'Cold drink, man?' 'Mi have ticket – you want ticket?'

It's Tuesday, day one of Champs, Jamaica's boys' and girls' inter-
schools championships. A schools athletics meeting like no other.
Security is tight. At the gate, there's a long queue, at the end of which
uniformed men and women check tickets and bags and even peel
labels off non-sanctioned soft drinks. My bottle of Pepsi is confiscated
while a guard pulls at the sticker. 'Why are you doing that?' I ask.

'Advertising,' he says.

'But Pepsi is one of the sponsors.'

'Oh . . .' His colleague nods confirmation. He hands the bottle back.

Inside the grounds of the National Stadium, more security guards carry walkie-talkies or wear earpieces. The stadium, opened in 1962, the year that Jamaica gained its independence, is a low-slung sand-coloured bowl that sits in a relatively affluent New Kingston neighbourhood. The Blue Mountains are on one side, the rump of the city – the ghettos and slums and garrisons – sprawling and shimmering all the way down to the sea on the other.

It's hard to believe, as I negotiate the throngs of people, and listen to the thrum of anticipation, that this is a schools championship. But Champs is the only show in town. The newspapers are full of it: front, back and letters pages. The radio stations are dominated by discussion of the young athletes – some of them already household names – who will star over the five days. There are public service announcements advising spectators to lock up and register their guns with the police. There is live TV coverage.

The man in charge of it all, the meet director, is none other than Usain Bolt's coach, Glen Mills. He is also one of the first people I spot when I enter the main stand and sit on the bench seat. He wears a pale blue T-shirt, loose-fitting jeans and trainers, and greets people with a shy, toothless smile (he is missing his front two upper teeth), but generally doesn't stop to talk, moving slowly up the stand. Mills doesn't look relaxed, he looks catatonic. Finally he reaches the top of the steps and the last row of seats and sits down heavily. I have been told that he will not be speaking to journalists during Champs (or at any other time).

Picking up a programme, I read the mind-blowing statistic that at the current time, every global male 100 metres champion, in every age group, is Jamaican: Olympic, world, Commonwealth, Youth Olympic, world junior and world youth. But on the very next page is something that jars with the celebratory, self-congratulatory tone. It says that from 2015 it has been propsed that drug-testing will be introduced at Champs, testing kids from ten years old upwards. 'It is such a pity that the hard work and natural talent of our young athletes are now being scrutinised with suspicion,' says the article, before going on to question whether drug-testing children is to ensure fairness, to protect 'Brand Jamaica', or to 'appease international critics'.

'Hey, you a coach?' an American voice asks to my left. We are sitting in the half-empty main stand before things hot up and the stadium fills later in the week.

He is unmistakably an American sports coach: neatly pressed polo shirt, college logo, knee-length shorts, baseball cap, sunglasses. He introduces himself as Keith Barnier, head track and field coach at Abilene Christian University (ACU) in Texas. He has come to Champs early, he tells me, to get a head start on the other US college coaches. Most arrive for the final day, the climax to the meeting, and then, Barnier says, 'get the hell back out as soon as possible'.

'They think Kingston is dangerous,' he explains. 'They say, "What the hell do you do there for five days?" But my wife is Jamaican, and I know you gotta be in the club of Jamaican people. You take care of them, they take care of you. Trust is everything here.'

Barnier clicks his tongue in appreciation as he watches Christopher Taylor, a fourteen-year-old from Calabar, win a 400 metres heat in 48.72 seconds. 'Forty-eight for a fourteen-year-old!' he laughs, as though the idea were preposterous (which it would be anywhere other than here). Taylor is small, wiry and smooth as silk. The crowd becomes excited to the point of hysteria as he glides down the home straight and lunges for the line.

Barnier says he's here mainly to study athletes in their final year, with a view to recruiting them for ACU. 'I look at the green bananas,' he says. 'But what I need are yellow ones.

'These guys are like soldiers,' he continues. 'And this, Champs, it prepares them for war. There's nothing like this anywhere else in the world. This is a freak show.' He means this in the nicest way. 'I'm serious. These kids are running for a better life and they are not messing around. The coaches are not messing around. And they are good coaches.' What makes them good coaches? 'They give a shit.'

Barnier knows most of the coaches and knows how they operate, explaining that they might initially send him a less talented youngster. 'They'll toss you a bone. It might not be their best athlete, but if you do well for them they'll send you a better one. That's what I mean about trust. When you make a promise to the Jamaicans, you gotta keep it. Americans say things they don't mean. My wife catches me for that.'

I meet Barnier the next day, and the day after, and the day after. He spends long hours at the stadium, but increasingly away from the main arena, in the stand by the side of the warm-up track; 'hustlin'', as he puts it. 'This is the boiler room,' he tells me, having sneaked me into what is technically a no-go area for journalists. 'This is where it all happens – not out there on the track.' Here, backstage, are coaches watching groups of athletes going through their paces; other athletes on tables, masseurs kneading their muscles, physiotherapists attending to injuries; and a lot of slow, languid movement. The athletes are different but the scene is identical to Moscow before the world championships, which tells its own story: the professionalism is striking (I don't remember sports masseurs and physios at my school).

Barnier picks his moments to approach the coaches – 'not just before a race' – at one point returning and holding up his wrist, where there used to be a watch. 'Traded it for an athlete,' he says. A joke. I think. But he does say that one coach offered his best athlete if Barnier could get his own son a basketball scholarship. In terms of what he is actually offering the athletes, Barnier says: 'I'm handing out $46,000 scholarships.'

At one time this would have been the holy grail. A scholarship to a US college was something every Jamaican athlete coveted – it was the whole point of excelling at athletics; it offered a ticket out of Jamaica to a better life. But there seemed to be a sporting cost attached: lots of promising young Jamaican athletes went to the States and were never heard of again. These days, a 'bone' might be all a US college gets. Some of the best Jamaicans are staying at home.

Barnier is familiar with the stories, and also the criticism that at US colleges Jamaican athletes are over-raced and burned out, or transferred to other sports that demand speed – perhaps basketball, or American football. In terms of popularity (and money), track and field lags a long way behind these sports in the US. (One theory is that if Usain Bolt had gone to an American college, he would have come under pressure to become a basketball player instead of a sprinter.) Change came in the early 2000s. Lots of young Jamaican athletes still go to the US on athletics scholarships, but they no longer have to. The best ones – Bolt, Yohan Blake, Asafa Powell, Shelly-Ann Fraser-Pryce, Warren Weir, Nesta Carter, Kemar Bailey-Cole – have opted instead to stay at home and train under Glen Mills or the other guru, Stephen Francis. Powell was the trend-setter. Or the trend-reverser.

It has made it harder for Barnier and his colleagues. But not impossible. 'What I'm selling,' he says, 'what I tell 'em, is: "I will not run you into the ground. I will help you run faster. I will let you run for your country if selected. And you'll get a great education in a beautiful school."'

A scholarship to a US college is still enormously appealing to lots of young Jamaicans. Some of them approach Barnier at the warm-up track. One very shy boy, who was hovering for a long time before plucking up the courage to approach me, eventually comes up and asks, 'Are you a coach, sir?' He looks crushed when I tell him I'm a journalist. He is a decathlete who missed out on selection for his school, Kingston College, in his main event but still harbours hopes of earning a scholarship based on his athletic ability.

The concept of recruitment is not new to a lot of them. 'All these kids, the good ones, are recruited by their high schools,' Barnier tells me. 'They understand that track and field can be their way out. And they're really easy to coach. They're not afraid of hard work. If you

get a bunch of 'em on your team, you're laughing. I would take any
five of these guys tomorrow.'

What exactly is he looking for – how does he spot talent? Barnier
laughs. 'I mean, the talent ID part is easy as hell. Look at these guys
jogging. They jog faster than my guys run. Beautiful.

'If you give them shoes, and a track to run on, they're very grateful,
they can't stop thanking you. The American kids are not like that. But
a lot of these kids we're seein' here are not getting three square meals
a day. Half of them have seen knife fights, they've seen someone get
shot. Hope is so important.'

That is what he is really selling, says Barnier: hope.

On the final day of Champs, towards the end of the closing session,
I sit on the baking concrete oval that ribbons around the athletics track.
It's a cycling track whose disrepair testifies to its lack of use; now it acts
as a buffer between the bleachers and the infield. All around me the
National Stadium is rammed: there are 30,000 people, and they have
been here since 4 p.m., five hours before the end of the meeting, when
the gates were closed.

The bleachers are bouncing. Spectators are arranged in blocks of
colour: yellow and red in one section; green and black in another;

purple and white; red; pale blue. Each block jumps and sways to its
own rhythm; each has its own band. 'The melodies of school songs
swirled and clashed in the air,' said Colin Channer, the Jamaican writer,
describing the atmosphere at Champs. 'Drumbeats from different
corners organised themselves into a bangarang . . . The stands were a
stand-in for Jamaica, a nation of passionate, noisy, tribal people. We
Jamaicans are most at ease in disorder.'

The atmosphere in the stadium is raucous. Despite the warnings
of fights and concealed weapons, it feels friendly, more a carnival than
a riot, but with the fervour of a big football match. Yet compared to
most British football matches, it is positively benign. There are whole
families: men, women, children and lots of babies clutched to mothers'
breasts. The vuvuzelas supply a constant high-pitched hum, like a
billion mosquitoes, a sound that mirrors that state of intensity. Perhaps
there is a parallel here with another Jamaican cultural phenomenon:
music. 'I don't know what it is about Jamaican music, but creatively
it just seems to take place at a higher amperage,' wrote the American
essayist John Jeremiah Sullivan. 'It may be an island effect. Isolation
does seem to breed these intensities sometimes.'

The flags around the top of the fifty-two-year-old stadium now lie
flat against their poles; earlier they blew furiously. Darkness is closing
in quickly, and the Blue Mountains, illuminated during the day by
blinding sunshine, are now ominous dark shadows that twinkle with
the lights from the homes of the people who live there. They include
some of the athletes so many of the schoolkids aspire to emulate – Bolt,
Blake and Powell all have large houses in the hills above Kingston.
Beverly Hills, where Bolt lives, is the most prominent area, with the
best views of Kingston, the ocean and the National Stadium.

In the bleachers and main stand there is frenzied chaos. But in
the track centre there is perfect order. It is as though the island's two
biggest influences – Africa and Great Britain – are represented by
this juxtaposition: the colour and vibrancy of Africa in the stands, the
restraint and authority of colonial Britain in the centre.

Records have been broken all week at Champs. Twenty-one will fall in total, but not all records are equal. The schoolboy feats of Bolt and Blake loom over this meeting like the Blue Mountains over Kingston. Zharnel Hughes destroys Blake's 100 metres record, set in 2007, running 10.12. Hughes is eighteen, from Anguilla (though his mother is Jamaican); he lives in Kingston and trains with Glen Mills's group. He is in Bolt's mould: tall at six-three, and like Bolt, he devours opponents over the final forty metres. Like Bolt, too, he is a product of the IAAF high-performance training centre in Kingston, where he has been since he was sixteen, training most days with Bolt and Blake. 'When I just got here and saw these guys,' he tells me after his record run, shaking his head. 'Bolt, man! I couldn't believe I had the chance to run with those guys.'

Blake was teasing Hughes before Champs. 'Big man, you can't beat my record, you can't beat my record. The closest you're going to come is 10.27.' Blake's record was 10.21. In the event, Hughes slices almost a tenth of a second from it. But the next day he pulls out of the 200 metres, feeling a twinge in his hamstring and deciding not to take any chances. He comes anyway to support his school, Kingston College, and says he isn't disappointed to miss out on the chance of the sprint double. 'No, man, every setback sets you up for a major comeback.'

It is difficult to keep track of all the outstanding performances. People are talking excitedly about young Christopher Taylor, the 400 metres phenomenon. 'I call him a freak,' smiles his coach at Calabar, Michael Clarke. 'He's small. I ask him, "Chris, how you generate so much power?" He's on the quiet side, but he's quietly aggressive.'

Then there's Jaheel Hyde. He has something about him beyond the fact that he sets a new national junior record in the 400 metres hurdles. He also wins the 110 metres hurdles. Recovering in his 'pen' afterwards, he carries himself with quiet, steely confidence; as self-contained as Usain Bolt is exuberant. His father, Lenworth Hyde, was one of Jamaica's greatest footballers, and Jaheel is said to be equally talented with a football – he was in the national under-17 squad – as he is on a track. To his father's disappointment, he has opted for athletics. Only in Jamaica would that be a rational rather than an eccentric choice.

Before the 200 metres comes the 400 metres final for the Class 1 boys. This is perhaps the most eagerly anticipated event on the programme because it features an athlete who is already a household name in Jamaica.

Six months earlier, Javon 'Donkey Man' Francis was selected for the senior world championships in Moscow. He was eighteen. But in a surprise move, Clarke, the Jamaican head coach, who also happened to be Francis's coach at Calabar, didn't just select him for the final of the 4x400 metres relay – he put him on the anchor leg.

On the night, in the old grey Luzhniki Stadium, Francis appeared unfazed as the Americans raced into a big lead. Behind them a small pack emerged: Russia, Great Britain, Belgium and finally Jamaica. With the Russians in contention for a medal, the atmosphere was as lively as it got in a city that seemed quite ambivalent about hosting the world athletics championships. Coming up to the final lap, and Francis's first appearance on the big stage, the runners jostled, stepping on each others' toes. The tall, slightly gangly Donkey Man bounced up and down as though the track was red hot, and urged his teammate on: 'Come on, come on,' he seemed to be gesturing with his hand. Then he settled into a semi-crouch, as though about to dive off a cliff, and waited still and poised, arms outstretched.

Francis took the baton with Jamaica lagging in fifth, slightly detached from the other medal contenders. He followed the others round the bend and then, on the back straight, attacked. He looked to be sprinting flat out as he passed the British runner, and then the Belgian. And then he overtook the Russian too. Jamaicans at home could only watch through the cracks in their fingers. What was Javon doing? The 400 was the most unforgiving distance: he'd die in the home straight, surely. He had hopelessly misjudged his run.

LaShawn Merritt of the USA was clear for gold. Francis had got the Jamaicans up to second. The Russian came back on the final bend, drawing level on the home straight. Now Francis would fade and die, and slip out of the medals. But incredibly, he surged again, and held on for second. His split was 44 seconds dead.

It would be an exaggeration to say that the world sat up and took notice of this extraordinary performance. But Jamaica noticed, and hailed the Donkey Man. It wasn't so much the time, though that was impressive; it was the way he attacked athletes older, more experienced and more respected; it was the aggression and the belief that flowed through him as he took off down the back straight, not merely to try and win a medal, but gunning for Merritt. The way that when the Russian came back, Francis didn't settle for bronze, but kicked again.

The reporters waiting in the mixed zone were unprepared, however, for Donkey Man's arrival. He entered this enclosed, claustrophobic part of the stadium – it felt like an underground car park – with the movement and swagger of a boxer. He danced towards a television reporter and took the microphone before speaking directly to the camera: 'A super donkey just did it!' he said, giggling, then turned serious. 'I listen to what coach say. To run my own race. Go out there. Last night me and him have a good discussion. Told him I wanted to get a medal to show my mum and dad. Now I got a medal to go home with.'

Francis was gap-toothed and goofy. For all his swagger, he had a sweet innocence about him. When his older teammates took their turn with the microphone – each one speaking shyly and uncertainly – he danced excitedly in the background and spoke over them in his thick Jamaican accent, lurching frequently into patois. Finally he grabbed the microphone again: 'I'm happy happy happy. I go home with a medal to show I am a future champion . . . I feel great about myself.

'A super donkey just did it!'

Now, back in Kingston, all eyes are on the super donkey, this latest golden child of Jamaican athletics. Francis grew up in an impoverished settlement, Bull Bay, nine miles up the coast from Kingston. When he was recruited to Calabar, he left his parents' modest home to move in with a guardian in the city. Despite his background, he is smartly and expensively attired: new Puma-branded green-and-black Calabar High School vest, shorts and spikes, tracksuit and rucksack.

The Calabar principal, Albert Corcho, is among the 30,000 spectators at the National Stadium as the boys' Class 1 400 metres finalists line up. Corcho recalls what Francis told him on the eve of Champs: 'Sir, I am going to break Usain Bolt's record. I am going for the record.' Bolt's record, set in 2003, stands at 45.35.

The gun goes for the start and Francis attacks. Here is the fearless athlete we saw in Moscow. Here, too, is an explanation for his coolness in Moscow, his ability to execute his race despite the atmosphere and sense of occasion. Because make no mistake, the world championships was nothing compared to Champs. Bolt has always said it: that if you can cope with Champs, you can cope with anything (he also suggested that it's why Asafa Powell has always frozen on the big stage – not enough experience of Champs: his school didn't always qualify).

From lane four Francis sprints around the first bend, hunting down the other runners then passing as though oblivious to them. By the second bend he is the clear leader. But he is not really racing the others; he is racing Bolt. Again there is that fear, or expectation, that he will run out of oxygen, his legs turning to jelly, running through mud up the home straight. Again it doesn't happen. Francis keeps attacking down the home straight, all the way to the line, over ten metres ahead of his nearest rival. He crosses the line with his arms stretched wide and his mouth open in a roar as the clock stops at 44.96.

The stadium erupts. The green-and-black block, housing the Calabar fans, bounces violently, as though it might burst open and spill on to the track. Donkey Man ignores the rest of the stadium and points to them, then drops to the ground and, mimicking the vanquished Bolt, starts doing press-ups. He manages three, then rests on his haunches, throwing his head back and stretching his arms out again, like Jesus. He gets back up but now seems to be in a daze. He mimics Bolt again with his 'To Di World' gesture, finishing it off with what looks like a salute, but he is staggering now, as though drunk. His time is readjusted to 45.00: a 0.35-second beating of Bolt's record.

And then Donkey Man collapses. He has been lurching around, trying to take it all in, while also milking it for all it is worth, when suddenly it overwhelms him. He crumples to the track. A stretcher appears. (Over the course of the five days, I count fifteen young athletes being carried out of the stadium on stretchers. When I ask one of the medics about this, I am told it has been a long season, with meetings every weekend, and that this is Champs: an injury is not going to stop an athlete competing.)

Francis is helped on to the stretcher. He lies there for no more than a few moments, blinking and recovering his composure, his chest heaving, before pushing the stretcher-bearers away and bounding back up. Maybe he has remembered that in two hours he has the 200 metres final. And that in 2003, Bolt, having set the 400 metres record that Francis has just broken, was back on the track three hours later to set a new record for the 200 metres.

'Ladies and gentlemen, please, we ask you to be quiet for the start of this event. Sssshhhhh.' The decibels drop a little, the low hum interrupted by a few isolated vuvuzelas. Then, from a distance, the far corner of the track, comes a clean, rasping sound: *poch.*

The boys' 200 metres starts and the vuvuzelas recommence, along with the brass bands and drums. Coming out of the bend, Javon Francis pulls up injured. It's a race too far for him. Jevaughn Minzie of Bog Walk, second to Zharnel Hughes in the 100, wins in 20.49, missing Bolt's record.

By 9 p.m., with Kingston now in total darkness and Champs winding down, sixty policemen have moved in to line the perimeter of the stands. They stand ten metres apart facing the crowd. The army appears for the closing ceremony as the schools re-emerge for the trophy presentations and fireworks. Calabar are declared boys' winners; Edwin Allen High School, from the farming community of Frankfield – in the dead centre of the island – win the girls' competition.

The fireworks are still going off as I join the thousands streaming out of the stadium, many of them heading to the after-parties. These are permitted again following a police ban that lasted several years. 'Promoters promise violence-free events' reads the headline in that morning's *Star* newspaper. The twenty-one Champs records will be on people's minds and in tomorrow's papers, but they also raise questions. If there is a doping problem in Jamaica – as the recent positive tests seem to indicate – does it also exist at schools level? While most celebrate the records, others wonder and some doubt.

Although the atmosphere at Champs was exuberant, an air of suspicion had descended on Jamaican athletics. It explained the pledge to begin drug-testing at schools level, as well as the defensiveness I encountered in some when I raised the topic. 'I'm not going there,' said Donald Quarrie, one of Jamaica's sprinting greats, when I asked him about drug-testing at Champs. Others professed surprise and confusion. Mark Ricketts, a friendly economist and former journalist who now lives in California, prowled the stands at Champs, hawking his book, *Jamaican Gold*, about the rise of the island's athletes. Ricketts said that the recent positive tests for Asafa Powell and Veronica Campbell-Brown 'baffles everyone's mind. But because they're kind of over the hill, people look at it and say, "Were they desperate, or did they make an innocent mistake?" '

My American coaching friend, Keith Barnier, didn't know what to make of it. 'You know the dirty coaches because they use all these long words you don't understand. They know what drugs do what.' Barnier looked thoughtful. 'Y'know, I kinda like it when people say my guys are on steroids. Means they're fast.'

Some Jamaicans were angry, but it seemed to me that many were less annoyed with the athletes who'd tested positive than with people like Renée Anne Shirley who asked awkward questions, or who claimed the cases pointed to a darker truth. Listening to the radio one evening mid-Champs, while driving back to my lodgings in Stony Hill, on the outskirts of Kingston, I heard the presenters grilling Anna Legnani, the IAAF's deputy director of communications. The main presenter seemed less interested in hearing what Legnani might have to say than in mounting a shrill defence: 'Bring in WADA [World Anti-Doping Agency] and the IOC!' he implored. 'Bring in the top officials and let them see what happens at this unique event in the western hemisphere! There's a difference between a doping violation and a culture of doping, and I know there isn't a culture of doping.

'It's good that Anna is here,' continued the presenter, well-spoken, with the perfect diction of well-educated Jamaicans. 'Let her see where it all starts, let her see that there isn't a culture of doping here. This, Anna, is the nursery for Jamaica's track and field.'

It seemed as though he was about to invite her to speak . . . but no, he carried on: 'There will be doping violations – we hope it doesn't happen – but this is where it begins. Your thoughts on what you're seeing, Anna; how long are you going to be here, by the way?'

'I'm leaving on Monday,' replied Legnani.

'When you are here on Saturday [the final day], you will see what we're talking about. You haven't seen anything yet. Your thoughts on what you're seeing, Anna. Have you seen anything like this in the world?'

'Erm, no. I mean the level and the depth of some of the performances we've seen—'

The co-presenter pitched in: 'Are high school kids drug-tested at meets like this in Europe and the States?'

'We don't have high school meets like this,' said Legnani. 'School sports are kind of disappearing in Europe, which is a shame. But it's such a reservoir of talent you have—'

'Are you saying that high school meets in Europe do not rise to this level, and wouldn't merit testing?'

'They are not at this level.'

'Why should we in Jamaica test when the rest of the world is not testing?'

'Um, well, that's a good point—'

'I don't see why we should be guinea pigs for the rest of the world.'

This was followed by a long, awkward silence, with shuffling and muffled talking; perhaps Legnani was gesturing that she had had enough of being grilled. Finally the main presenter spoke again: 'Yes, I . . . I want to move from that because I think we've exhausted that . . . And Anna, I know she's a good jumper, but she's going through the hoops, and she's not going to answer that, so we're flogging a dead horse.'

The radio presenters were right about one thing: there is nothing like Champs. It is surely the world's biggest schools athletics meeting, and perhaps also the oldest. 'For over a century it hasn't missed a beat,' I was told by the former prime minister, P. J. Patterson.

Over the five days of the meeting, I spoke to coaches, athletes, journalists and seasoned observers. Where had the Jamaican athletics' success started? I asked. Who or what was responsible? Lots said Champs. Nobody said Usain Bolt. Donald Quarrie, the Olympic 200 metres gold medallist in 1976, said that if there was one person who deserved more credit than anybody else, it was Herb McKenley, the hero of the Helsinki Olympics. 'Every Jamaican athlete has a bit of Herb in them,' said Quarrie (an accidental double entendre in the land of the 'holy herb'). Mike Fennell, president of the Jamaica Olympic Association, agreed: 'Herb was first. He used to seek opportunities for the youngsters. He was a fantastic individual.' Even Bolt, when asked in 2014 who his Olympic hero was, didn't hesitate: 'Herb McKenley.'

There were other names, some from further back: Gerald Claude (G. C.) Foster, who sailed in a banana boat to the London Olympics in 1908 only to be told he couldn't compete. These days, the G. C. Foster College is where the island's athletics coaches are all trained. Other names: Norman Manley, the father of independence, a schoolboy champion who held the Champs 100 yards record for forty-four years; Jamaica's first Olympic champion, Arthur Wint; George Rhoden; Don Quarrie; Bert Cameron; Asafa Powell. Not forgetting the women: Merlene Ottey; Grace Jackson; Juliet Cuthbert; Deon Hemmings; Cynthia Thompson, the 100 metres sprinter, the first Jamaican woman to reach an Olympics final and the first to break an Olympic record at the 1948 London Olympics.

And the coaches, Glen Mills and Stephen Francis, who oversaw the two leading Jamaican clubs – MVP and Racers. 'You have a lot of brilliant people in Jamaica,' Mark Ricketts told me. 'Mills and Francis are brilliant people. Francis is very well read and intelligent: a genius.' I had spotted Francis – who coached Powell, Shelly-Ann Fraser-Pryce and others – at Champs, sitting watching in the main stand, wearing a wide-brimmed hat. He was even bigger than Mills, and more serious and intimidating-looking.

'Mills is withdrawn,' Ricketts continued. 'He's so quiet, unassuming. You see him sitting up there.' He pointed to Mills in his favourite seat, high in the stands. 'He wanted to be an athlete and recognised he wasn't going to be an athlete, so he has studied everything. Like a surgeon. Like a neurosurgeon. Like a brilliant scientist. He has done everything to be the best sprint coach in the world.'

In Jamaica I wanted to meet as many of the key people as possible, though I ended up travelling to the Caribbean more in hope than expectation. I realised, having tried to set up some interviews, that this is not how they operate in Jamaica. A typical conversation would go like this:

'When did you say you get here?'

'Next week.'

'Call me next week, man.'

That was fine. Until a phone call on a Monday, attempting to arrange a meeting for later in the week, would go like this:

'What day?'

'Wednesday.'

'Call me Wednesday, man.'

There was a certain thrill, a sense of exhilaration, to this. I had much to do, lots of people to see in Kingston. But my first stop after Champs was the countryside. I was heading to the other side of the island, to rural Trelawny, home to the Maroons, the tribe of people who escaped slavery and survived on their wits, strength and endurance in the lush, mountainous and harsh interior. And also home to Usain Bolt.

3

BOLT'S OWN COUNTRY

William Knibb knew, long before Jamaica at large was aware,
the special talent it had in its hands.
Letter to the *Jamaica Observer*, 2 April 2014

I stop the car, wind down the window and say: 'Mr Bolt's house?'

The routine is repeated five times. Each time an arm extends, a finger points, instructions are offered. The first time it is a woman emerging from a shop that I think might be Wellesley Bolt's general store, not realising that there are identical stores – huts opening on to the road – every few hundred yards. The second is a Rastafarian youth sitting on a tree stump. The third and fourth are workers who have stopped for a break. Then there's a man walking along the road holding a machete. 'It in Coxheath,' he says.

Coxheath is out the other side of Sherwood Content, just before the bumpy road peters out altogether. When I arrive at the Bolt family residence, I realise that stopping and asking was unnecessary. You can't miss it. It's the only house enclosed by a large and recently added wall, with an iron gate, and, on the roof, an enormous satellite dish.

The gate is open, and at the end of the small path, the front door to the house is ajar, the sound wafting out that of a football match on television.

As soon as I appear at the gate, Mr Wellesley Bolt materialises, filling the doorway. He steps out to the porch, waves me forward, extends his hand and invites me to sit on one of the two chairs. He is wearing a baseball cap, and a T-shirt with a picture of his son on it. 'Bolt', it says.

Wellesley says that neighbours regularly drop by to watch games beamed in from England. As for Usain, he lives in Kingston and returns home when training allows. Given how hard he trains, that isn't often, says his father. We sit down, the door remains open, and it's possible to make out the outline of a man on the sofa. Is it . . .?

The thirty-minute drive to Sherwood Content from Falmouth, the coastal town where Bolt attended secondary school, plunges you deep into lush forest. Initially you follow a river on one of the sinuous, heavily potholed roads that dominate the interior, and which make driving so treacherous. (That, and the driving habits of some locals. Another hazard is that they drive on the left in Jamaica, except on blind corners. 'Undertakers love careless overtakers' reads one billboard.)

From the air, much of the island looks uninhabitable. Apart from its pale, sandy fringes it seems to be mainly thick green tropical forest on triangular mounds that resemble moguls on a ski run (for giants). The forest is at its densest in the north-west, in and around Trelawny. This is Cockpit Country, where, most famously, the Maroons camped out. A popular if unproven theory is that the people of Trelawny are endowed with the toughest, strongest and, evidently, the fastest genes of all Jamaicans due to the fact that so many of their ancestors survived in such hostile terrain.

It seems to be borne out by the number of athletes who come from here. As well as Bolt, there is Warren Weir, Steve Mullings, Veronica Campbell-Brown, Omar Brown, Voletta Wallace, Lerone Clarke, Inez

Turner and Debbie-Ann Parris, with Merlene Ottey and Yohan Blake from the neighbouring parish. Together they come from an area with a population of 74,000. That's the size of Carlisle. It's the same number of people as live in a *square kilometre* of Manhattan Island.

When you get to Sherwood Content, it would be impossible to be unaware that it is home to Usain Bolt. A large white triangular sign has a hand-drawn cartoon of Bolt doing his famous pose. And beneath the picture, the message:

Welcome to Sherwood Content
Home of the World's Fastest Man
Usain Bolt
World record: 9.58 in (100m) 19.19 in (200m)

As you drive through the village, there's another big white board, with another almost passable likeness of Bolt, same pose. 'Welcome to Usain Bolt Apparel Gift Shop' this one reads. This is the home of his Aunt Lilly, whose Bolt-themed gift shop opened a few months before my visit.

Just before you reach the scattered houses that make up Sherwood Content, home to a community of 1,500 people, you pass Waldensia Primary School, a collection of colourful buildings with corrugated tin roofs perched on a grassy hill. And on a small clearing before the slope begins to rise, seven parallel lines are scorched into the grass: Bolt's first six-lane running track. Not an oval – there isn't space – but a straight, no longer than fifty metres.

Sherwood Content seems like a sleepy place where, ironically, given that its fame now rests on being home to the fastest man in history, nothing happens very quickly. One house might have a satellite dish that wouldn't look out of place at NASA headquarters, but the water still comes from the local river rather than through pipes and is stored in large drums in people's gardens. The Bolt association has brought new sports facilities (a multi-purpose court, branded with Digicel, the

phone company and Bolt's long-time sponsor), but there is still no mains water, despite Bolt himself highlighting the issue, Red Stripe donating £100,000, and pipes being laid: they've been arguing for it for more than forty years. According to local legend, it worked for one week only – the week that followed Bolt's world records at the 2009 world championships in Berlin.

Wellesley Bolt is tall. Not as tall as his son. 'I'm six-three,' he says. 'My father was tall. I am not sure how tall was my father, but taller than I am. So was the mother's father.' He frequently refers to his wife,

Jennifer, as 'the mother', and to his son simply as 'Bolt'. It's a Saturday, so Jennifer is at church. She's a Seventh-day Adventist.

You don't imagine that Wellesley has changed with his son's success. The Bolts still live in the same house, doing the same things, and Wellesley seems as laid-back as the youth I passed sitting on the tree stump. But life is different in some ways. 'Well, financially, yes, it has changed,' he says. 'Because it was difficult when he was going to school. I was working in the coffee industry, then I was made redundant and so I travel abroad, do some work, come back to put him to school.

'But things has changed. The house wasn't this big.' He flashes a grin and leans back to take it in – it's a large house, perhaps not the biggest in the village, where there are several old Victorian houses, but it's no mansion. Bolt's neighbours are, according to Wellesley, relaxed about having such a famous, and wealthy, family in their midst. There's the wall around the property. But the gate is wide open.

Wellesley was the victim of crime on one occasion, in Falmouth in June 2013, when thieves broke into his Toyota pickup and stole $4,000. But he seems perfectly happy to welcome a stranger if not quite into his home, then at least on to his porch. (Aunt Lilly, who I visit later, is more circumspect. Initially, as she opens up her gift shop for the potential customer, she is friendly and chatty, but she becomes guarded on learning the visitor is a journalist. When I ask if she travels to watch her nephew run, she replies: 'I stay home and keep the journalists away.')

'We have the dish,' Wellesley continues, gesturing towards the roof as the football commentary drifts out to the porch (Chelsea vs Stoke City). 'And I have two vehicle. A motorbike. So, you know. A lot of changes.'

When his son attended Waldensia Primary School, Wellesley went and watched him compete at sports day. 'Ricardo Geddes, he's the only person who beat him at school,' he recalls. 'And he cry, he cry when Ricardo beat him. I said to him, "Don't worry, man, you'll get him the next time round." And he put that in his head and Ricardo never beat him again.'

Wellesley continues: 'I would go and watch the kids, and think, Hey, he's winning almost all the races. Probably this guy may have some talent. Time goes by, and at twelve, I realised he was doing well at track. He was awarded a track scholarship to William Knibb' – the high school in Falmouth. Was it a big decision to send his son away? 'Well, he has to go somewhere. He has to travel from here to somewhere: William Knibb or Clark's Town or Wakefield. But William Knibb was the closest, so he accepted the scholarship.'

That meant daily taxi rides. Apparently Mr Bolt would wake his son at 5.30 a.m. 'Yes,' he nods, 'I don't believe in lateness to school. You go to school and you must get every ounce of your lesson.' Wellesley has an older son and a daughter, each to a different mother, but he kept a very close eye on his younger son, turning up in Falmouth randomly and unannounced. 'I always go to William Knibb once per week to see him train,' he says. 'In the early part he would try to skip training sometimes to go and play those video games in Falmouth. So I always had to be on top of that.'

He kept on top of that by not telling Bolt when he would turn up. 'After a while he realised that's what I was doing.' Wellesley slaps his hands together. 'He couldn't take the chance. Coz I was vicious, then.'

What was the punishment when Wellesley caught his son skipping school or training? 'I would strap him. Because I told him, "It's difficult to find money to send you to school." He was wasting that. He didn't like it. But now he say I'm the best father. He said if I was the type of father who let him do that, probably he wouldn't be where he is now.'

For a thirteen-year-old boy from rural Trelawny, Falmouth represented the bright lights, the big city.

I went to Falmouth a couple of days earlier. It's a twenty-mile drive up the coast from Montego Bay, Jamaica's second biggest city and a busy, bustling place, popular with tourists. The road to Falmouth is dominated by large luxury resorts, where security guards prowl the grounds and patrol the gates, with the beach divided up and enclosed by fences. Presumably to keep the locals out.

You turn off the main highway at a junction marked with a huge billboard showing Bolt from behind, topless, arms outstretched against a backdrop of the Jamaican flag. 'Living Legend', it reads: an advert for Digicel. Ten minutes later you enter the town of Falmouth, the capital of Trelawny Parish, and it's like stepping back in time. It resembles a nineteenth-century film set, with dusty, bumpy roads, crumbling buildings and hand-painted signs above the shops. You half expect to find horses and carts instead of cars.

As I drove into Falmouth, there was another sight, one that was utterly incongruous. Sitting in the harbour, towering over the town, was the *Freedom of the Seas*: one of the world's largest cruise ships, capable of holding over 3,500 passengers. Two days later, there were two of these Caribbean cruise behemoths moored in the harbour. That should have meant up to 6,000 visitors, yet the streets of Falmouth were virtually empty.

There are market stalls, shops and restaurants, all empty. Locals beckon you to their stalls or into their shops, not aggressively, but with an air of desperation. An old man with white dreadlocks and gold teeth sneered when I said 'No thank you' to his offer of accompanying me to the shop selling Falmouth's best jerk chicken. 'This is Jamaica,' he pleaded. 'People friendly here. Don't be unfriendly.' He continued shouting as I walked away. But he was right – people were friendly, though many seemed to have given up and sat slumped in the shadows, escaping the heat. It was a mystery. Where were the tourists?

It was as if the clock had stopped around 1810, when Falmouth had its heyday as a busy port. In one direction went sugar and rum to Britain; in the other came slaves from Africa: up to thirty boats a day sailing in and out of the harbour. The town, built on a grid system similar to New York's,[1] boasts the finest Georgian architecture in the Caribbean, the *pièce de résistance* being the courthouse, the first building you would see when you arrived in Falmouth by sea. Not a coincidence, perhaps.[2]

Close to the courthouse is Market Street. This is where Ben Johnson lived before moving to Toronto when he was fifteen. It's one of the main streets in Falmouth, with shops and businesses as well as homes. The businesses are eclectic: there's a 'Miracle Medical Lab' (which might have been of interest to Johnson in his drug-fuelled pursuit of glory), as well as a 'Dr C. A. L. Behasse, Clinical Christian Psychologist'.

I had arranged to meet Devere Nugent, pastor of the William Knibb Memorial Baptist Church: the man who spotted Bolt's talent, and who, as Bolt says in his autobiography, bribed him with food ('jerk chicken, roasted sweet potatoes, rice and peas') as he encouraged him to swap cricket, which he loved, for athletics, towards which he was initially indifferent.

On the phone, Nugent had told me to meet him across from the church in the William Knibb Educational Centre. But it appears to be a building site, all bare concrete and exposed metal rods, with workmen adding a second floor. On closer inspection, however, the ground floor is intact – and in here, despite the noise and commotion overheard, it is business as usual.

The pastor's office is in a small room in the corner of a big hall, where I wait while Nugent finishes a meeting. He is well turned out in jeans and a Ralph Lauren shirt, and when I am called to see him,

---

1 Falmouth was different in one respect: it had piped water before New York. The town had the first piped water in the western hemisphere, introduced in 1799, which only makes the lack of water in Sherwood Content and other rural villages seem more ridiculous.

2 As well as being a major slave port, Falmouth also became a focal point for revolt. A leading abolitionist in the first half of the nineteenth century was the man whose name now adorns the church and the high school, the Baptist minister William Knibb.

he explains that the building we are in hosts an academy, which he set up four years ago. They hold evening classes for schoolchildren wanting extra tuition in, as the sign outside indicates, 'Math, English, Business, Accounts, Human & Social Biology, Social Studies, Physics, Chemistry, and others on demand'. Students attend these classes in their own time – the academy is entirely voluntary, but they struggle to accommodate all the young people who want to come. Hence the extension.

Like Bolt, Nugent comes originally from Sherwood Content. He also went to the same secondary, William Knibb Memorial High School. But he was never an athlete. 'In my mind I was,' he tells me, 'but as a child I grew up with bronchitis and because of that my mother never allowed me to exert myself too much physically. But I grew to love track and field when I got to high school.'

Charismatic and engaging, Nugent continues: 'You know, Usain Bolt is not our first Olympian; neither is he the first William Knibb past-student to have made the 100 metres finals of the Olympics. There's a guy, I don't know if you've ever heard of him, named Michael Green.'

Green, who made the 100 metres final in the 1996 Olympics, was a few years older than Nugent. A new coach also started at the school while Nugent was a pupil there. Pablo McNeil was an ex-Olympian who ran in the Jamaican 4x100 metres team that was fourth in Tokyo in 1964. 'When Pablo came to William Knibb I would sit behind the auditorium,' says Nugent, 'and watch him evening after evening just taking the students through their paces. I began to have an appreciation for that.'

When he finished high school, Nugent returned to Sherwood Content to work as a teaching assistant at Bolt's primary, Waldensia. 'I knew Bolt from when he was a baby,' he says. 'No, before – I've known Bolt from when his mother was pregnant.'

He began to look after the sports programme at Waldensia. It was a big school, 300 pupils from six up to fifteen, and Nugent's goal was the district athletics championships, which they won. But the school

then downgraded to a primary, losing the older pupils. It meant that
Nugent began to take an interest in the eight-year-old Usain Bolt,
who was part of the cricket team but didn't play because he was too
young. 'The next year, he was a Grade 4 student and he was batting
at number three with the Grade 6 boys. He was my gully fielder and I
remember it like yesterday, for two reasons – his height and his athletic
abilities. He could cover that span, that area, in absolutely no time and
for me had the best square cut. For a schoolboy he had one of the best
square cuts that I have seen.'

Bolt played cricket in the first part of the year and did track and
field in the second. According to Nugent, he was 'a decent athlete
and he liked the competition'. Nugent encouraged the rivalry with his
classmate, Ricardo Geddes. 'That for me created the passion inside of
him to not allow anybody to beat him.' He admits that he did bribe
him with food. It was a way, he says, of saying: 'Give me everything
you have, lay it all on the track.' And Bolt did. He had boundless
energy. 'That fella never really walked as a child, not a day in his life.
He ran to school, he ran to the shop, he ran, he ran. He had a wheel,
one of those bicycle wheels where the spokes were removed and he
would run it with a stick.'

Nugent coached Bolt until he left for theological college at the end
of Bolt's penultimate year at primary school. Despite not being around,
he kept in regular contact with the family and took a keen interest in
Usain's schooling. Bolt's father told him he was thinking of sending
Usain to Cedric Titus school in Clark's Town. Nugent advised against
it. 'I told him, "No you cannot send him to Cedric Titus." Cedric
Titus never had, in my mind, a decent enough sport programme. The
only school in the parish that had a decent programme at the time
was William Knibb. So I said to him, "Let me speak with the coach at
William Knibb." That would have been Pablo at the time.

'I went to Pablo and asked whether or not he would take a look at
him. The next day Pablo had a look at him and got him into school.'

*

Searching through the records of Champs, the first mention of Bolt is in 2000. He was thirteen, running for William Knibb in the Class 3 (youngest) category, and he placed fifth in the 200 metres in 24.03. First was a local rival, Keith Spence, who went to Cornwall College, along the coast in Montego Bay. (These days, Spence is a fitness instructor in a private gym in Kingston.) Otherwise, Champs was notable not for the debut of a boy named Bolt, but for crowd trouble during the medley relay: 'A melee in the bleachers splashed spectators on to the track.'

The following year, 2001, now in Class 2, Bolt was seventh in the 400 metres in 51.16. Veronica Campbell, another sprinter from Trelawny, was the standout performer, winning the girls' sprint double. Still a schoolgirl, she was, incredibly, already an Olympic medallist, having been a member of the 4x100 metres relay team that won silver in Sydney the previous year. She was also the junior world champion over 100 and 200 metres.

Finally, in 2002, in his all-white William Knibb kit, Bolt tasted victory at Champs. The meeting was held not at the National Stadium, which was being refurbished for the world junior championships in July, but at G. C. Foster College in Spanish Town, along the road from Kingston.

The star of the meeting was Steve Mullings, yet another Trelawny product, who won the sprint double in his final Champs before heading to the US and a career as a professional. Bolt, 'the gangly William Knibb Memorial product, was almost as good [as Mullings]', reads *Champs 100*, the commemorative book. Bolt was denied a possible 400 metres record when a power cut stopped the electronic timing. He was hand-timed at 47.4 seconds – the Champs record was 47.49. In the 200 metres he equalled the record, winning in 21.61. Interviewed afterwards, he said: 'I train hard but not as hard as you would expect from one doing such fast times at my age.'

Then, as now, a record at Champs had the whole country buzzing. Already they were asking: what could this kid do at the world juniors, to be held on Jamaican soil, at the National Stadium, just four months later?

Lorna Thorpe, head of sport at William Knibb, realised early that in Bolt the school had a major talent on its hands. She had seen him run at the local primary school championships, held on the grass track at the high school he would later attend. 'I was introduced to him, a tall, lanky young man,' she says.

Thorpe was head of sport at William Knibb for thirty-four years and retired recently. She now works for the Member of Parliament for North Trelawny, Patrick Atkinson QC, Jamaica's Attorney General and a member of one of the country's two main political parties, the (left-leaning) People's National Party. I meet her in the PNP's Falmouth office, around the corner from the William Knibb Memorial Church, where she sits behind a desk, showing admirable patience in dealing with the issues, complaints and gripes of an ever-renewing line of local people. Judging from those in the waiting room, they include some of Falmouth's most colourful characters.

Thorpe speaks about Bolt with motherly affection – Bolt has described her as his second mother – and, in her gentle way, shrugs off the wayward behaviour that could earn him a beating from his father. 'That's any teenager. When you're always at training and you see your friends doing something else – football, basketball – you want to be part of that. So sometimes Usain would run away from track training just to be with some of his friends, to play different games.'

Being responsible for the sports programme at William Knibb meant Thorpe had to 'make sure that they go to training, they get their meals, they get their uniform, their running spikes. I was always there for them, to hear their complaints and make sure whatever they were supposed to get, they get it.' She was also Bolt's form teacher. 'The bond get closer and closer. He would come for advice. I would encourage him: about track and field, outside of track and field. Having that relationship with him, telling him that the sky's the limit,

I was always there. We still share that relationship. I am in touch with him a lot. He comes back when he can. Holidays, he comes back, visit his parents, stays at home, like any normal person.'

Bolt was a pupil who needed additional support, the school thought. As his athletic talent shone more brightly, he struggled to balance training and school work. The principal, Margaret Lee, tried to find him a mentor. She approached a former pupil, Norman Peart. 'As the principal saw it, we had this special one, and she wanted to make sure he was on the right path,' Thorpe explains. But Peart resisted the overtures from his old school. He had finished college in Kingston and returned to nearby Montego Bay to work in the tax office. When I speak to Peart, he tells me, 'I was single, no kids, and the principal called me one day. "I hear you're down this side of the island. Why don't you come and help the team?"

'I said, "No, I'm finished work at five o'clock. You'll be finished training then."' But Lee didn't give up. A few weeks later she called Peart again. 'She said, "There's this special one. Very talented. I want you to help him because I want him to get a scholarship." She wanted him to get a scholarship to the States.' This time Peart said: 'OK, I'll help this guy.'

But first he called one of his old teachers, still at the school. 'Is this guy OK?' asked Peart. 'Because I don't want to fight with no kid now.'

'No, no, he's fine,' he was told. 'Quite humble.'

Peart is thirteen years older than Bolt. Did they connect? 'Erm, no,' he laughs. 'Not really. He wasn't a talker . . . then. He saw me more as a second dad. I let him do things his dad didn't.'

Mainly Peart helped him with his school work. 'He did OK in his studies but had his troubles. I didn't realise when I got to him, but I don't think he was ready to go to college, for more reasons than one. But pretty much the big decisions for him came within twelve months of knowing him, because I met him in February of 2002' – a month before his success at Champs, and five months before his first major meeting: the world junior championships in Kingston.

Thorpe says that she didn't ever believe that going to a US college would be an option for Bolt, even if the principal thought otherwise. She is adamant that he would never have become the athlete he became if he had left Jamaica. American colleges started approaching him; sending brochures, care of the school. Most ended up in a drawer in Thorpe's desk – some might still be there, she says – or in the bin. 'As soon as they come he would pass them to me. He just did not want to leave Jamaica. He loves Jamaica.'

It was July 2002 when Bolt announced his talent to a wider audience, though the most passionate one was packed into the National Stadium in Kingston. The stands were predictably full, the bleachers bouncing – unusual for a world junior championships. And on the new track, in lane three for the final of the 200 metres, was the home favourite: the Champs hero.

The TV camera panned along the eight finalists, but leapt up when it reached Bolt's lane and found only his chest. He looked about a foot taller than the other athletes. Already six-three (though accounts vary about his height at the time; in some he is already six-five) and with the build of a bean sprout, he was just a frame, with no muscle.

Bolt was introduced to the crowd. There was no showboating. He cracked his knuckles. He looked serious and nervous, even a little afraid, rocking from side to side, fidgeting, unable to keep his hands still. But when the race started, he was quickly up, stretching to full height, accentuating his height advantage – though it seemed like a disadvantage on the bend as he drifted to the outside of his lane, as though his head, which was cocked to the right, was pulling him.

Entering the straight, he was alongside the runner on his inside. He was ungainly, ragged, head tilted back as the runner in lane five, Brendan Christian of Antigua and Barbuda, began to challenge.

Christian was catching; he almost drew level. But Bolt held on, winning in 20.51. At fifteen, against runners up to three years older, he was the junior world champion – the youngest in history.

He was watched from one of the boxes at the back of the stand by the country's prime minister, P. J. Patterson, a former Calabar High School pupil and keen athletics fan. Patterson was sitting with Donald Quarrie. 'I said to Quarrie, "You've got to take this fella under your wing," ' Patterson recalls. 'Because if he can run a curve like that he'll be a world beater.'

Now it wasn't just colleges that were after Bolt, but big companies too. Another observer was a French marketing executive from a German company. Pascal Rolling was there representing Puma because the sportswear brand was interested in aligning itself with Jamaica; or more accurately with the Jamaican culture and lifestyle. They were on the verge of signing deals with the Jamaica Athletics Administrative Association (JAAA) and Jamaica Olympic Association. 'At the same time,' says Rolling, 'we were looking for an athlete we could use in our communications.'

And there before him was a fifteen-year-old world junior champion who, after winning, seemed in his celebrations to forge a bond with the crowd. There was a connection there, thought Rollings. 'I had seen Usain before, but at the world championships he not only made the show on the track but also off the track, after the race. I thought, This is the perfect ambassador to represent our new relationship with Jamaica.'

They didn't set out to sign someone so young, Rollings continues: 'It wasn't a specific age we had in mind, just someone who could represent the brand. Usain, with his charisma off the track, was a perfect representative. You didn't have to be a genius to see that this guy has market potential because of his size and how he dominates the junior level. But equally important for us was the fact that this fifteen-year-old kid had such a connection to the public and a way to entertain.'

Jamaica attracted Puma because the sportswear company was interested in more than sport and elite performance. 'We were balanced between sport and lifestyle,' Rolling says. 'Jamaica had a culture of track and field since the late forties, and consistently produced top sprinters, but we were interested in the culture of Jamaica, too. They are everybody's second favourite team at the Olympics, aren't they?'

Within a few months of his world junior title, Bolt had signed with Puma. Lorna Thorpe recalls, 'When he signed his first contract he put in a clause where a certain amount of goods would come to William Knibb each year. From 2002 the school has not bought a pair of spikes because of Usain Bolt.'

Bolt was far from being the first world-class sprinter to emerge from his corner of Jamaica, but his junior world title was the biggest thing to happen to Falmouth since Ben Johnson won the Olympic 100 metres in Seoul in 1988. Thorpe recalls that night well. 'Oh boy, that was a night. I know Ben Johnson quite well; his father, his sisters. When the holidays are here, he comes. William Knibb is where Ben come and train, still.'

Thorpe said I should visit the high school. It's on the outskirts of town, a collection of purple-and-cream buildings – the school colours – with a guardhouse at the entrance, and a sign: 'Ignorance Enslaves. Knowledge Liberates.' I had been told to visit during lunch break; somebody from the sports department would see me then.

Gloria Grant appears, munching a sandwich. She graduated from G. C. Foster College in 1985 and coaches the girls' athletics team, but she remembers Bolt, especially his first Champs. 'He was late for one of his races, so he ran from where we stayed. I think that was why he did not win.' They were staying, as they usually do, in the theological college, close to the stadium.

She plays down the school's part in making Bolt. 'Usain was just natural. He just developed. He used to hide from training sometimes, because Pablo McNeil took training very, very serious. He was firm with them; he would push them. He was a disciplinarian. But I don't think Usain was pushed after a while, because he was motivated.' McNeil, who refused to let Bolt see his stopwatch when he was training, died in 2011. He had been in poor health after suffering a stroke in 2007 (he had been working on a book, *The Bolt of Lightning and Me*, which has never been published). Bolt had another coach at William Knibb, Dwight Barnett, who is said to be at another school in Jamaica – strangely, nobody I spoke to seemed to know which one.

I ask Gloria if there are currently any promising young athletes at the school: anyone to follow in Bolt's footsteps. There are some boys nearby, all in the khaki uniform that every Jamaican schoolboy wears, with purple-and-white epaulettes denoting William Knibb. She looks up. 'Come here, Ben!'

One of the boys comes over. 'Hi, Ben,' I say.

'Bent,' Gloria corrects me.

'Christopher Bent, sir,' the boy says. He says that he's a sprinter too. How did he get on at Champs? 'It wasn't that impressive.' He speaks hesitantly. 'It could have been better. I have to work on certain areas. Go back to the drawing board.'

He was fourth in his heats in the 200 metres, so didn't qualify, though his time of 22.34 was nothing to be ashamed of. And still he hoped that athletics would be his passport to a college in the US or Canada. 'I would like to get to a college overseas to do studies and track and field.'

Bent met Bolt when he returned to the school to donate a bus in December 2012. 'But I've not had a conversation with him. It's a great thing, you know. Usain Bolt has given us a lot of motivation. The way he performs, he's a great man to look up on in terms of achievement.'

Bent seems as reserved as Bolt is outgoing: what does he make of his showmanship? 'I don't really enjoy his showman stuff. His performances are great, that's what I like.' He seems a little embarrassed about Bolt's excesses, which doesn't surprise me. Jamaican schools like William Knibb were modelled on British public schools, and many of the traditions – the deference, politeness, restraint – seem to have been preserved.[3]

Gloria Grant regards Bolt's pre-race and post-race exhibitions with the kind of amused bemusement that a parent might demonstrate towards a child showing off. 'Oh, his antics!' She explodes with laughter. 'I think that is what helps to calm him down. When he does that, I think he gets more relaxed. But Usain wasn't like that at school.'

Back in Devere Nugent's office, across the road from the William Knibb Memorial Church, the pastor shares a secret: 'I have a theory that I have not necessarily brandished about the place.' Then he leans forward, putting his elbows on the desk. 'Usain went through something that a lot of folks did not go through. If you are a doctor practising surgery every day for fifty years, after fifty years you are going to be good at what you are doing. Well, since this fella has been about eight or nine years old, he has been running at the highest level of his age group.

'Since he has been eight years old he would have been running at the National Stadium every year. I don't think there's another athlete in the Jamaican set-up right now with that kind of experience under their belt. I don't think there is.' These were the formative years, says Nugent. 'Because if you look at him as a [sixteen-year-old] Class 1 athlete, he's a very lanky fellow with no muscles, which indicates that up to that point he was just running off raw talent: raw, raw talent.

'There's a second aspect to him that is under-discussed,' Nugent

---

3 In *Beyond a Boundary*, his memoir of growing up in Trinidad in the early part of the twentieth century, C. L. R. James writes: 'I learnt and obeyed and taught a code, the English public-school code.' This code manifested itself in particular in sport: 'We lived in two worlds. Inside the classrooms the heterogeneous jumble of Trinidad was battered and jostled and shaken down into some sort of order. On the playing field we did what ought to be done.' That translated as fair play, sportsmanship, respect for authority: something I observed at Champs, even if it was not always apparent elsewhere in the 'heterogeneous jumble' of Jamaica.

continues. 'I call it a reverse preparation. When he was in primary school he ran 100 and 150s at his age. So when he went to William Knibb he went feeling in his heart that he was a 100 metres runner. But the coach, looking at his height and his physique, decided that this fellow is not suited for the 100. So he takes him from the 100 and pushes him up to the 400 and says, "Now you've got to run the 400 or the 200." But in his heart and in his belly as a child he's always been a 100 metres runner.'

Running 400s built a foundation of strength and endurance that Bolt wouldn't have had if he'd always focused on the shorter events, Nugent believes. 'I think what that did was to somehow – and while I cannot prove it from a scientific perspective, it's just my layman's theory – develop him in another kind of a way. He always had the speed, but that kind of endurance built up the muscles, developed him in a kind of different way. Which is the reason he does not break down as easily as most sprinters.'

Yet, as several people observed, Bolt was not at one of the major schools. Although exposed to the highest level of schoolboy competition in Jamaica, he was at a school that did not measure itself by how well it did at Champs, perhaps for one simple reason: they had no chance of winning. 'There was a big to-do at one stage because when he began to be seen as a good athlete, some schools in Kingston wanted him,' Nugent says. The likes of Calabar and Kingston College were sniffing around, trying to recruit him, but Nugent felt that he would be better off staying where he was. 'I explained it in this way: 1988 boys' championship, Daniel England, Calabar, is in the 100 metres finals. Michael Green of William Knibb is in the 100 metres finals. Michael Green runs eighth in the final. Daniel England wins. But more than that, Daniel England won that year the 100, the 200, the 400, he won the 4x100 and the 4x400 for Calabar. Jump to 1996: Michael Green is in the Olympic finals in Atlanta. Daniel England is yet to make an Olympic team.'

When approaches were made by the big Kingston schools, Nugent continues, 'I told Bolt's father, "If you are going to send him to a school in Kingston he is going to board with somebody else. You don't know what he does, where he's going."'

He says he wasn't worried about Bolt going off the rails or falling in with the wrong crowd. Despite perceptions, he was always level-headed. 'A lot of people will look at him and see him playing around and even behaving as if he's an imbecilic person. He's not – he's a very disciplined guy. If he respects you he gives you 110 per cent. If you have not earned his respect, you can't get anything out of him. To this very day, even though he's a big superstar, when he sees me he still says "Mr Nugent" as if he was a student of mine. Still says "Mr", and he's still very humble and cordial with me. Even with the colossal-ness of his . . .'

Nugent can't find the word, but he adds that Bolt's success can be attributed to three things: talent, parents and discipline. 'I don't think he understood his talent and that probably was a good thing. Because very often when they know how good they are, they see the light even before they reach it.'

You wonder if there is a fourth factor, too. The coaches and teachers who worked with the young Bolt, then passed him along to the next one, like a sprinter handing over a baton. Nugent and Thorpe, both formative influences, come across as fundamentally decent, sensible people; moreover, people whose lives are devoted to helping others – it is what they still do, sitting in their offices, dealing with others' problems.

These days, Nugent is too busy with the church and his academy to do any sports coaching, which is a source of regret. 'It's something I've missed. Especially cricket coaching, because I think you get a chance to pass on valuable tips and not just about the game but about this game called life,' he says, adding that he enjoyed telling people 'they can', and 'watching the light bulbs come on in their heads'. It is often just a case of believing, he thinks, telling anecdotes about children he has helped make something of themselves by planting an idea in their heads – Bolt isn't his only success. 'We get so much opportunity I believe to help children believe in themselves,' Nugent says. 'I never understood it until a few years ago. One of my former students from Waldensia came to me and he said: "Sir, I want to thank you." And I said: "For what?" He said: "Do you remember the day you came to class? You came into the class and you began to tell us what you saw us doing in the future."

'And I said: "Yes, I remember," but I didn't remember what I told him. He said: "Yeah, you came in the class that day and you told me that you saw me as a businessman in my jacket and my tie going into my office to work. That was the day you put it in my head. So I did business in high school. I went to UTech [University of Technology in Kingston], I did business because you placed it in my head. Now I am working with Scotia Bank, where I have to wear my jacket and tie to my office." '

Before leaving Nugent to deal with the lengthening queue of people outside his office, all waiting in the hall with the building work still going on overhead, I ask him the question that's been bothering me about Falmouth. With two cruise ships in the harbour, why is the town deserted?

'Oh,' he says, 'that's a different thing.' For the first time he looks deflated and downbeat. What happened, he explains, is that Royal Caribbean International (a cruise company based in Miami) approached the town with a proposal: they would redevelop the old pier, which was dilapidated. The quid pro quo, the town assumed, was that the boats would sit there for days and the passengers would disembark. Local people were encouraged to open restaurants, shops and market stalls for all the tourists who would throng the old streets.

'I knew from day one,' Nugent says. 'I recognised that the persons who were leading the process have never been on a cruise ship, so they really never knew how a cruise ship would work. Now, when you pay

$600 for a cruise, it's all-inclusive, so why would people come into the town and pay more money?'

But it turned out to be worse than that. When the pier was redeveloped, shops and restaurants were built in what Nugent calls 'a demilitarised zone'. It's a mini-town, modelled on Falmouth, built in an enclosed area on the pier. 'It is literally a replica of the town of Falmouth. It is basically designed like Falmouth. It has the square and it has the . . .'

A fake Falmouth on the pier itself? 'On the pier itself. Ten acres. So the people on the boat don't really have to come into Falmouth.'

The shops and restaurants in the replica town are staffed not by locals but by employees of the cruise company. A fence keeps tourists in and locals out. As in the expensive resorts, fear is driven into tourists; it is fear that keeps them (and their money) within the confines of the hotels, the ships and the replica town. 'I can understand the security concerns,' Nugent says. 'But I think the days when ships are not in, the pier could be open even if it's at a cost. So that folks could walk over there and enjoy the aesthetics, even; just enjoy the aesthetics of the pier. The other problem is that there are not too many attractions in Falmouth.'

Well, other than the fact that it is where the fastest man in history went to school. Nugent says that the town – like Bolt himself – does not really appreciate what Bolt could and should mean to Falmouth. 'Those who come in on the boats and really want to see Jamaica are bussed out of the town,' he says sadly. 'Falmouth has become a dumping ground.'

It literally has: the boats dump their waste and stock up on water. How depressing, I say.

'We will overcome,' says the pastor as he stands to see me out.

4

THE BROTHERHOOD

There's no miracle in Jamaica. We've always been doing this.
Albert Corcho

The name was ubiquitous at Champs, sounding particularly resonant in the precise, lilting Jamaican accent of the stadium announcer, his emphasis on all three syllables: Cal-a-bar.

Calabar athletes looked a cut above the others in their green and black Puma kit. They were slick, professional, menacing – especially the captain, Romario McKenzie, who wore a black Batman mask throughout in homage to his older brother, Ramone, who used to do the same.

There was an air about Calabar. As Champs built towards its climax, they seemed to win virtually everything; they had momentum behind them on the track and in the stands, where their supporters were the loudest and most passionate. They had an aura that other schools lacked. I found myself intrigued, fascinated, impressed. By the final day I even found myself quietly rooting for Calabar.

I began to look into the school's history. Its athletics pedigree is astonishing. When Jamaica won a gold medal in the men's 4x400

metres at the Helsinki Olympics in 1952, three members of the team – Herb McKenley, Arthur Wint and George Rhoden – were from this one school. Since then there has been a steady stream, the legacy continuing all the way to the present day, with 200 metres runner Warren Weir, the bronze medallist at the London Olympics, the latest star alumnus. And yet, as I was repeatedly told at Champs, the current crop of schoolboy superstars may turn out to be the best yet: Javon 'Donkey Man' Francis, Michael O'Hara, fourteen-year-old Christopher Taylor, to name a few.

They were visited by Weir on the eve of Champs. It was dark and flash bulbs illuminated Weir, who wore a white Adidas tracksuit top as he addressed the athletes. Impossible to believe he was only twenty-four; he spoke with the authority of a veteran coach; with the motivational qualities of Martin Luther King. 'My favourite time of the year,' he said. He sounded serious and statesmanlike, and was confident enough to pause after important points, to let them sink in. 'Favourite time of the year, no matter how old or young you are.

'One thing we go out there for, and that's to win. To win. To win. To win. To win. To dominate. To crush them.' He said 'dominate' the way the stadium announcer said 'Calabar'. *Cal-a-bar, dom-in-ate.* 'To repeat also,' he continued, 'and carry on the legacy, the big legacy of *Cal-a-bar*. Win. *Dom-in-ate.* Make people inherit that this week – this weekend – nothing shy of that. Go out there and represent yourselves good . . . As Martin Luther says, be the best you can be. Never stop being that. The best sprinter, best middle distance, best hurdler. The best you can be.'

Weir was interrupted by a shout from the crowd, which was the cue for wild chanting, ending in the Calabar Lions' motto: 'The utmost for the highest.' The passion and intensity – the fervour – was comparable with that surrounding high school football in Texas, as depicted in the book *Friday Night Lights*, 'where high school football went to the very core of life'.

Two weeks after Champs, I meet Weir for lunch in one of the plush hotels in Kingston's business district. He is softly spoken, boyish-looking and seems even younger than twenty-four. He turns up with his girlfriend. She snuggles close to him, while he turns and speaks quietly to her at regular intervals. (Efforts to market Weir as 'the Weirwolf', not least by Weir himself, seem a bit ambitious. Similarly with Yohan Blake's nickname, 'the Beast'. Perhaps only Bolt has the profile and the personality to carry off such a nickname – the irony being that he is so transcendent he doesn't need one.)

Weir is one of the new breed of Jamaican athletes, those who eschewed the US colleges to live and train at home. He lives in a smart area in the Kingston hills overlooking the National Stadium, drives a nice car, has some of the trappings of modest wealth: expensive-looking watch, jewellery, smartphone. He is sponsored by Adidas, but, like most professional athletes, he is not a millionaire. The $40,000 that came with winning the Diamond League 200 metres title in 2013 would have been quite a windfall.[4]

Like Bolt and so many other top athletes, Weir comes originally from Trelawny. There is actually a small community in Trelawny called Calabar, where Calabar Theological College was established in 1839. It was named after the slave port in Nigeria; the community in Jamaica was close to Falmouth, one of the major ports of embarkation for the thousands of slaves shipped through the Middle Passage from Africa. In 1868, Calabar College moved to Kingston, and in 1912, Calabar High School was established in the city by two Baptist ministers for the sons of other ministers and for the ever-larger population of poor Jamaicans, many of them descendants of former slaves, living in ghettos – or garrisons, as some areas would eventually come to be known. In 1952, Calabar High School moved to its current grounds at the foot of Red Hills Road, in west Kingston.

It was here that Herb McKenley, the hero of Helsinki – still the only athlete ever to reach the finals of the 100, 200 and 400 metres at an Olympic Games – was head coach for more than thirty years. Here that he led the school to no fewer than eighteen Champs titles. And here that, upon his death in November 2007 at the age of eighty-five, his body lay in an open casket.

McKenley is the one they all talk about, yet his career as an athlete is only the beginning of the story. It is as a coach and motivator that he is recalled with even greater reverence. 'People tell you that if you go to your grave having not heard Herb in his final pep talk before boys' Champs, especially if he has a glimpse he can win, you haven't heard the best of Herb,' said Neville 'Teddy' McCook, one

---

4 How much athletes earn is shrouded in mystery with shoe deals generally undisclosed, with the exception of Usain Bolt's $10m-a-year from Puma. A 2014 survey by the Track & Field Athletes Association and the USATF Foundation revealed that more than 50% of athletes ranked in the world top 10 in their event earn less than $15,000 a year. It is worth putting that in the context of earnings in Jamaica, however, where the minimum wage is £31 per week and the average worker earns £2,600 a year.

of Jamaica's great sports administrators, who died in 2013. 'He saw his athletes right to the gate, telling them, "You can win, you can win, you can win."'

In his pre-Champs talks, McKenley would sometimes reduce himself to tears. 'The boys would realise that, they would see the tears trickle,' said McCook.

Warren Weir was McKenley's final gift to Calabar: one of the last athletes he recruited. 'Mr McKenley got me in 2001, when I was in primary school, then he got a stroke in the summer, so he was mainly in the background,' Weir tells me. 'I didn't get to know him personally, but the little words he spoke to me was very encouraging. No matter how down you were feeling he'd always have words of encouragement.'

The curious thing, says Weir, is that he was not an outstanding athlete at primary school. As well as Calabar, other leading schools, such as Kingston College, Wolmer's and St Jagos', have highly active recruitment programmes run by alumni, sometimes offering inducements (refrigerators, for example) for the parents of talented athletes. But no one showed much interest in Weir. 'I was pretty much a normal athlete, but Mr McKenley saw something.' He was a hurdler at the time rather than a 200 metres runner, but at Calabar, under head coach Michael Clarke, Weir began to blossom. He ran at Champs, experiencing the extraordinary atmosphere and finding it terrifying, but also inspiring. Where does it come from, I ask him: the tribalism, the intensity?

It comes from the high schools wanting 'bragging rights', he says. 'Everybody wants to be the top school. Even if you don't attend one of the top schools, you tend to be a fan of that school, because there's a hype and a certain tension. And that's what drives us Jamaicans to be so successful, because even after the high school level, we're still driving for that . . . bragging rights, or driving for that goal.'

Weir was at Champs in 2014, in a box at the back of the stand with his Racers clubmate Yohan Blake, watching some extraordinary performances. He is still processing what he saw. 'To see high school kids run 10.1 seconds [for 100 metres], 45-zeros [400 metres], the four-hurdles in 49; to see fourteen-year-olds running 21.7 [200 metres]; to see fourteen-year-olds running the four by one in 41 . . . that's really, really fast. Extremely fast. A fifteen-year-old ran 10.3. That's quick.'

But best of all, Calabar won. The school is like a fraternity, says Weir. And it endures; his status as a Calabar old boy seems even more important to him than his national identity, or his membership of Glen Mills's Racers Track Club. 'Every year I go back there, because I left maybe, like, four years, five years ago, and so there are still students there that I knew. I'm still familiar with some of the athletes, but even when I don't know anybody there, I'll still go back and support them, because it's like a brotherhood.'

He echoes McKenley, who said, in a documentary film made shortly before his death, that when he was approached to become a pupil at Calabar, the headmaster 'told me how important it was to have a sense of belonging to Calabar . . . that I should feel about Calabar the way I feel about my parents and brothers and sisters'. And yet, like Weir, McKenley did not strike many as a world-class athlete: he was consistently in the top two or three, but lost his first ten races at Champs.

There is footage in the film of one of McKenley's famous pre-Champs motivational speeches. What strikes you, apart from the logic of what he says, and the sense of morality underpinning it, is his sincerity – that, and the boys' rapt attention. 'Remember to do your best,' McKenley tells them. 'Your best does not necessarily have to be better than somebody else's. But your best is what you have. Your best today can be superseded tomorrow because of what you do between now and then. Your best in every way: in academics, your behaviour.'

Then he recites from memory (so not entirely accurately) his favourite quotation: 'Sports is an occupation of the whole man, for it not only develops the body but makes the mind, what, a more refined instrument for the search and attainment of truth and helps man to achieve love, the greatest of them all.'[5]

McKenley's speech is quite different to Weir's, with its emphasis on winning and 'crushing' the opposition. Yet there is the same idea of being 'the best you can be'. McKenley concludes: 'If you do those things, transfer them, then you will be such a great champion in every way. A champion who everyone will admire.'

There were extraordinary scenes at Calabar on the Monday morning after the school's third consecutive victory at 2014 Champs – their twenty-fourth success in total.[6] The celebrations got under way at 8 a.m., when the chairman of the school board, the Reverend Karl Johnson, addressed most of the 1,700 boys – plus parents, family and old boys – during morning devotion. There wasn't room for everybody in the chapel; they had to move outdoors, where the Mortimer Geddes trophy stood on a table draped in the green of Calabar. 'Ever so powerful, ever so strong,' Johnson told them, his voice rising. 'One, two, three, C'bar. Three, two, one, yow!' The address was greeted by a storm of cheers and vuvuzelas.

Then it was the turn of the principal, Albert Corcho, to speak from the stage. 'I am glad the media are here,' he said. 'We want to send a very strong message to all the other schools that participated at Champs that the Mortimer Geddes trophy will live at 61 Red

---

5 McKenley was paraphrasing Pope Pius XII's speech at the Sport at the Service of the Spirit Award in 1945: 'Sport, rightly understood, is an occupation of the whole man, and while perfecting the body as an instrument of the mind, it also makes the mind itself a more refined instrument for the search and communication of truth and helps man to achieve that end to which all others must be subservient, the service and praise of his Creator.'

6 They might have won more Champs titles, but in 1981, while leading, there was a scuffle during the medley relay, when athletes from Calabar and deadly rivals Kingston College clashed, prompting a track invasion by spectators. According to the book *Champs 100*, 'ugly pandemonium' ensued. Both schools were banned in 1982.

Hills Road.' More cheering; more blasts from the vuvuzelas. Corcho continued: 'It doesn't matter where athletes are imported from, one thing I can tell you is that the programme is the best programme in this side of the hemisphere.'

Romario McKenzie, the captain, in his Batman mask, introduced the winning team. 'It was a rough championship,' he said. 'After the first two days without a point, my phone kept ringing because persons wanted to know what was happening. The team was worried, I was worried, but as a leader you can't show signs of weakness, so I kept them motivated.' McKenzie then handed the microphone to Michael O'Hara, which was symbolic: O'Hara would take over as captain in 2015. But O'Hara, who struggled with injury at Champs, wasn't as composed as McKenzie. He began crying and couldn't speak. The microphone was handed back to McKenzie, who ran through some of the heroic performances by the Calabar Lions, saving the best until last, introducing the Donkey Man, Javon Francis, to huge cheers. Like O'Hara, Francis then burst into tears. It fell to his guardian, Andrea Hardware – also the team manager – to speak: 'I am the proud manager of this track team. I am the proud guardian of Javon Francis and I am the proud grandmother of Dejour Russell.' Russell was another promising young sprinter and hurdler.

The celebrations continued, and when I visited Calabar ten days later, there remained a lingering sense that something good had recently happened. There was a feeling of confidence and optimism about the place.

The Red Hills Road compound is on a dusty, arid expanse of land just off Washington Boulevard, the main arterial road that enters Kingston from the west, from Spanish Town, Jamaica's original capital. It was the scene of one of the island's most remarkable and bizarre recent episodes, with gunfights in 2010 involving the police and supporters of the powerful Kingston don Christopher 'Dudus' Coke.

Coke, wanted in the US for gun and drug trafficking, was believed to be protected by one of Jamaica's two political parties, the right-leaning Jamaica Labour Party. (At times it might perhaps have been more accurate to say that the party was protected by him.) Coke was the Don for the Tivoli Gardens garrison, about five miles from Calabar in west Kingston, but during a state of emergency dons and gunmen from other areas took on the police in sympathy with Coke, including men from a garrison near Calabar. At least seventy-three people were killed in a five-week US-led hunt for Coke, not to mention those who over many years were allegedly executed by the don in his makeshift jail, using a hatchet and a power saw. Yet like other dons, some of them still at large in Kingston today, Coke was a hero to many: a Robin Hood figure who redistributed his ill-gotten gains among the poor.

Coke was eventually caught at a routine roadblock, in a car driven by an evangelical priest. He was dressed in women's clothing, wig and all. He said he was on his way to the US Embassy to turn himself in. In 2012, he was sentenced by a New York court to twenty-three years in prison.[7]

Driving into the school compound, I negotiate my way past the guards at the entrance by saying I'm meeting the principal, and park near a green-and-cream building with a large sign. There are signs everywhere in Jamaica, warning against everything from unprotected sex to drunk driving, frequently in patois, often in graphic and blunt terms. The schools are no different. 'Calabar High School Dress Code', reads this one. 'No Setters (Rollers). No Spaghetti Straps. No Halter Tops. No Midriff Blouses/Shirts. No Tights, Shorts. No Low Cut Pants/Jeans.

7 During his trial, a link emerged between Coke and schools athletics – though not Calabar. Anthony Brown, a former assistant coach at St Jago, the Spanish Town school with its own great sprinting tradition, thanks to Yohan Blake, Nickel Ashmeade and others, told of a US visa racket between 1997 and 2001. Brown said that he charged $1,500–$3,000 to help people get visas through the athletics programme to travel to the US. The head coach at the time was Bert Cameron, Jamaica's 1983 world 400 metres champion. Cameron said he had no knowledge of the scheme.

No Bathroom Slippers. No Flip-Flops. No Handkerchief on Head/ Around Neck. No Merinos. No Vest. No Clothes Displaying Explicit Graphic Information. No Exposed Undergarment. No Bare Feet.' And underneath, the school motto: 'The Utmost for the Highest'.

I can see, beyond a high fence, the sports facilities: a field with isolated patches of grass and a dirt running track. The buildings are scattered and sand-coloured. Some used to be dormitories, but there are only fourteen boarders now. The pupils, all wearing uniform – the usual khaki, army-style, with Calabar-green epaulettes – stand in clumps, eyeing the stranger with curiosity.

The principal's secretary instructs me to take a seat in the reception area, telling me that Mr Corcho will see me soon. The Mortimer Geddes trophy takes pride of place in here, but it is in good company: the shelves sag with silverware; medals dangle from cup handles. A steady stream of people file in, all of them addressing me – 'Good morning, sir' – until eventually Mr Corcho appears: clean-cut, businesslike, in a tailored light tan suit, offering a universal 'Good morning' as he breezes past.

Once he has seen the other people who have been waiting, I am summoned. 'All right, what can I do for you?' says the principal as I enter his office. 'Welcome to Calabar.' Same lilting pronunciation as the stadium announcer: *Cal-a-bar*.

Corcho has only been at the school since May 2013, when the previous head, Austin Burrell, resigned after receiving death threats. That followed the fatal stabbing of a pupil, sixteen-year-old Narrio Coleman, during an argument with another student. The head of the local police force was angry, complaining that the school failed to report the incident: they learned of it from medical staff at Kingston Public Hospital. As for the death threats, the Ministry of Education took them seriously enough that Burrell, once removed, was only able to retrieve his belongings by sneaking back into the school.

Corcho was principal previously at Munro College, another school with a strong reputation for athletics. Munro have the advantage of boarding facilities, he explains, which means they can attract youngsters from abroad. 'It's something Calabar needs to do in the next couple of years. We have land on this compound.'

The school is not obsessed with athletics, he says, insisting that they strive hard to keep a healthy balance between sport and academic work.[8] But the recent success at Champs is reward for a strategy put in place four years ago. 'Let me give you some history,' Corcho says, bringing his hands together and relaxing into his leather chair. 'Before my time, four years ago, the board sat down. The school celebrated a hundred years two years ago and they wanted to do something long-lasting in terms of the centennial.

'The chairman sat with the coach and said, "Listen, we want to reorganise our programme: we want to win Champs." ' Calabar, in the period after Herb McKenley's death, seemed to lose its way – which only highlighted the great man's contribution. 'So,' continues Corcho, 'they sat and they crafted a programme. It's for five years. What you're seeing now is year three. You saw that we dominated the thing, but more so we dominated Class 3' – the youngest age group. *Cal-a-bar, dom-in-ate.*

The issue of recruiting talented athletes from beyond the Calabar catchment area, and indeed from beyond Kingston, is controversial. But Corcho says that it's just as likely that parents will approach Calabar looking for a place for their son. They call and say, 'We want our son, we want our nephew, to be part of the programme.' But it is true, he concedes, that the school 'may identify an athlete, and say, "Listen, Calabar is available if you're interested." But I can tell you that since Champs I've had about thirty, thirty-five people calling, sending letters, saying, "Listen sir, come September we want to be part of the programme." '

---

8 The academic attainment of boys in Jamaica is a national crisis, with dwindling numbers progressing to further education. According to Corcho, 'only about 10 or 15 per cent of the [Jamaican university] population is male'.

The brightest star in the Calabar stable is the Donkey Man, of course. Javon Francis was recruited. 'We facilitated that,' says Corcho, and he pays tribute to former pupils, the 'old boys' association', who 'do a fantastic job in offsetting some of the costs for boarding, if boys are coming from rural areas. They help provide for books, tuition, food. They do a lot of fund-raising. The old boys love track and field. If we weren't getting the support from our alumni, we wouldn't be able to perform the way we do.

'And we have a food programme. We try to make sure the boys get fed.'

What does the Puma sponsorship provide? I ask, and Corcho springs forward: 'Oh, let me tell you, I'm glad you brought that up. One of the reasons we have done so well is our main sponsors, Puma. Puma provide all the gear.' Calabar have a five-year contract with the German company (I find myself wondering how many British schools have such arrangements), and Corcho is confident it'll be renewed. 'Let me tell you,' he says, 'we have not purchased any gear for the track and field programme. We could not afford it. I feel for some of the other schools who compete at Champs because they don't all have sponsorship.

'We say to our boys, once you put on the Calabar top, it's not just about the school; you're representing our sponsors. I meet with them on a regular basis.'

For some reason, the latest Champs victory sparked the biggest celebrations yet at Calabar. Perhaps it was the quality of some of the individual performances – Francis beating Bolt's 400 metres record stands out – or that they had to come from behind. Corcho is still basking in the warm glow. 'The reception here was enormous,' he gushes. 'Enormous! We couldn't hold it in the chapel, we had to do it outdoors. Un-believable. They stood in the sun. Parents were there, friends, well-wishers, old boys, past teachers. Everybody came back. Because this victory was very special. There was talk that other schools would win. That it was going to be close. But we threw down the mantle and made it quite clear that we were not about to lose our title. We had some hiccups. Some never performed: Michael O'Hara; Javon in the 200. But it shows the depth of our Calabar programme.'

The highlight was certainly Francis's 400 metres. 'He said long before, he said, "Sir, I am going to break Usain Bolt's record. I am going for the record." I watched that race about ten or twelve times. From when the gun went off, you saw it was on his mind . . . On his mind from the moment the gun went. Proud of him.'

I head back out into the blazing sun and suffocating heat to meet one of the coaches, Omar Hawes. He scowls beneath his baseball cap but appears relaxed, peppering our conversation with 'Yeah, man', as most do here, but occasionally seeming exasperated. Then it becomes 'Yes, man!'

Omar has promised to talk me through the programme and show me the facilities. I meet him on the sports field; the running track is just about visible: an oval of scorched dark lines on a grass track without much grass. Really, it is bumpy, dry mud. 'The track,' I say to him, 'it's—'

'Bumpy,' he interrupts. 'Yeah, man. But this is where we start. What it does for us is show . . . Not blowing our own trumpets, but I think we're doing pretty well in terms of the techniques we use, and how we utilise what we have . . .'

He can say that again. It is frankly amazing to think that athletes who are already world class train here. Not just Javon Francis, but also Jason Livermore and Romario McKenzie, both now professionals who continue to train under the Calabar head coach, Michael Clarke.

Sometimes, when speaking to someone like Omar, you are brought up short. The smart Puma gear – the slick green-and-black vests, shorts, tracksuits and rucksacks – and the professional air of Calabar at Champs is misleading. 'A youngster can be running well but he doesn't have shoes,' Omar mentions. 'Once he earns the shoes, there's a lot of shoes for him from the sponsors . . .'

'Some of the kids don't have shoes?' I say.

'Yes, man!'

'Silly question?'

'YES, MAN! A lot of kids come here and they'll train, but they don't have shoes. But they want to be part of the Calabar team. And once they earn the stuff, we give it to them. Everything in life, you have to earn it.'

It must be an ambition to have better facilities, I say. 'Yes, man! For years. For years. We just need somebody to push it forward. Probably a Javon Francis. If he goes out, it can make a difference, because this is where it started for him. And Warren Weir is very, very passionate.'

I tell Omar that I met Weir, and that he said he was surprised to be recruited by Calabar; that he considered himself only modestly talented. 'Warren came here with a youngster by the name of Roger Tennant,' Omar explains. 'We went to Waterford [primary school] for Roger Tennant and he say he has a friend called Warren. Warren wasn't the prime target.' What happened to Tennant? 'He got an injury.'

Omar, himself a Calabar old boy, recalls McKenley with fondness and reverence, as they all do. 'He was more of a motivational person than a coach. A coach too. But he made persons do things they couldn't have done otherwise. Brought the best out of persons. He was great at bringing talent to the forefront; and he had an eye for talent.' And when he decided he wanted an athlete to come to Calabar, he 'went all out. He was a person that came to your house, Mr McKenley. You saw him at your church.'

When it came to recruiting Javon Francis, Omar says that he was identified at Junior Champs – the primary schools' championship. 'For the most part, he . . . how would I put it? He was a bit, um, more talented than the other athletes there; he stood out in terms of talent. But when most schools have gone to recruit him for their institutions their response to him was . . . inferior, because he wasn't as articulate as some persons. But,' Omar quickly adds, 'very talented.'

The plan with Francis was to develop him, to work on his running and his education. 'Over the years he has moved leaps and bounds in terms of how he answers a question,' says Omar. 'You speak to him; he can answer a question properly.'

I had spoken to Francis, the so-called Donkey Man. The nickname had in fact been the subject of some discussion in the *Jamaica Observer*, and even a little soul-searching (was it derogatory? demeaning?). Noting Francis's tough upbringing in Bull Bay, the newspaper claimed that it originally came from a football coach who said Francis resembled a boy named Donkey. But it really caught on at Calabar, for entirely unrelated reasons. As one coach explained: 'We allowed a younger runner to run off seconds before him and told him to chase him.' Francis failed to catch the youngster, and the coach asked why not. 'Him fast, sir.'

In fact, the runner he was chasing was – unbeknown to Francis – one of the school's most promising young athletes. Again Francis was told to chase him. This time the greyhound almost caught the hare. But not quite. Feigning outrage, the coach asked: 'How you don't catch him?'

'Mi a nuh donkey, sir,' replied Francis ('I'm not a donkey, sir').

From that day on, he was Donkey Man.

5

DONKEY MAN

He knew of no candle that burned out more
quickly than that of the high school athlete.
Friday Night Lights

They rejoiced when Javon Francis took the baton at the world championships in Moscow and, with talent, guts and determination, dragged Jamaica to a silver medal.

They despaired a few months later when, at Champs, he broke down. There was outrage at the decision to put him in the final of the 200 metres just a couple of hours after his beating of Bolt's record in the 400 metres. He had collapsed to the track, at one point being helped on to a stretcher before staging a Lazarus-like recovery.

To see him pull up injured, his face a picture of agony, was heartbreaking. It became a huge talking point throughout the country, even warranting a solemn editorial in the *Jamaica Observer*: 'This newspaper was jarred by the perception that student athletes are being overworked in pursuit of glory.' To underline the seriousness of the matter, he was 'Mr Francis' throughout. Noting that after the 400 metres he 'had to be helped off the track', the article continued: 'It seemed logical that, given this hiccup, Mr Francis would be pulled from remaining competition. Not so. Less than three hours later – with Calabar holding an unbeatable points lead in the race for the boys' championship title – Mr Francis was on the track lining up for the 200 metres final.

'To the utter dismay of most of us watching, Mr Francis pulled up, grabbing his hamstring 20 to 30 metres from the finish line. Jamaicans will be keeping their fingers crossed that this athlete, among this country's most promising, wasn't badly hurt.'

Francis grew up in Bull Bay, nine miles along the coast from Kingston, where children play on the beach and catch fish in the river. To call the dwellings of this community modest would be an understatement: many are no more than shacks with wooden walls and tin roofs.

He went to St Benedict's Primary School and dreamt of becoming a footballer. But in Jamaica, football comes second to athletics. His football coach, seeing his speed, took him aside one day. 'You know, Javon, you have good potential – have you tried track and field?'

'No, sir,' said Javon. 'I don't want to try track and field. I want to be a great footballer like Ronaldinho.'

'But you can be the next Usain Bolt or Herb McKenley.'

'OK, coach, I give it a shot.'

The Javon Francis who relates all this, grinning as he recalls the exchanges, is nineteen and about to turn professional. He sits in the grounds of Calabar High School, where he still trains with his old coach, Michael Clarke, and speaks with an endearing sense of innocence, giggling and opening his eyes wide to convey wonder.

At his sports day, after the eleven-year-old lined up against the school's fastest sprinter, and beat him, it was the turn of the athletics coach to have a word. 'Bwoy, you really fast! Footballer, come to track and field.'

'Sir,' said Javon, 'I am going to sit down and decide what I want to do.'

He talked to his father. 'Whoa, dad, it's hard. I want to be the next

Ronaldinho.' His father told him it was up to him. 'Then I go round,' says Francis, 'and ask lots of questions, make people tell me how it feels to do track and field. My cousin used to do track and field and he said to me, "Well track and field, it's nice, but the training is very hard. But you can go to places, the Penn Relays, the Miami Classic."

'"Wow! Those places? Cuz, if you go on a plane, how does it feel?"'

'"Well, it's nice, you go up in the air, look down."'

That was it, says Francis. 'I make up my mind. Track and field is what I'm going to do: be a superstar. But my first day, training hard, I throw up. And say, whoa, this is hard.'

While Francis talks, his guardian, Andrea Hardware, gazes at him and smiles, swatting flies and mosquitoes as they land on him. Beside her is Noel Facey, who recruited Francis. Facey and Hardware are both parents of Calabar pupils or former pupils; Hardware, director of human resources at Digicel (who sponsor Bolt and now Francis too), also manages the school's athletics team.

Facey recalls the moment he spotted Francis. He was sitting watching a meeting with Clarke. 'Michael Clarke has an eye for talent. Not for the winner. He'll look at the boy who comes third or fourth, looking at stride pattern, muscle build-up. I don't question Michael. I was beside him when Javon ran and he said, "Facey, this is the boy I want."'

Facey's job then was to recruit him for the school. 'It's a whole lot of work,' he says, 'but everything we do is with the head coach. He picks them out, and my job is to go and get them. I talk to the parents, tell them about the programme. I generally sell Michael: his track record. But the parents have got to say yes. Javon's parents said yes.'

Omar Hawes had stressed how humble Francis's upbringing was. Francis himself mentioned that the first time he ran the 100 metres, he was in his stockinged feet. 'His parents are not well off, but they're trying to make sure he gets the best out of life,' said Omar. Unusually, his parents are still together. 'Most of the athletes who have talent here in Jamaica, you find they come from broken homes. Most of them have a reason to excel in whatever strength they have. To help the family out and help themselves.'

Francis's father is a fisherman, while his mother, says Hardware, 'does anything she can find herself to do to make a living'. Javon is the youngest of six children: five boys, one girl. Which is interesting. An extraordinarily high proportion of top male sprinters seem to be late-born, or youngest, in their (often large) families: Usain Bolt (youngest of three), Ben Johnson (youngest of five), Carl Lewis (third of four), Asafa Powell (youngest of six), Calvin Smith (sixth of eight), Yohan Blake (seventh of eleven), Justin Gatlin (youngest of four), Maurice Greene (youngest of four), to name just some.

This phenomenon was discussed by Daniel Coyle in his book *The Talent Code*. 'History's fastest runners were born, on average, fourth in families of 4.6 children,' writes Coyle, who argues that 'deep practice' is the key to sporting excellence (excellence in any field, for that matter). The pattern of late-born sprinters suggests, he asserts, 'that speed is not purely a gift but a skill that grows through deep practice, and that is ignited by primal cues. In this case the cue is: you're behind – keep up!'

In a nutshell, speed is honed by younger children trying to keep up with their older siblings.

There may be something in that. Or perhaps not. David Epstein, author of *The Sports Gene*, notes that the leading female sprinters are nearly all first- or second-born in the family. Is it because females are less competitive, less ego-driven? Again, maybe. But Epstein doesn't think that's it. 'To me,' he writes in an email, 'when you see a male/female disparity – handedness, dyslexia, etc. – it often points to a pre-natal effect.'

The Coyle theory, that the social effect is the determining factor, is also slightly undermined by the fastest man of all time. Bolt was third-born, but didn't really grow up with his older siblings (a brother and a sister). In fact, several of the youngest-born sprinters mentioned above, including Gatlin, did not grow up in the company of their siblings.

Epstein carried out his own informal survey into the phenomenon and considered that the gender of the older siblings seemed to be significant. 'We know that the environment of the womb changes with each successive boy birth, but not each girl, and my survey found that the boys particularly had lots of brothers. So in my opinion, the weight of evidence is for a biological effect, not a social one.' (Although being a good scientist, he is reluctant to draw any firm conclusions, given the limitations of such a small sample.)[9]

So Francis may have got off to the best possible start in his athletics career by being the youngest in his family, especially by having four older brothers.

Although he started out running all the sprint events – the 100, 200, 400, 4x100 and 4x400 – he found himself gravitating towards the one-lap race, or the quarter-mile as people still call it here, in which Jamaica has such a strong tradition – on which the island's reputation was originally built. 'The 400 is an event I love with a passion,' Francis tells me. 'I go out there in Moscow or at Championships, and say, Hey, I want to make a big statement out there, so everyone say: "Young Javon Francis is coming up."

'I wish my idol, Herb McKenley, was alive to sit and talk to,' he continues. Francis was thirteen when McKenley died, and never met him, so presumably he is only aware of his reputation through attending Calabar. 'Yes, sir,' he says. 'I hear that Herb McKenley is a great guy and I look up to him.'

---

9 Epstein adds something else: 'Actually, there's at least one other very well known effect of older brothers, and it doesn't matter at all if the younger bro grows up with his siblings, only that they once occupied the same womb.' This is the 'older brother effect': the more older brothers a man has, the greater the possibility that he will be homosexual. Again, there is no equivalent correlation with women. It's thought to be connected to the hormonal conditions in the womb; as Epstein explains, the idea that 'the mother's body has an immune response only to male fetuses, and there's some imprinting of it with each successive boy', is scientifically unproven, but 'gaining conceptual strength'. A logical follow-up would be to ask: how many leading male sprinters are homosexual? Not many – at least publicly.

When he first started at Calabar, he commuted from Bull Bay by bus: a journey of between forty minutes and over an hour each way depending on the Kingston traffic, on roads that, in the miles close to Bull Bay, deteriorate terribly. It took its toll on the fourteen-year-old. 'Training finishes at six o'clock,' says Hardware, 'so that would get him home pretty late. The affordability was a big challenge for his parents. They're very proud. They wouldn't ask for help and they could only afford public transportation, not a taxi. So he was getting home late. And for development meets at weekends it became a big challenge for them to afford those. So he'd be missing those, and those meets are important; they're where you get ready for Champs.'

Hardware was already acting as a mentor to Francis. 'Each year we take in a cadre of boys. About fifteen of us manage the team and each of us gets two or three boys to mentor. Javon was my mentee.

'We realised that coming to Calabar, he needed all kinds of support: educational support, financial support, and through our committee and myself that was provided for him,' she continues. 'But I got very concerned when I got a call telling me he's coming to school late, he's sleeping in class, he's not keeping up – that sort of thing. Mr Facey said, "You have to do something more for this boy." '

'After Javon came to Calabar,' Facey interrupts, 'Andrea loved him so much she let him move in.'

Hardware nods in agreement. 'It was very easy for me to say, "Come, Javon, stay with me." My sons both went to Calabar, but they were away.'

When she spoke to Francis's parents, 'They were immediately open to the idea. I remember the conversation I had with his mother. She said, "Thank you, God bless you. I know he needs the support and I can't do it for him." She was very, very appreciative.' Francis has lived with Hardware in her home in Kingston for the last four years. She treats him like one of her own sons, and he looks on her as a second mother. 'He calls me Mum,' says Hardware. 'But when I get angry at him he calls me "Andrine". He's part of our family; they

all get along very well. He's quiet, so they pull him out of his shell, take him places.'

There is an innocence about Francis that makes him difficult to read, particularly when he can be such a showman on the track. It's hard to reconcile the quiet, diffident boy with the pumped-up extrovert who appeared in the mixed zone in Moscow, announcing: 'A super donkey just did it!'

'That's just him,' says Hardware. She means the sweet, innocent boy who has jogged away to start training, leaving with a handshake and a 'Thank you, sir.' 'That's who he is,' she says. 'It's one of the qualities he has that really endears him to me. Because he's so humble, so appreciative. I don't think he's aware of the immense talent he has.'

Later, I speak to Michael Clarke, the head coach, who I had met in Moscow at the senior world championships. In smart shirt and trousers, with obligatory baseball cap, he strolls slowly around his athletes as they go through their drills, sometimes pulling them aside to have a quiet word. Then he peels off to speak to me, also very quietly – and with a Zen-like calm. Clarke went to Calabar in 1973, having been recruited by Herb McKenley; then, in 1980, he was among the first batch of students to be trained in sports coaching at the new G. C. Foster College. For the last thirteen years he has been head coach at his alma mater.

The first time he saw Francis run, he recalls, 'he didn't do anything spectacular. He was third, beaten by some distance. He ran 52.7. But I wanted 400 athletes and what struck me was his build: he was tall, sinewy, lanky, but he had some speed. He was sought after by a number of other schools, in fact.'

Clarke can reel off Francis's times, illustrating his improvement once he joined Calabar: 'First race he ran here was 49-something, then he was in the 50-range, then he did a 48, then a 47.'

It was Clarke who took the bold decision to select an eighteen-year-old for the anchor leg of the 4x400 metres in Moscow. Francis, when he found out, went straight to his guardian, who was on the team bus, travelling to the stadium. Hardware recalls how the conversation went: 'Mum, me coach make me anchor for the race!'

'What?' said Hardware.

'Mum, I'm going to run the race, I want to win a medal.'

'If you win a medal, I get you a car,' she told him. ('I still haven't got him that car,' she admits.) 'He said he didn't have a race plan,' Hardware tells me. 'He said he just wanted them to give him the baton in the pack. I was standing in the stand, and when I saw him blaze out, I was like, "No, Javon, you're going too fast!" I was literally shouting, "You're going too fast! You're running too fast!" But when he came off of that third bend, I knew he was going to finish it. He maintained his composure; such a mature thing for him to do at eighteen.'

Now Clarke tells me that he chose Francis for the anchor leg because of the heart he'd shown at the Penn Relays earlier in the season. 'He was coming off chickenpox, and he ran down a guy, Delano Willliams, from a twenty-metre lead. I said, "Wow." It was an outstanding time: 44.6. He has the record for Penn Relays.

'He has something special,' continues Clarke. 'He's a chaser. He displays an intellect on the track that belies his real intellect off the track.' Expanding on this, Clarke explains: 'He's a simple youngster: simple, jovial, very candid about things. He has tremendous charisma.'

He can see similarities with Bolt, as everyone can. They have been looking for the next Bolt or Shelly-Ann Fraser-Pryce: another athlete who can dominate at world level. But so many athletes who seem poised to do just that don't make it, often because they break down with injury. On the comparison with Bolt, Clarke says: 'Both are candid. They both have charisma. They like to perform. Javon is not as eloquent yet, but he's getting there. We're trying to help him. But he has personality. Now in Jamaica when we go out in public every-body – kids, adults – they flock around him. People recognise him, they are endeared to him.'

I was still coming to terms with the quality of the facilities at the centre of world excellence that is Calabar High School. I had asked Omar Hawes how many other coaches there are at the school. 'Let's see,' he said, and began counting on his fingers. 'There's a coach for the throws, horizontal jumps, vertical jumps, hurdles, quarter-mile programme, sprints, distance . . . That's seven. And Mr Clarke is overall coach.' Eight dedicated athletics coaches. But what I only learn later is that they are all volunteers – parents of pupils, or old boys, like Omar. In his day job, I discover, Omar is a policeman.

There is a darker story I want to ask the coaches about. Demar Robinson was a Calabar schoolboy who in 2013 – within weeks of leaving the school – tested positive at the Jamaican national championships for androgen receptor modulator (SARMS), a steroid. Robinson was a high jumper who captained the school at Champs in 2012. He was given a one-year ban: a light sentence for such an offence, but the rumour (unconfirmed by Jamaica's anti-doping agency, because his hearing was in camera) was that he had offered useful information. Robinson is now at college in Kansas.

When had Omar last seen him? 'It would have been at Champs. He came to say hi to the youngsters.'

Omar told me he didn't know why Robinson had tested positive, and hadn't spoken to him about it. 'He had his lawyers. I wish him the best. It was an unfortunate situation. I don't know how that got into his system.' He did speak to him at Champs, but didn't discuss the positive test. 'I asked him how he was dealing with the pressure. He said "All right." It sounded like he wanted to return.'

I want to ask Michael Clarke about Robinson too. It seems like a blot on the Calabar name, and indeed has fuelled a certain amount of suspicion. At another school I visited, Cornwall College, in Montego Bay, the head of sport, Gregory Daley, was critical of what he described as the 'win-at-all-costs' mentality that prevails at some schools. 'It is hard to say, but I am going to say it anyway,' he said. 'Schools like Calabar, KC, JC [Kingston College and Jamaica College] will always have the best athletes. They will do things we won't do or we can't do. There are schools who will come to a parent and say, "The boy can run, and I want him to come to our school – here's a fridge."

'Most often these boys are from the, I don't want to say ghetto, but they are from the lower strata of the financial scale. So the parents will always say, "What? Fridge? Stove? Yeah, man," and the boy's gone.'

On this specific point, Noel Facey, who recruited Javon Francis, says it's not common practice. 'I can say that's a rumour for Calabar. Everything at Calabar is for the boys, not for the parents. So we cannot give the parents this.'

Daley said he had personal experience of Calabar's recruitment policy. When he was at another school, Herb McKenley came for one of the most talented young athletes he had ever seen: Ali Watson. 'Herb McKenley came for him at Grade 4,' said Daley. Watson was eight years old. 'The father and myself, we're very good friends, he came to me and said, "Grade 4? Why's he want a Grade 4?" The fella went to Calabar and in Class 3 at Champs he won the 100, he won the 200, he won the 400 in record times.' Class 3 is the youngest age group. But it was as good as Watson got; he never won again.

As for drugs, Daley said he had not encountered any at schools level. 'But I doubt if it does not exist.'

Clarke says he believes that doping is unlikely to exist in schools, mainly because of the cost. 'Those performance-enhancing drugs are expensive, very expensive, to get initially, and to sustain it is even more expensive. The coaches can't, I certainly can't [afford it]. And even if I could, I wouldn't, because it is unethical.

'I've been coaching for thirty years and I don't think any one boy should risk putting thirty years on the line,' Clarke continues. 'For me that's a no-no.'

Nonetheless, he admits that the Robinson case did leave a cloud over Calabar. 'He had just left school. You hear a lot of discussion about it in terms of what the real truth is; I don't know what the real truth is. But given his humble beginnings, it would be difficult to think that he could afford it. So obviously somebody must have given it to him in ignorance, from what I gather.'

He looks reflective. He is still Zen-like. 'That left a bit of a blemish, yes,' he adds. 'I guess we can hide behind the clouds and say it wasn't during his time at Calabar.'

Now Clarke is coaching not just high school athletes but professionals too – the latest being Javon Francis. Given the positive tests there have been in senior athletics, and rumours that the sport has a serious doping problem at international level, is Javon going to have to make a choice at some stage?

'Well, he listens to me attentively, and to his guardian,' Clarke says. 'We discuss whatever supplements he takes. He doesn't like taking pills, doesn't like taking these things, but he needs to. I get them checked out. We don't push anything. He follows my instruction where that's concerned.'

*

There were other questions for Francis – and for Clarke. I kept hearing about Jamaican athletes who had been high school stars – Ali Watson, Daniel England – only to fade away as seniors. It brought to mind another passage from *Friday Night Lights*, concerning the father of a teenage star who 'saw the irresistible allure of high school sports, but also saw an inevitable danger in adults living vicariously through their young. And he knew of no candle that burned out more quickly than that of the high school athlete.'

There were so many examples of this happening to athletes in Jamaica, I was learning. And it was bound to get worse. The achievements of Bolt, Yohan Blake, Shelly-Ann Fraser-Pryce, Asafa Powell and others only intensified the pressure on the young stars of Champs: the stakes were higher than ever. At Calabar, as Omar Hawes suggested, it was hoped that Francis's success could help the school get better facilities, perhaps even a new track. Bolt, in his minor school in the backwater of Trelawny, had had it easy; he was protected, wrapped in cotton wool, by Devere Nugent, Lorna Thorpe and his parents.

Would Francis be the next Bolt or an Ali Watson? Perhaps the season stretching out in front of us would offer some clues. I said to Francis, just before he joined Clarke for training, that I would be returning to Jamaica in a few months and hoped to see him again. 'Yes, sir,' he nodded.

More immediately, I had another appointment, with somebody at the other end of the age spectrum. I had been told about him repeatedly at the National Stadium during Champs. His name was the answer most frequently suggested when I asked the question: 'Who is responsible for all this?' He was yet another Calabar man, and the original Herb McKenley protégé, and he was known throughout Jamaica as 'DJ'. As Mark Ricketts, the economist and writer, told me: 'Without DJ, there would be no Glen Mills and no Stephen Francis' – the two leading coaches. 'And without Mills, you don't have Bolt,' added Ricketts.

Could he put me in touch with Dennis Johnson? He gave me

Johnson's number. I called and asked if I could come and hear his story. 'Yes, man,' said a voice at the end of the line. 'Come on Sunday at eleven o'clock,' he added, and hung up.

6

THE ARCHITECT

I tell you, man, Jamaica is not going to lose any
sprints for the next fifty years.
Dennis Johnson

His sprawling house sits on the outskirts of Kingston, overlooking the city. It's on Stony Hill, one of the more salubrious parts of the capital, but the steep, hairpinned road leading there is rutted and not so much potholed as cratered, as though it has been shelled.

Several cars are parked in the driveway, some in as poor condition as the road. The garden is a little overgrown and scruffy, and on the large porch, sitting on a chair by a table, is a man who is clearly not Dennis Johnson. For one thing, he is white. 'Looking for DJ?' he asks as I approach, then shouts: 'DJ? Somebody here to see ya . . . DJ!'

As well as the table and chairs, the porch is cluttered with potted plants and large birdcages full of budgies hopping from bar to bar, chirruping.

Johnson shuffles stiffly in, sliding across the hard floor in flip-flops, shorts and a faded yellow T-shirt that says 'Director – Sports'. He has a shock of white hair, a bushy moustache and a tuft of hair below his

lower lip. It is clear that he also has no recollection whatsoever of our appointment.

Before I can explain – even before I sit in the seat he indicates – he launches into an impassioned defence of Asafa Powell and the other sprinters who tested positive the previous year, clearly continuing a conversation he and his friend had been having. 'They took a supplement and in the supplement is a banned thing!' Johnson protests. His friend looks at him with a mixture of bemusement and irritation. 'He can't know that!' continues Johnson, who seems a little breathless. 'WADA, I think, is out of order. The IAAF think so too. You understand?'

The friend shakes his head in quiet resignation. Then Johnson turns to me. 'Now, what do you want?'

Well, I say, I would like to hear his life story. But on the other hand, it sounds like I've interrupted an interesting conversation. (The friend,

I later learn, is David Mais, until recently chairman of the G. C. Foster sports college.) So what does Johnson think happened, and why are the anti-doping authorities out of order?

'It's simple,' Johnson says, settling back in his chair. He speaks slowly and frequently closes his eyes, as though keeping them open is too much effort. 'Let me think of an example.' He tilts his head back. 'OK, I'm from Mars and I don't know what calculus is. What is calculus?'

Fortunately, he isn't really interested in an answer. 'The reason I ask is that even the people who do maths don't know what calculus is. I'm telling you, ask a maths teacher: what is calculus? It's finding the area of an irregular shape – that glass or something.' He reaches for a glass on the table. 'Easy. This?' He leans forward and picks up a plate. 'Easy. But a teapot? A pentagon? A nineteen-a-gon? You get what I'm saying?'

'Um . . .'

'You cannot tell an underdeveloped country to work out calculus when only 10 per cent of the population is literate!'

'Aha, so you think the rules are too complicated? It shouldn't be one size fits all?'

'Yes, man! It should be made simple! You cannot have a universal rule! They want to stop doping so they go to the extreme. It's like the false start rule. Nothing wrong with it, but give people a way out, threaten them. Should be about stopping people cheating, not punishing them if they make a mistake! You understand?'

Johnson's booming voice, his bombastic presence, fills the porch of his house, which, it becomes clear, is where he holds court, receiving visitors much like a member of the Jamaican royal family, if such a thing existed.

He was born in Kingston in 1939 and went to Calabar, where the coach was Herb McKenley. McKenley started the athletics programme there in 1953, the year after his defining achievement as an athlete, when he almost single-handedly won the 4x400 metres relay gold medal for Jamaica at the Helsinki Olympics. He received the baton twelve metres down on the Americans but ran his leg in 44.6 seconds, to hand over to George Rhoden with a one-metre advantage. Had it not been part of the relay, his time would have stood as a sea-level world record until the late 1970s. The wiry, sharp-featured McKenley was credited with revolutionising the 400 metres: he ran the distance flat out, like a sprinter, rather than conserving energy and saving it for the finishing straight.

At the 1948 Olympics in London – Jamaica's first Games – McKenley had been favourite for the 400, but took silver after being overtaken close to the line by his fellow Jamaican Arthur Wint.[10] McKenley said that for years afterwards he was haunted by the sound of Wint gaining on him: 'Boom, boom, boom.' With first and second in the individual event, they were favourites for the relay until Wint collapsed with cramp.

They made amends four years later, when McKenley also became the first – and still the only – athlete to reach the finals of the 100, 200 and 400 metres, winning silver medals in both the 100 and 400. Many

---

[10] Given Herb McKenley's profile, Arthur Wint might be considered the forgotten man of Jamaican athletics, though the National Stadium sits on Arthur Wint Drive (near Herb McKenley Drive), and an enormous statue outside the stadium, 'Athlete' by Jamaican sculptor Alvin Marriott, is clearly modelled on Wint's Bolt-like six-foot-five frame. Confusingly, the head is McKenley's. It was Wint who originally inspired McKenley, when he appeared at Calabar High School in his Jamaican team uniform and panama hat. 'He looked really splendid,' said McKenley. 'Regal.' Wint was a surgeon, an RAF pilot and a diplomat, who served as High Commissioner to Britain, before returning to work as a doctor in rural Jamaica; he was a noble, upstanding and principled man, known as the Gentle Giant, apart from one curious incident. This features in *The Longer Run: A Daughter's Story of Arthur Wint*, Valerie Wint's fascinating biography of her father. In 1941, when he was twenty-one, Wint accidentally shot and killed a colleague: a thirty-year-old woman. He didn't know the gun was loaded and was given two years' probation. It was, perhaps, his most formative experience. Of his sport, he said in 1985: 'Today running can make you well off. In my era it was the thing that taught you about the limits of money. It lifted you to heights and rewards money could never buy.' Wint died in 1992, aged seventy-two.

maintain that he should have been given gold in the 100. He started as favourite alongside another sprinter originally from the Caribbean, the Trinidadian McDonald Bailey, representing Great Britain. Lindy Remigino of the USA later recalled being visited by McKenley before the final in the locker room. 'I was laying on a table, getting my thoughts about the race,' said Remigino, 'when Herb comes up to me. He's a very jolly fellow, and he said: "You know, Lindy, McDonald Bailey is ready to be had, he's so nervous. I think we've got him out of the way."'

McKenley got a poor start while Remigino, in the lane alongside him, was off to a flyer. But McKenley finished fast and was closing the gap when Remigino dipped too early. They crossed the line together: a photo finish. Remigino was convinced McKenley had won. 'I went up and congratulated him. I said, "Herb, I think you won this doggone thing."'

'It was close,' McKenley replied, 'but I think I got it.' Meanwhile the officials were still studying the photo finish, and eventually showed it to the two athletes. 'It was the closest thing I ever saw in my life,' said Remigino. He got the verdict and the gold medal. 'When I look at the film,' said McKenley fifty years later, 'I still think I won.'

One remarkable aspect of Jamaica's first two Olympic Games is that they foreshadowed Beijing and London by sixty years. In 1952, for the second Games in a row, there was a Jamaican one-two in the 400 metres, George Rhoden winning, with McKenley second again. The athletics medals table in Helsinki makes for surprising reading. With its population at the time of 1.5 million, Jamaica took silver in the men's 100, gold and silver in the 400, and gold in the 4x400 (and Wint also claimed a silver in the 800).

On the night of their triumph, the relay quartet celebrated in their living quarters with a bottle of Scotch and a member of the British royal family, Philip Mountbatten, the Duke of Edinburgh.

At Calabar in the mid-1950s, Johnson the schoolboy athlete and McKenley the coach formed a close bond. 'We became friends, Herb

and me. He would take me to his house in Mona.' Mona is at the foot
of the hills on the other side of Kingston. 'I had dinner at Herb's. I
had a bed there. If he was going to a picnic with his family, they would
take me, and after training he'd go buy me a milkshake. You know? We
became friends for life.'

Johnson echoes everyone else when he describes what McKenley
was like. Warm, enthusiastic, encouraging, driven by a passion for
athletics and coaching. 'Herb was something else. You'd like him
immediately. Charming; a beautiful guy; just a fine human being.
But no nonsense. I took my dog to the vet one Saturday morning and
he came storming in. I was missing training, you see. He had made
arrangements for the dog, but I didn't know that. I was sitting at the
vet's having an ice lolly. "Not on my time!" he said.

'We were friends, but he was very strict when you were working.'

Before Champs in 1957, Johnson was the favourite for the sprint
events. Mark Ricketts was also competing, and remembers his teacher's
response to Johnson's final leg in a relay: 'That was a lightning bolt.'
In his book Ricketts recalls Johnson as 'a cocky young man . . . As he
walked, he half rotated his upper torso, swinging it from side to side.
This confident swagger, this peacock-like strutting, was reminiscent of
wrestlers readying for battle and fearing no one.'

'A very bossy young fellow' is how P. J. Patterson, another Calabar
old boy, remembers Johnson. 'You would hear him before you saw
him, but he's one of the early great successes of Jamaican athletics. I
don't think he gets his due.'

Despite his confidence, Johnson could only finish fourth in the boys'
100 yards and third in the 220 yards at 1957 Champs. But there was
a reason for that. He had a broken arm. With the rest of the Calabar
team, he had been at McKenley's house on the eve of the final day
of competition to 'map a winning strategy'. He and a friend left at
10 p.m. to drive home, but they were involved in an accident; their car
overturned. Johnson was taken to the nearby University of the West
Indies hospital for surgery. The surgeon was Arthur Wint.

A year later, Johnson made amends, taking the sprint double. His winning time for the 100 yards (about 91 metres) was 9.8 seconds, then a Champs record.

McKenley had been the first Jamaican – the first from any Caribbean island – to get an athletics scholarship to a US college, in his case to Boston College in 1942, before transferring to the University of Illinois in 1945, coming under the spell of an influential coach, Leo Johnson. McKenley encountered racism, even if it only dawned on him slowly – during a train journey with segregated carriages. He said he overcame it thanks to his British passport.

It was as a coach himself that McKenley helped to open the floodgates. It is said that he arranged college scholarships for 1,000 Jamaican school-leavers. After his Champs double, Johnson was one of the first. He had little say in the matter. McKenley had contacts all over the US and set it up for him. 'All right, Dennis,' he told him, 'you are going to Bakersfield.'

So Johnson went to Bakersfield, California, on a scholarship that was not as glamorous as it might sound, nor as generous as those being offered by Keith Barnier of ACU at Champs in 2014. 'The old boys put you up,' Johnson tells me. 'In my case, in a fire station. My job was to clean the place, do odd jobs, and you'd get your meals and fifteen dollars every couple of weeks.'

At a track meeting in his first year at Bakersfield, Johnson was approached by a coach from another college. He had caused a stir, winning the national junior college title, and he was getting offers from some of the top universities – Stanford, UCLA, USC. But it was a coach from San José who said to him: 'Come up to San José and see if you'll be comfortable.' The coach sent Johnson an air ticket, met him at the airport, and took him to dinner. Then he made a formal offer. Johnson accepted immediately.

The coach was Bud Winter, one of the most famous names in sprint coaching. Winter worked at San José State College for twenty-nine years, from 1941 to 1970, building his reputation as his athletes sped to thirty-seven world records. The stadium at San José became known as 'Speed City'. Thanks to Winter, it was also the first to have a synthetic track – initially just a single lane – years before the rubberised material was used in competition.

Winter was progressive in lots of areas, but particularly when it came to coaching black athletes. After Johnson, he coached Tommie Smith and John Carlos, the 200 metres gold and bronze medallists at the 1968 Olympics in Mexico who became even better known for their Black Power salute on the podium. It took courage for Winter to actively recruit not only African Americans (and Jamaicans), but also Hispanic athletes. Johnson says his old coach was colour-blind; when it came to athletes, he only saw ability.

Once he had them, what was his secret? I ask Johnson. Was he scientific? 'No, man! Bud was a journalist. Then he was a social professor at the school. When it came to coaching, Bud was simplistic. Very simple. The strange thing about Bud was the things he thought was good, the method he came up with, they were hunches. And it turned out, as time went by, that he was right.'

Winter focused on the mechanics of sprinting: correct form, and the importance of maintaining it over the course of a sprint, blowing his whistle at eighty metres, at which point the runner would have to snap back into shape. The mechanics of sprinting are something Johnson is also obsessed with; he points out that it is not simply about moving one's legs quickly; that the sprinting action is not natural, but has to be learned. In fact, he adds, sprinting is not really about moving the legs quickly at all: it's about minimising contact with the ground while applying as much force as possible.

Form depended on 'a half-dozen or more essentials', said Winter, 'starting with high knees'. As he put it: 'A man doesn't walk with his knees up, so first you have to develop the muscles for it. The second and most important essential is foreleg reach. The knees have to be pumped high; but they can't be pumped straight down unless what you want is to run in [one] place. Watch a whippet sometimes, or a racehorse. They're extending their legs as far as they can.' Then there was 'Good arm action, lean forward, run tall, and "dig a hole" in the track with each foot as it comes down.'

But Winter was concerned with more – far more – than the mechanics of running. He was equally focused on the mental approach of the sprinter.

'Bud had an interesting job in the war,' Johnson says. 'He used to teach pilots to relax.'

How? Johnson blows out his cheeks, exhales, shakes his head. 'Read my book,' he says. 'You'll learn something.'

I couldn't find Johnson's book, but I did find Winter's – not his most famous, *Relax and Win*, but his other one, *So You Want to be a Sprinter*, where he explained his wartime job. 'In the Navy we were dealing with the cream of American youth,' he wrote. 'We provided them with the best planes in the world, the best education in the world, but at no time were we shooting live bullets at them. In their first mortal combat some of them tied up mentally or physically, or both. We lost the man and the plane.'

Winter could see that they needed to be as relaxed in combat as in drills, but this, of course, was easier said than done. So he set about devising a relaxation programme in consultation with 'the best minds in the country on the subject'. It had 'startling results'. Winter explained: 'Fatigue was alleviated, coordination got better, speed and reaction time improved, the learning of physical skills was accelerated and self-confidence was established.'

In a 1959 interview with *Sports Illustrated*, Winter went into more detail about his wartime work. He explained that they were losing pilots who were good in training because they tensed up in combat. They were sleep-deprived thanks to 'nuisance bombers' sent at night by the Japanese to fly over their Pacific base. They were understandably tense. And when they were tense, their physical coordination deteriorated.

'We had to figure out some way to relax them,' he said. 'We worked out a programme that taught pilots how to relax themselves, and we ran a test on two platoons, 60 men in each platoon. The 60 who learned how to relax did better in everything which requires physical coordination.'

There was no secret or quick fix, claimed Winter in his book: 'The course took six weeks, three hours a day. It taught you progressively how to relax every muscle group in the body. Then you were given a conditioned reflex with one word, "CALM". By repeating this word, you could elicit a relaxed state immediately . . . You could get to sleep in two minutes any time of the day or night – even with amplified machine gun noise in the room.'

After the war, working with sprinters, Winter noticed the same inability to relax under pressure, with the same effects on physical coordination, albeit with less catastrophic consequences. He paid special attention to the jaw and hands. When the sports writer Tex Maule spent time with him in 1959, observing a training session involving Ray Norton, Winter told Maule: 'Watch his lower lip. That's what we work on. The lower lip and the hands. If his lower lip is relaxed and flopping when he runs, his upper body is loose. If his hands are relaxed, his arm muscles are relaxed. You got to run relaxed to get maximum speed. If you have antagonistic muscles working against each other, you're working against yourself.'

Maule described Winter as 'a sun-scorched, intense man who talks very rapidly, as if his ideas outpaced his words'. There is footage of Winter: he fizzes with energy, though in his breeches and hat he looks more Victorian dad than pioneering coach. He told Maule that his favourite exercise was to time a sprinter making three efforts over thirty yards, then tell him to do it one more time at four-fifths speed. Flat-out, a good sprinter would do thirty yards in three seconds.

'Don't strain,' he would instruct his athlete before their final 80 per cent effort. As he told Maule: 'So he runs it at four-fifths speed, and we time him and he comes up to me and I say, "What do you think your time was?" And he'll say, "Oh, maybe 3.4, Coach," and

I'll show him the stopwatch. You know what? Nine times out of ten, he's run it two tenths of a second faster. He's run 2.8. You believe that? It's true.'

Relaxation did not appear to be much of a problem for Johnson.

'A New Sprinter for the Speed Master' read the headline in the 22 May 1961 edition of *Sports Illustrated*. The subject was Johnson, 'the latest of a long string of distinguished runners whom persuasive – and sometimes hypnotic – Coach Bud Winter has attracted to California's San José State College'.

Johnson quotes the introduction of the article to me from memory: 'At 8.24 last Saturday night, a tall, lithe Negro from San José State College . . .' The description seems to tickle him, still. The article carried on: 'Dennis Johnson jogged easily in the dim light behind a wire fence set at the head of the 220-yard straightaway in Fresno (Calif.) State College's Ratcliffe Stadium. When Starter Tom Moore called to the eight finalists in the West Coast Relays 100-yard dash, "Runners to your blocks," Johnson took off his sweat suit, stepped through a door in the fence and walked slowly to the starting line. The man who many now think may be the fastest runner in the world was the slowest to get ready.'

Johnson remained relaxed as they were called to the 'set' position. While the others got ready, he stayed on his haunches. Then, just before the gun, he sprang up and launched forward. The starter called them back. But this was Johnson's style: a style that, according to the magazine, 'made him as controversial as he is fast'.

A rival coach, Chuck Coker, accused Johnson of a 'rolling start'. 'Oh, that was ridiculous!' Johnson says now, throwing his head back and closing his eyes. 'There was no rolling anything. When the man said "On your marks, get set," I did not listen to the instructions immediately. I got up slowly. When everyone is in the set position the starter fires the gun, unless the starter is an idiot.' But why did he get up so slowly? 'I couldn't hold the set position because I broke my arm three times.'

At the time, Johnson didn't mention his arm, responding to the accusation of a rolling start by saying: 'It's so stupid. Rising slowly has very little to do with my style. It just keeps me relaxed by leaving me straining at set for less time than the others. The short piston arm stroke is what's important.'

Now he says, 'Oh, one guy, Coker, made heavy weight of it. Did I ever get kicked out of a race for false-starting? Never. Not once.' (Well, there was that one time at Fresno State, I think, but he wasn't kicked out of the race, so I don't bring it up.) 'I was a good starter. But starting doesn't mean moving first. It means accelerating quicker than everyone else, which involves mechanics and leverage. You cannot move without levers. Levers! It all depends on that.'

Johnson never scaled the very highest peaks in major championships: at the 1960 and 1964 Olympic Games he reached the 100 metres quarter-finals; and alongside Pablo McNeil, who later coached Bolt at William Knibb, he helped Jamaica to fourth in the 4x100 metres relay in Tokyo in 1964.[11] But in a six-week period in 1961, he equalled the then world record of 9.3 seconds for 100 yards on four occasions.

'Jamaican Fast as a Jet' read the *Toledo Blade*'s headline after his second run, at Stanford on 15 April. The article noted that 'an oversight by the Stanford hosts – failure to have a wind gauge alongside the track – was the only thing that prevented the San José State sprinter from getting his world record equalling time into the books. There was virtually no wind . . . two of the three official clocks had him at 9.3 [this being before electronic timing and times to a hundredth of a second]. The third showed 9.2.' That would have

---

11 A teammate at the 1964 Olympics was Vilma Charlton, who says that Jamaica's reputation for track and field was already established – in Japan, anyway. 'We went to the opening ceremony and the Japanese children, who ran alongside our bus, knew about Jamaica and knew about Herb McKenley. So this was their chant: "Jamaica, Jamaica, McKenley, McKenley". That made me feel special. We were resting on their shoulders: they were the giants.'

been an outright world record, but Coach Winter was – as you would expect – relaxed. 'He'll get the world record sometime this year,' he said. 'He's a wonderful fellow to work with – eager to learn and very pleasant.'

Johnson never did get the outright world record. Still, the figure sitting before me now, his hair white and bushy, his paunch straining at his T-shirt, his atrophied legs and flip-flopped feet below the table, could once claim to be the equal-fastest man in the world.

Back in 1961, Johnson was twenty-two and was, as he says, as close to Winter as he had been to his first coach, Herb McKenley. In the *Sports Illustrated* article the reporter observed this closeness first hand, writing that athlete and coach had a tendency to 'smother each other with verbal posies'. Johnson's scholarship was worth $160 a month and covered his tuition; he also had a job, working in the Santa Clara Youth Village. He needed the money because he was married and had a baby daughter. They had managed to rent a small apartment near the campus; before that, they lived in a hotel. 'No one wanted to rent to Negroes, because "the neighbours might object",' Johnson said, with, the reporter noted, 'some bitterness'.

Johnson's wife has passed away. 'She's over there,' he tells me, gesturing at one of the plant pots.

In 1966, Johnson finished at San José and returned to Jamaica to be interrogated by his father. 'What are you going to do?' he asked. 'Teach people how to run,' Johnson replied.

'The man laughed,' Johnson says. 'He had a fit! Then he said, "How?" I said, "Watch me." '

Johnson's plan was to introduce Bud Winter's techniques to Jamaica by holding training sessions around the island. He wrote a proposal that he presented to one of the island's cigarette companies, Carreras, asking for sponsorship for an island-wide athletics programme. His goal was 'to have workshops and clinics in every school. The guy said, "Does that sell cigarettes?" I said, "No. It's what you call niche marketing. PR. You're getting PR from me, a world record holder. And you're doing a good thing for the country." '

But he told them he could sell their cigarettes, too. 'Give me six vans with cigarettes and I'll take them to the shops as I go around the country. And in the evenings I'll show track and field films.' Carreras went for it, and so was born the Carreras Sports Foundation, as well as Johnson's mission.

A common sight in Jamaica these days is large marquees hosting temporary churches, often Jehovah's Witnesses or Seventh-day Adventists, attracting new recruits with lively, impassioned services. Perhaps there are also parallels with the Jamaican music scene, which began to thrive from the late 1950s, when the 'sound men' took their equipment out of Kingston and toured the island, finding big and appreciative audiences in the most remote communities.

Johnson was no less evangelical as he travelled round the country in the late 1960s, visiting schools by day, showing films from his van-cum-mobile-cinema in the evening.

But as he's telling the story of how he founded and ran the Carreras Sports Foundation, Johnson is interrupted by his friend David Mais. Mais says it was in fact his uncle who started the Carreras Sports Foundation. Johnson is having none of it. Mais protests, but Johnson butts back in: 'Anyway, that's neither here nor there. What is here or there is the VISION. You need to know what you're doing.' And Johnson was using Winter's techniques, focusing especially on relaxation and the mechanics of movement, to teach Jamaican youngsters to run with grace, style and speed. And form. Nobody slipped through the net, he says. Anybody with talent would be discovered.

After a year of his running roadshow, Johnson was called into the offices of his Carreras paymasters to be told: 'Dennis, we no longer need your services.' Yet the man was smiling as he delivered the message. 'Dennis,' he continued, 'when you took over, we had 33.3 per cent of the market. Now we have 66 per cent.'

'Why are you firing me, then?' said Johnson.

'We need you at the Rothmans Foundation.' Carreras had merged with Rothmans in 1958, and the company eventually became Rothmans International. For Johnson, it was a promotion. 'I had this dream,' he says. 'I wanted to be like Herb. I wanted to become like him. I said to people, "We're going to produce international runners right here." Because I had this vision. That's what sustained me and kept my sanity. And I did it! You understand?'

Something else Johnson did once he was back home was invite his old San José mentor, Bud Winter, to Jamaica to take part in a two-week conference on coaching. 'And you know who came to Bud's seminar?' Johnson says. 'Glen Mills and Stephen Francis.'

In 1971, Johnson was appointed part-time lecturer and director of sport at the University of Technology in Kingston. In the 1970s, Ricketts had told me, Johnson became known on campus for his 'ever-present smile and his swagger'. He was a maverick with a rebellious streak who always said that his dream was to produce world-class Jamaican athletes right there in Jamaica.

There were obstacles, but Johnson was enterprising and resourceful. Before one of his first big meetings as a coach at UTech, he asked if his athletes would be allowed to train at the National Stadium. No, he was told. (For a country famous for being laid-back, there is a lot of petty bureaucracy in Jamaica – another legacy of British colonial rule, no doubt.) Regardless, Johnson instructed his athletes to meet at the stadium at 4 a.m.; they scaled the walls and, before the sun crept over the Blue Mountains, did their training before making their getaway.

Johnson remained at UTech until 2006, by which time the university had fulfilled his vision, becoming the base for the world's top track and field club, MVP (Maximising Velocity and Power), with its stable of home-reared global stars. The club was – still is – run by Stephen Francis, who became Johnson's assistant at UTech, taking over as head coach at the university when Johnson retired in 2006. A partnership began between the university and Francis's club, building on what Johnson had established: namely, home-based support to rival – or improve upon – what was available elsewhere. It was the first programme designed to support world-class athletes who wanted to live and train in Jamaica, finally offering an alternative to a US college scholarship. In 2001, Asafa Powell declared: 'I am going to stay in Jamaica and beat the world naturally.' Four years later, when he ran 9.77 seconds in Athens, MVP and UTech had the fastest man in the world: proof that it was possible.

Yet that was only the start. At the 2008 Olympics in Beijing, ten MVP athletes made the Jamaican team and seven won medals. The most impressive single result was in the women's 100 metres, won by Shelly-Ann Fraser, with Sherone Simpson and Kerron Stewart both awarded silver medals: one-two-two in the women's 100 metres for Jamaica, and Fraser and Simpson from the same club.

There is no false modesty from Johnson, who argues that it is merely the realisation of his original vision. 'We established a programme here that's probably the best in the world,' he reflects. 'I don't know if there's another college anywhere that's produced the world-beaters we have. Can you think of one?'

'Not off the top of my head,' I reply. Wrong answer. 'Try six months of thinking!' Johnson blasts back. 'Think of the Olympics: one-two-two. This isn't a backyard thing! The Olympics! That's where it all started, and the high performance centre, with Bolt and everything. All the sprinting technique, all came from there. I tell you, man, Jamaica is not going to lose any sprints for the next fifty years.'

'Fifty?'

'Yes, man.'

Johnson enters an almost meditative state, even becoming a little glassy-eyed, when he talks about the top sprinters who have emerged from Jamaica in the last decade, partly because he appreciates their talent, but also because he views this golden generation as his legacy (his Wikipedia page describes him as 'the architect of the Jamaican athletics programme'). He says he coached Usain Bolt briefly – he isn't specific about when – but the emotion isn't far from the surface when he speaks about Mills, the coach who led Bolt to greatness. And he explains that he can tell a Mills-coached sprinter simply by watching him run. 'Oh yes, easily, easily. When Mills's sprinters run, when they perform, if you're into sprinting, you'll cry.

. 'The feet just touch the ground. They just kiss the ground. The people don't look haggard, they look like they're dancing. If you appreciate movement, the dance, anything poetic, like I do . . . When I watch Champs, I cry sometimes. Where in the world do you see movement – form – like that?'

Like all the best coaches – like Winter – Mills is a hypnotist, says Johnson. 'Coaching is hypnosis. When you believe in a coach, you go out there with all sorts of confidence.' As an example, he cites a schoolboy athlete he coached. It was Champs, and Johnson needed the athlete to finish the 5,000 metres to score the one point his team needed. The athlete started the race in a suitably hypnotic state, with one thing on his mind: to finish. Even when, mid-race, he suffered a sudden, violent attack of diarrhoea, his focus didn't waver. 'He was dehydrated,' Johnson explains. 'Started shitting himself all the way around the track. Plop plop plop plop. The most embarrassing fucking thing I've ever seen. And people saying, "Stop him; take him off," and the boy says, "DJ says I need one point, one point, one point." ' Recalling the episode, Johnson wheezes with laughter.

On Mills, he says: 'Mills is more Bud Winter than Bud Winter. Glen Mills used to come here every Sunday and listen how you're listening now.'

I had read that Mills was interested in maths and numbers. 'No,' says Johnson abruptly. 'He's not that intelligent. He's got street smarts, and his sprinters look beautiful. He got that information from me, not in a formal way. So did Stephen Francis; they learned at the same time. It all started when I brought Bud over to Kingston.'

Francis is better known than Mills as a Johnson protégé. He certainly was interested in maths and numbers, having worked in corporate finance. 'Stephen is not intelligent,' Johnson says. 'He's super-intelligent. I wish I was as bright as him. First-class honours; a scholar at Michigan [where he did an MBA]. He has a computer in his head. Super-bright. I have a good library. One of the best. And Stephen's library is bigger and better than mine.'

Francis also seems more versatile than Mills, and he has developed a reputation for polishing rough diamonds. 'Hurdlers, triple jumpers, high jumpers, women and men. Mills just teaches sprinters. Good sprinters. But most of Stephen's people – like Asafa – are people who never won Champs.'

Johnson describes himself as a 'connoisseur of sprinters'. He explains: 'Frankly I don't give a shit about nothing else. I like sprinting. Like the idea of getting from one point to the next as fast as possible. I think outside the box as far as sprinting is concerned. For example, energy.' He looks thoughtful, unsure whether he should carry on. Then he carries on regardless, explaining a theory he has been developing (if only in his own mind). 'If you're in the desert dying, if the first energy source dies – the glucose system – fat takes over. And we store more fat than Carter has peanuts. I'm trying to figure out how I can get to that energy source.'

This sounds interesting, if ambitious, but Johnson dismisses it. 'What I'm saying is foolishness, madness. Because right now it's impossible. But that is where my eyes are.' It would mean, he thinks, 'tricking the body into saying, "We need this energy" ' – the energy stored in fat.[12] 'I don't have any secrets, but I've been discussing this with the Prof, Errol Morrison. He's the best physiologist in the world.'

---

[12] Perhaps it isn't madness. In early 2015, it was reported that scientists at the University of Oxford have been developing an energy drink using ketones, chemicals produced naturally by the body, which encourage the burning of fat as an alternative to glucose.

Morrison, the president at UTech, has worked with the physiologist Yannis Pitsiladis, originally of Glasgow University, more recently of Brighton, in studying the Jamaicans' sprinting success, including trying to identify a gene that might explain it – a speed gene. I mention to Johnson that I'd like to meet Morrison; is he easy to contact? 'Yeah, man,' says Johnson, reaching for his phone, dialling his friend's number. 'Prof, got someone wants to speak to you . . .' – looking up, addressing me. 'What's your name, my friend? . . . Richard. Here,' and he hands me the phone.

'One final question,' I say to Johnson when I've arranged a time to meet Morrison, but he interrupts: 'No, relax! I'm not in a hurry.' And on cue, a teenage boy appears with a tray of cold drinks. His son, says Johnson. A promising sprinter.

One thing that Johnson has been insistent on is that as well as technique (the number one thing), the physiology of the sprinter is important, and that the physiology of humans has not changed over the years. Therefore, training and coaching hasn't changed. A curious but related claim he makes is that sprinters are not any faster now than in his day, despite the times coming down. What does he mean? 'The fundamentals are the same,' he says. 'Physiology doesn't change, unless we grow horns or fins.'

But times do seem to have improved; how does he explain that? 'That's a very interesting question,' Johnson says. 'Are you ready for the answer?'

'Yes.'

'Nothing has improved since 1948.'

He thinks the faster times can all be explained by improvements in tracks, shoes, timing methods and other non-physiological factors. So, I ask him, who would win if both were at their peak – him or Bolt? He takes a circuitous route to the answer – hardly 'getting from one point to the next as fast as possible'. 'I was the first man in the world to run on an artificial track – a Tartan track. The Minnesota Mining and Manufacturing Company [these days known as 3M] came to

San José and put down one lane. One lane! Sixty yards long. The guy wanted to know how fast I ran. I alone ran along this track. I also had the world record for 60 yards: six-flat. Hand-timed. But when I did this experiment, with a guy called Arthur from Los Angeles, he had an automatic timer, but not like a stopwatch – it was one of those computers that fill a whole room. Anyway. The long and short of it is that I run 5.8 seconds. That means the track is two tenths faster than the dirt.

'Now, sixty yards is about fifty-five metres,' Johnson continues. 'The world record as we speak is 5.80. You can check that on your Google. So I ask myself the question: how much longer would it take me to do the next forty-five metres, bearing in mind I'm going at twenty-five m.p.h.? I'm asking you – I have forty-five metres left, I've passed the point at 5.80. My time for 100 metres. Come on.'

'I'll say around 9.8,' I suggest.

'Exactly!' says Johnson. 'And that is the ballpark in which they run today. When I did it, my shoes don't resemble what they look like today. We were running on dirt. I was a student with a job. You understand?'[13]

But Bolt has gone quicker than 9.8, I say – 9.58 is his world record. 'Bolt doesn't run 9.5 again,' Johnson says, 'or anywhere near it. Nobody is running that or close to it every day. Nine-point-eight is the ballpark.

'But Bolt is the best,' he concedes. 'The best ever. Undoubtedly. I know him fairly well. What is good about Bolt is not his blinding speed. What is good about him is his head. You understand? You can't beat somebody like that.'

Before I leave, Johnson mentions a sports science conference in the Pegasus Hotel in Kingston in a couple of weeks. 'The Prof', Errol

---

13 Once again, Johnson may be on to something. An academic study attempted to compare times set today with those of yesteryear. Allowing for the cinder track, shoes and other factors, Bob Hayes' 1964 world record of 10.06 seconds is equivalent to 9.66 (9.72 with no wind), reckons Dr Brian Maraj of the University of Alberta.

Morrison, will be there, among others, and he says I'm welcome to come along.

A fortnight later, I take up his invitation. During a break in the conference, I spot Johnson deep in conversation with a young man in a suit. It looks pretty one-way, with Johnson doing all the talking. And as I get closer, I can hear what he is saying: '... a sixty-yard track, about fifty-five metres, and I did it in 5.8 seconds. Five-point-eight-zero. The world record today is 5.80. Check that on your Google.

'So I'm asking you . . .'

7

CUBAN SWIMMING POOL CRISIS

Jamaica's prowess in global athletics is no fluke . . . or, as some would wish to convince the world, the result of officially blessed and systematic cheating . . . That dominance rests on natural talent, a tradition of excellence that has its roots in more than a century of Champs and the return on investment more than three decades ago in establishing the G. C. Foster College for Physical Education and Sports.
Editorial in the *Jamaica Gleaner*, 2 April 2014

If Dennis Johnson did more than any other individual to take sprint coaching around the country, and Herb McKenley developed a culture of excellence at one school, it needed something else, an institution, to bolster, spread and sustain their work.

Heading out of Calabar High School, turning right on to busy Washington Boulevard, takes you in the direction of Spanish Town. And when, after half an hour, you reach Spanish Town, you find G. C. Foster College.

Or you try to find it. It isn't easy. It's actually in the north of Spanish Town, in the Angels district. The college sits in expansive grounds, but these grounds are hidden on the other side of a railway line, in the middle of a community that resembles a shanty town: houses and shops constructed from wood and old bits of metal. You get lost in a maze of small, bumpy streets, until, about to give up, you abruptly emerge into open space, with plains and sports fields stretching out in front of you.

'It's in a terrible place,' I was told by Hugh Small, a judge and former politician who served as youth sports minister. 'It's not what it was or what it could be. But it needed a significant amount of land and the only available land was in Spanish Town.'

Small was one of the politicians who in the late 1970s worked on the plans to establish a sports college in Jamaica modelled on the centres of excellence that existed in Cuba, East Germany and the Soviet Union; centres integral to the systems that brought these countries phenomenal success at the Olympic Games. It was no coincidence that inspiration came from behind the Iron Curtain.

Jamaica in the seventies had a socialist government, led by the charismatic five-times-married Michael Manley of the PNP, the People's National Party. Manley forged a relationship with Fidel Castro's Cuba that alarmed the US, who feared the spread of communism so close to their shores. As a consequence, the CIA increasingly involved themselves in Jamaican politics, backing the rival right-leaning Jamaica Labour Party (JLP), led by the reggae-loving Edward Seaga (also a record company owner who contributed much to the burgeoning music scene). Less than two decades after gaining independence, the island was becoming bitterly split along party lines. Communities in Kingston were turned into garrisons affiliated to one political party or the other; guns began flooding into the country; gangs were allegedly armed by politicians.[14] The violence kept escalating

---

14 Almost inevitably, a culture developed where local 'dons', like Christopher 'Dudus' Coke, became all-powerful in the garrisons. As Mark Shields, a British police officer seconded to Jamaica in 2004, told the *Guardian* in 2012: 'It's criminal terrorism. People literally live in fear. If they run a shop, they have to pay protection. If the don wanted their youngest daughter, they would have to give her up so he could take her virginity. The community was completely under the control of the local don, and the police were deeply frightened about going in there.'

even as Bob Marley, living in exile in London after being shot in his home on Hope Road in 1976, put Jamaica on the world stage with his songs about love and peace.

Marley's One Love Peace Concert at the National Stadium in 1978 was intended to signal his return to Jamaica and put an end to the violence. At one point he called the two political rivals on to the stage to stand alongside him, joining their hands above his head, the politicians stern-faced and awkward as they towered over the diminutive singer. 'We gotta be together,' said Marley. 'I just want to shake hands and show the people that we're gonna make it right, we're gonna unite, we're gonna make it right, we've got to unite . . .' (It didn't have the desired effect: in 1980, when Seaga replaced Manley in a bitter election, 800 people were murdered in the course of the campaign. The violence was shocking. But it has since got worse: there are around 1,500 gun deaths a year in Jamaica, almost a fifth at the hands of the authorities: in 2013, 258 people were shot dead by police, though, encouragingly, it was closer to 100 in 2014.)[15]

The Manley name is synonymous with Jamaican politics. Michael Manley's father, Norman, who founded the PNP, was hailed in 1962 as one of the founding fathers of independence. It seems more than a coincidence that he was also one of Jamaica's first world-class sprinters, whose national 110 yards record of 10 seconds flat, set at Champs in 1911, stood for forty-one years. Later, as a barrister, he represented future Olympic champion Arthur Wint when the young Wint was on trial after accidentally shooting and killing his female colleague. Yet Norman Manley, having fought so hard for Jamaican independence, never served as prime minister. His cousin, Alexander Bustamante, who set up the rival JLP, was the country's first elected leader, serving from 1962 to 1967. Manley's son, Michael, was then elected in 1972.

Michael Manley was inspired by the strong emphasis Cuba put on sport, with athletes identified at a young age – a Junior Olympic Programme was established in Cuba in 1963 – and given specialist coaching. Results followed. By the seventies, Castro's Cuba was an Olympic powerhouse.

Hugh Small told me that in the late 1970s, when he was Jamaica's youth sports minister, he visited Cuba to inspect their then state-of-the-art sports facilities. He also travelled to East Germany and the Soviet Union, and to one non-communist country: Great Britain. 'I went to Loughborough,' he recalled. 'I met Seb Coe and his father, Peter.'

Even back then Jamaica already had a disproportionate number of world-class runners: after McKenley, Wint and Rhoden came George Kerr, a double Olympic bronze medallist in 1960, Lennox Miller, an Olympic 100 metres medallist in 1968 and 1972, and Don Quarrie,

---

15 According to Laurie Gunst in *Born Fi' Dead*, her disturbing and controversial 1996 book about gang culture in Jamaica: 'The politicians and their gunmen took over where the slave masters and their overseers left off: the practice of intimidation was a logical outgrowth of the brutal intimacy that had always prevailed between the powerful and the powerless.'

the 1976 Olympic 200 metres champion. But Manley wanted to establish a system, open to rich and poor, but especially poor, to put Jamaica on a par with other small nations – Cuba and East Germany being the obvious examples – that didn't just punch above their weight but were sporting superpowers.

P. J. Patterson, the foreign minister in Manley's government, recalls a visit by Castro. 'Fidel offered six schools,' Patterson told me. 'Michael said he wanted one for people to be trained in physical education. That became the G. C. Foster College, and out of it has come a flow of coaches.'

You enter its grounds and drive past a disused Olympic-sized swimming pool and diving pool. Both are fading white edifices, dry as a bone, with weeds sprouting through the cracks. The sports fields are large, but they too seem neglected. The buildings that make up the campus look as though they were built in 1980 and have barely been touched since. A large sign at the entrance, with a picture of a smiling Gerald Claude Eugene Foster, offers some historical background. The first sports college in the English-speaking Caribbean opened in September 1980, 'the original buildings and equipments [...] gifts from the government and people of Cuba to the government and people of Jamaica'.

Foster, after whom the college is named, is another major figure in Jamaican sport. Dennis Johnson mentioned him as the only coach, apart from Herb McKenley, worthy of the name when he returned to the island in 1966. He was an old man then; he died that same year, aged eighty.

Foster is best known for his efforts to compete at the 1908 London Olympics, crossing the Atlantic in a banana boat only to be denied the opportunity because Jamaica, as a British colony, was not a member of the IOC in its own right. Foster remained in England and took part in post-Games meetings, where he showed his talent, beating some of the sprinters who had excelled at the Olympics. He had attended

Wolmer's Boys' School – still a powerful force at Champs – and was marked out as a gifted athlete when, as a fourteen-year-old, he was given a ten-yard handicap against Kingston's best sprinter, M. L. Ford. He won by three yards. When he was eighteen, he ran 100 yards in 10 seconds: comparable with Archie Hahm's 11 seconds over 100 metres to win the Olympic title in the same year, 1904.

While I was in Jamaica, staying in Bull Bay, I mentioned that I was researching a book on athletics and was asked if I had heard of G. C. Foster. 'His daughter lives two doors down,' I was told. Pat Lightburn was her name, and she was eighty-eight and frail, living in a small, run-down house by the beach, surrounded by family – four generations at least, with a not untypical mix of ethnic influences, from the pale-skinned Mrs Lightburn to her black great-granddaughter.

Here was a living link to the original roots of Jamaica's sprinting culture. It was quite mind-blowing, especially to realise that it was almost fifty years since G. C. Foster had died. His daughter recalled him as vividly as she could: as an energetic, enthusiastic and relentlessly positive man who poured all his energy into sport. He was also a first-class cricketer before becoming an athletics coach, but he coached everything – she remembered him firing the starting pistol at the cycling track at the National Stadium to cries of 'Let them go, Mr Foster! Let them go!' She added: 'He coached at every school at one time or another, and they all won Champs when he coached them.' Indeed, he led Calabar to their first Champs title in 1931, then took Jamaica to the island's first international games, the 1935 British Empire Games in Hamilton, Canada, and to the 1948 London Olympics.

At the entrance to the college posthumously named after Foster, I am met by Maurice Wilson, the head coach, who takes me on a tour, pointing out, beyond the running track, a curious structure that looks like a funfair ride made out of Meccano. '*Cool Runnings*,' he says. This was where the Jamaican bobsleigh team trained for the 2014 Winter Olympics.

Wilson tells me that he has been head coach at G. C. Foster for eleven years. But like so many other coaches in Jamaica, his responsibilities range from schoolchildren to the best in the world. He is technical director of the country's governing body, the JAAA, and acted as head coach at the 2002 Commonwealth Games in Manchester, then again at the 2014 Games in Glasgow, having done the same job at the 2011 senior world championships in Daegu, South Korea. At G. C. Foster he is also principal lecturer in sports and recreation. 'But I'm a specialist track and field lecturer,' he adds.

Wilson talks the way an athlete limbers up, stretching his vocabulary. 'The persons who come under my guidance are versed in the major disciplines of track and field,' he explains when we are in his office. 'They must be able to coach to a level, and to pass on the information to other coaches.' His office is next to a classroom in which the students are becoming rowdy. 'I need to talk to them,' he says, and disappears, then quickly reappears, closing the door. 'My job is to make sure they become experts in the different disciplines; they are then distributed and dispersed all across the island to spread the philosophy of G. C. Foster. So it filters through the system.'

How would he sum up that philosophy? 'The basic techniques, the basic training methods, are given to these youngsters early. This is why you're seeing these performances. We do not leave, for example, technique, and mobility, and coordination, just to be learned. We help to correct deficiencies, and so on. This is done at an early stage. This is why Jamaicans are able to pass a baton without even having a training camp. It's drilled into them; from primary school.'

He echoes Dennis Johnson when he says that as far as he's concerned, it's all about technique. Not that Jamaicans know how to sprint while the rest of the world does not, but that the correct techniques are so ingrained because they are taught so early.

I was struck at Champs by the fact that the schools all had coaches who were, clearly, coaches, as opposed to teachers performing extracurricular duties. It is difficult to explain why this was obvious;

it just was, from their uniform – baseball cap, polo shirt, stopwatch, whistle – to the way they carried themselves, to the deference shown by their student athletes. The coaches took what they did – and by extension their athletes, and themselves – seriously. Wilson says that all of them will have passed through G. C. Foster; indeed, it is now a requirement of the secondary schools' association that organises Champs that school coaches must have a G. C. Foster qualification.

The college doesn't just churn out coaches. It produces people with other sports-related qualifications: sports masseurs, for example. Usain Bolt's personal masseur, Everald Edwards, trained at G. C. Foster. So did Shawn Kettle, who works for Yohan Blake, and Patrick Watson, a long-time member of Asafa Powell's team.

Wilson himself was a 400 metres runner at school, but, like Glen Mills and Stephen Francis, he was not an exceptional athlete. He excelled academically; he has a masters degree in science, as well as an undergraduate degree and a teaching diploma. This is another feature of quite a few of the top coaches: they are highly educated. Wilson believes that as well as being good athletes, his countrymen have a flair for coaching: 'I think we're naturally good coaches. Like Englishmen are good bankers . . . or seafarers.'

Where does it come from, this aptitude for coaching? 'I think although sometimes we don't pay attention to detail, anything that intrigues us we do well at. And running is a national obsession.'

On a tour of the grounds, Wilson laments the state of the running track and hopes a new one can be installed soon. He seems apologetic or embarrassed by the non-pristine condition of the place, and doesn't lead me anywhere near the swimming pool. But even if the infrastructure is crumbling, the wide-open space is invigorating. And compared to the facilities at Calabar, this is state-of-the-art.

We arrive at the office of the principal, Edward Shakes. He too speaks slowly, deliberately, in similar velvety tones; but initially, and at some length, about British football. 'I'm a Man U fan,' he says sombrely. 'Me, Chelsea,' offers Wilson, who sits in the corner of the principal's office and inspects his phone.

Shakes's background is in engineering – he studied in Britain for a while. 'I didn't come here as an expert in sport,' he says, 'I came in as an education administrator.' There are around 500 students at G. C. Foster, slightly more men than women. All will leave as certified coaches, and in many cases, as qualified teachers too.

'Prior to the college, there were only a few schools who performed very well and most of the outstanding athletes came from those few schools,' Shakes explains. 'Kingston College, Calabar and so on. But with the advent of G. C. Foster College, we train and disperse persons right across the country. We have trained persons placed in the schools in very rural areas. So someone like Usain Bolt, for example, who comes from rural Trelawny, he would have been exposed to a G. C. Foster coach at a very young age, and it would have been that person who discovered his talent and gave him all the early grooming.'

Shakes acknowledges the benefits of having an international coach on his staff – one of Wilson's athletes, Rasheed Dwyer, would go on to be crowned Commonwealth 200 metres champion in 2014, winning ahead of Warren Weir. Wilson is a Level V IAAF coach: the highest qualification. 'When you have that combination – someone like Maurice who is an academic as well as an internationally qualified coach, and a practising coach – you ensure your standards remain relevant. We have other international coaches on staff. We try to maintain standards. And they are practising what they teach.'

In a sense, the college has achieved what it set out to do, training coaches to a high standard and, as both Shakes and Wilson say, dispersing them around the country, like seeds blowing off a dandelion. Naturally it took a few years for these seeds to find fertile ground and flower; then a little longer for the athletes to progress through the schools system and emerge on the international stage. But it certainly happened. And now the challenge, for Shakes, is maintaining standards, keeping G. C. Foster College fit for purpose – not letting the Jamaican system, of which the college is such an integral part, decline as the Cuban one has.

Shakes mentions the swimming pool, describing it as 'one of two big projects', along with the athletics track, requiring attention. He says he wants to 'resuscitate our pool. One point I was making was that we have the opportunity to do in swimming what we have done in track and field.'[16]

I ask when the pool was last used. Shakes sighs deeply. 'Interesting story. It was built by the Cubans. But as happened in the UK, governments change. And in 1980, the socialist government in Jamaica was voted out and a more conservative government was voted in on an anti-communist, anti-Cuba platform.

'So immediately after the election, the new prime minister [Seaga] ordered the Cuban technicians that were here to go home. And so, although the pool was built, it was never commissioned.'

'You mean it's never been used?'

'No. It was well built. And now, refurbishing it and getting it going is what we want to do.'

The Cuban technicians were just days away from completing their work. Could Seaga not have let them stay to get it finished? 'In the Cold War, a lot of crazy things happened, you know,' Shakes says. There was considerable pressure on Seaga from the US, he adds. 'If you wanted their money . . .' So it was American money or a swimming pool? 'I wouldn't put it that way, but the government acted because of pressure from the US.'

*

16 Why not? In December 2014, a Jamaican, Alia Atkinson, became the first black woman ever to win a world swimming title, at the world short-course championships in Doha. Atkinson won the 100 metres breaststroke. She trains in Florida.

'Irrespective of what you may think of Jamaica, you have to come here to see,' Maurice Wilson tells me after we have left the principal's office. 'We have many more Usain Bolts. It is not a fad. It is something that is ingrained in us. You have to be at boys' and girls' Champs to understand it.'

I tell Wilson that it's all very well me reporting back on Champs, and the extraordinary performances I witnessed, but many have made up their minds – that the explanation for Jamaica's success is drugs.

'Let me say something on that,' he replies. 'When you look at the drugs that was involved [in recent cases], let us be reasonable. When you talk about a stimulant, that has no effect on you during competition . . . yes, you have violated a rule, but why make it appear as if those guys are on steroids? There is no distinction made!'

Wilson, like Dennis Johnson and others involved in the sport in Jamaica, is frustrated at the perception that their athletes are systematically cheating. He does not think the transgressions are the 'tip of the iceberg', as one Jamaican drug-tester has claimed. 'We have never had a top-notch athlete coming out of Jamaica that has tested positive for a hard drug, like steroids, where you know that they definitely went out there to cheat,' Wilson says. 'And I know that a lot of times people throw cold water on performances. In other words, "I cannot believe that in a population of three million these guys are topping the world." But I do believe that Scottish people are great bankers . . . I do believe that the Irish do well in business. So how is it that you cannot believe we are great athletes?'

Perhaps it was a natural evolution from G. C. Foster's production of so many home-grown coaches to have home-grown stars too. 'It was Stephen Francis', Wilson says, 'who decided, after Carl Lewis made a statement that they [the US] were training our athletes, that the job could be done here.'

8

SHIFTING THE PARADIGM

*We no longer saw track and field as an individual sport. We saw
it then and still see it today as a team sport.*
Bruce James, President, MVP

They meet at 5 a.m. at the East Stadium, which sits beside the National
Stadium like its little brother. This was the warm-up track – the 'boiler
room', my American coaching friend called it – during Champs.

The first question is: why so early?

'I do this', Stephen Francis has explained, 'to control the night-time
activities of my athletes.'

By 7 a.m., the sun is creeping up from behind the Blue Mountains,
casting long shadows across the faded red track and patchy grass of the
infield. The light is pale gold.

Sitting watching in the stand, it's like observing a factory floor, with
groups of workers performing highly specific tasks, watched over by
the foreman, Francis. There are close to 100 athletes, all in little knots:
a hive of activity and noise, the coaches' whistles providing regular,
jarring variations to the hum of the morning rush hour.

Francis is slumped on a bench in the infield wearing ill-fitting black
tracksuit trousers, a green polo shirt and a sun hat. He has a black 'man

bag' slung over his shoulder. The bench faces away from the track, but Francis has twisted his body – no mean feat, given his build – to be able to see the home straight. But as waves of athletes pass, sprinting or running with exaggerated knee-lifts, Coach Francis seems hardly to notice; he looks indifferent. Eventually he gets up and lumbers towards a group of four female sprinters gathered at the bend. Four other sprinters pass him and, without appearing to be watching them, he barks, 'Shoulders, Shamira!'

A sprint hurdler is next down the straight and past the slow-moving Francis. 'Trail leg!' he shouts after her, again without turning.

But now he goes to work, helping the female sprint teams prepare for the upcoming Penn Relays: a huge date in the Jamaican athletics calendar ever since Herb McKenley began taking teams there in the early 1960s. Today, in one of their final sessions before Pennsylvania, the baton changes are not as slick as they could be. 'Reach!' yells Francis after one sloppy change. After another failure, he stretches to full height with his hands in the air, then places them slowly behind his head in an attitude of pure exasperation. He raises his voice again: 'Tell her to reach!' When the men have similar problems, he seems to lose his temper: 'What did I say? What did I say?'

Francis turns his attention to a young male sprinter. 'Relax your shoulders, man . . . Let's go, boy. Heels!' Then, to a female sprint hurdler: 'Lean forward! Forward . . . Forward . . . Forward! . . . Good, I like that.'

The track is full of sculpted, muscular bodies, now starting to overheat as the sun rises further in the sky. It's still only 8 a.m., but Francis blows for a final time on his whistle, the activity abruptly ceases, and he wanders into the bowels of the stand. Soon he will make his way to the car park and his gleaming white BMW X5 to drive to his home in the surrounding hills, where he will read scientific papers or pore over data on his computer. Training will resume at 3 p.m. with a weights session in the gym at UTech.

The fifty-year-old Francis's reputation precedes him. In reports his name is frequently prefixed with 'controversial', mainly because he seems to be permanently at war with the administrators: the Jamaica Athletics Administrative Association, the Jamaica Olympic Association, the government; pretty much anyone in authority. 'We have never received one cent from any of them,' he once complained. In interviews he comes across as blunt and outspoken but not rude or aggressive. In contrast to Glen Mills, with whom Francis has a strained relationship, at least he *gives* interviews.

Watching Francis with his athletes, blasting on his whistle and barking instructions, the impression is of a formidable, imposing and intimidating figure. Not somebody you would pick a fight with. Then again, perhaps his reputation owes too much, and unfairly, to his physique. He is a generously proportioned man. A 2009 article in the Australian newspaper *The Age* described him, a little unkindly, as 'one of the unlikeliest sights in sport . . . A bear of a man who can barely manage a brisk walk, he spends his days bellowing through a megaphone at some of the fleetest athletes on the planet. They appear terrified of him.'

That was tame. In 2013, the *Gleaner* published a comment piece about Francis, under the headline 'He ain't pretty but he's pretty damn good.' It opened with some general observations on the relationship between a person's looks and their popularity, in particular the unfortunate fate of the 'ugly man'. It went on: 'It can be argued that Stephen Francis, a genius of coaching and moulding athletic talent, does not get due respect and acknowledgement from the Jamaican public, perhaps because he's not a pretty boy.'

The article continued: ' "Frano" could hardly have been more unfortunate in the looks department. A corpulent man who makes the shade black look black,[17] Francis knows what it takes to make athletes run pretty quickly with poise and beauty. Much of the reason for some people disliking him is the fact that he's often brusque with the media and doesn't indulge their prying into the business of him and his athletes.'

It ended with a plea for respect. It was an article in *defence* of Francis.

First impressions can be misleading. The day before my early-morning appointment at the East Stadium, I visited Dr Rachael Irving, a scientist at the University of the West Indies. From her office on the sprawling, well-maintained Mona campus we could just about see the pristine blue track where Mills and his Racers Track Club, including Bolt, train every morning.

Irving has been involved in a project to find the 'speed gene' that might explain the Jamaicans' success, though originally she was more

---

17 The remark about Francis's colour provoked some angry responses in the *Gleaner* but it hints at an enduring preoccupation with the colour, or shade, of someone's skin, and some of the complex, contradictory attitudes surrounding this issue in Jamaica: attitudes exemplified by the dancehall star, Vybz Kartel. In 2011 he bleached his skin and launched a range of skin-bleaching products even while singing that black people should be proud of their colour. During my first visit to Jamaica the news was dominated by Kartel's conviction for murder; he was sentenced to thirty-five years in prison.

interested in the original trailblazers, Francis and his MVP club, than in Mills's Racers Track Club. She was charged by scientist Yannis Pitsiladis with collecting DNA samples from some of the top athletes, including those at MVP.

She only knew Francis by reputation. 'I was a little afraid. I went there to watch them training, the early mornings. I sat there in the stand for a month and just watched. Stephen came to me one morning and said, "Why are you here every day looking at us?"

'I said, "Well I'm supposed to be involved in this project but I'm afraid to talk to you."

'Stephen said, "Why are you afraid of me?" ' She explained the project and Francis, to her surprise, was curious. He told her to phone him when he returned from a trip to Europe. She would do that, she said, adding that she already had his number. 'That's the number I give to people I don't want to talk to,' said Francis.

When it came to collecting the samples, Francis couldn't have been more obliging. While Irving hovered with her swabs to collect saliva samples at the end of training, Francis ordered his athletes, including Asafa Powell and Shelly-Ann Fraser, to assist her. 'Give Dr Irving some support!' he barked if they showed any reluctance.

'We developed, I wouldn't say a friendship, but he's somebody I can talk to,' Irving told me. 'He has a rough exterior. Well, persons say that, but they don't know him. I think he's fantastic!'

Beneath the stand, in the shade, the athletes file past, panting and sweating, in various states of distress. Francis, having stopped to speak to a couple of his assistants, watches them, offering words of encouragement or mild, tongue-in-cheek rebuke. The athletes include some of the best in the world: double Olympic 100 metres champion Shelly-Ann Fraser-Pryce; Nesta Carter, a double Olympic 4x100 metres gold medallist and 9.78-second 100 metres man; Shericka Williams, an Olympic relay medallist.

Francis looks relaxed. It might be a good time to approach. Can he spare some time? 'Sure,' he says.

Like Glen Mills, Francis was not a star athlete as a schoolboy (another thing he has in common with Mills is that he is a bachelor. He explained in 2006: 'In my twenties I was too much of a party person to marry. In my thirties I could not afford it. Now that I am in my forties I travel too much').

'I was a thrower at school,' he tells me, 'but not very good.' He was a pupil at Wolmer's Boys' School (the first ever Champs winners, in 1910). He was more academically inclined, captaining the Schools' Challenge Quiz team (a big deal in Jamaica: basically Champs for brainy kids). He went to the University of the West Indies in Kingston to do management studies, with accountancy and economics. Later he went to the US, to the University of Michigan, to do an MBA in finance. Bright, then.

While doing his undergraduate degree in Kingston, Francis began to take an interest in the athletic career of his younger brother, Paul, who was also at Wolmer's, and a decent thrower. He volunteered to help coach at the school. 'I got the coaching bug after a while,' he says. 'I went to the US to do my MBA, then returned and started coaching again part time at the school.'

Back in Kingston, he worked as a management consultant for KPMG. But it was increasingly coaching that consumed him. He would go and watch Dennis Johnson's training sessions at UTech. A voracious reader, he devoured books on athletics and coaching. He was interested in the theoretical as well as the practical. (Which brings to mind a Ronald Reagan quote: 'An economist is someone who sees something that works in practice and wonders if it would work in theory.' Francis is an economist.)

'You start first by reading books on track and field,' he says, his voice so deep that you can almost feel the stand vibrating. He has a tendency to refer to himself in the second person. He says he read 'Sprinting books, throwing books. Um, and then you realise you have to move to different areas: physiology, biomechanics, anatomy. To be a really knowledgeable coach you need to read a lot more than one would think necessary.'

Any key books? 'A lot,' Francis nods. 'I think the most important book in my early career . . . I had a friend at Wolmer's who went to study coaching in Cuba. He came back with a book about coaching that he said had all the secrets. But it was in Spanish.' Which Francis didn't speak. So how did he read it? 'I sat down with a dictionary and a typewriter and translated it over a period of a month or so.'

It didn't contain all the secrets, but it had some useful information on 'the whole question of recovery; how they did periodisation; increasing [training] load. Those things were not as clear in most of the American textbooks I was reading at the time. You had other people like Frank Dick in Britain, who wrote some good books, and some American authors. A wide variety. Now a lot of the reading I do is research papers, research journals.'

It's not all he reads. 'I'm a very avid fan of novels. I read a lot of non-fiction, mainly legal, mystery-type theories. I do a lot of reading.'

As for favourite authors: 'I like to think I discovered Michael Lewis,' Francis says, 'because I read his first [*Liar's Poker*] in 1989.'

This is interesting, because Lewis's books are concerned with the worlds of finance and money, or, as in the case of *Moneyball* and *The Blindside*, sport. There are differences between them, though. In his books about finance, he is concerned with exposing corruption, greed and nefarious practices; in his books about sport, he tends to be more interested in innovative coaches who discover and develop previously hidden, underrated or underperforming talent (the subtitle of *Moneyball* is: 'The Art of Winning an Unfair Game').

In fact, you could say that most of his books are essentially about people who beat or subvert the system: schemers. In the world of finance they tend to be malignant; in sport, benign. It could be a coincidence, of course. But there seems to be a moral distinction, one that maybe says more about Lewis's cynicism towards the world of finance (a world he knows well having worked as a bond salesman) and his idealism when it comes to professional sport, with which he is perhaps not so intimately acquainted.

By the late 1990s, Francis had itchy feet. His job at KPMG paid well, but his passion was for athletics, or rather coaching. He believed that Jamaican athletes were being lost, slipping through the cracks in the system, although his main bone of contention was that there was no system in the first place. He felt that complacency reigned. (In the best tradition of those who see themselves as operating outside and against the system, he cannot resist digs at the Jamaican sporting establishment, even as he praises Champs as the island's greatest institution: 'Jamaica's athletics success has always been about Champs. It was not designed by anybody, though the British have a lot to answer for. And so far Jamaicans have not been able to destroy it – but I think they're working hard at that.')

Jamaica's problem was that they had always done so well: they consistently won more medals than an island their size had any right to expect. Francis believed that success bred complacency. There was a reluctance – a refusal – to think about how they could be even better.

Jamaica was a good nursery, but the finishing schools were in the US. As well as the home-grown, overseas-reared athletes, the success of other expats – including the Olympic 100 metres winners from 1988–96, Ben Johnson, Linford Christie and Donovan Bailey, even if the first two now have doping offences against their names – reinforced the idea that the existing model worked: teach kids how to run, then send them away.

Francis thought differently. He wondered if, in fact, talent was being lost. 'The research thing for me', he explains, 'was to compile a list of people from Jamaica and see what happened to them four years down the road compared to Americans, Kenyans, Australians . . . whatever. It was always something I discussed at various levels with the

JAAA and with other coaches. At the time, everyone was very fearful of taking the step [of coaching Jamaican athletes at home], because it was all they knew: they run, they get a scholarship, and if you do hear from them again you get them to run for Jamaica as seniors. That was how it was.

'DJ tried to change that up at UTech, but there was something missing when he was there in terms of connecting what he was doing at UTech to the top level of the sport.'

The frustration for Francis came in realising how many talented athletes had left for the US and then disappeared. 'It was difficult to understand. I mean, I believed that a lot of the kids who didn't make it in the States were either sidelined or there was maladjustment: missing their parents, missing their food, being stuck in the cornfields of Iowa, or the cornfields of Kansas, or being in the city and being caught up in the whole gangster and drugs stuff.'

There were advantages in the States in terms of facilities and regular competition. But not coaching – he believed they could be coached better in Jamaica, where their focus wouldn't be running all over the US chasing points for their universities in the national colleges competition. Moreover, he adds, 'I felt that if you could give them a relatively comfortable situation, the fact that they are where they're accustomed to would more than make up for the deficiencies in proper weights facilities and so on. It would at least give them an equal chance. The problem was to get people to try it out.'

In September 1999, the Francis brothers and two friends, David Noel and Bruce James, who worked at Citibank, sat discussing the issue in James's flat in Kingston. From this discussion they decided to start their own club. They called it Maximising Velocity and Power (MVP) Track and Field Club. At the same time Francis made a major decision: to quit his job and try coaching full-time. A radical, bold – or foolish – step. 'Oh yeah,' he says, 'a big move. There were many ramifications. A lot of lifestyle changes and questioning as to whether it was a sensible thing to do.'

Presumably it meant a big drop in earnings, too. 'Oh, huge, because up to that point nobody had made a living out of full-time coaching seniors in Jamaica. The only person at the time who'd made a living as a coach was the national football coach, who was a Brazilian.' That was René Simões, who led the national team, known as the Reggae Boyz, to the 1998 World Cup finals in France.[18]

For the new MVP, the challenge was to recruit athletes. Was it a hard sell? 'It was a no sell,' Francis says.

The first member was Brigitte Foster, a twenty-five-year-old sprint hurdler who had followed the familiar path. She had been a promising schoolgirl – though she never won at Champs – but had lost her way when she went to university in the US. In 1999, after four years away, she was back in Jamaica. As Bruce James explained in a TEDx talk in 2011 about the origins of MVP: 'She was in search of a coach, and we were in search of an athlete.'

Francis began working with Foster, and within a year she was an Olympic finalist. She finished eighth in Sydney after hitting a hurdle, but the telling statistic was the improvement she made in twelve months, her time dropping from 13.30 for the 100 metres hurdles to 12.70. Foster said that what most impressed her about Francis was his 'constant grasp for knowledge'.

Francis thought Foster's performance in Sydney would put MVP on the map. Instead there was resistance at home to what they were trying to do. Bruce James believed that their vision, to coach senior Jamaican athletes in Jamaica, was actually unpopular with the powers-that-be: 'We soon discovered that not everyone loved our idea. In fact, they

---

18 Dennis Johnson was absolutely scathing of the Reggae Boyz. 'The Reggae Boyz!' he spluttered. 'The Reggae Boyz was born to lose. When countries go to the World Cup, them eyes on the prize! You know what we went to do? Get on to the field of play!' Johnson overlooks the fact that Jamaica became the smallest nation ever to win a World Cup Game, beating Japan 2–1 in their final group match. The Reggae Boyz might not have been in France thinking they could win the tournament, but they were hardly *Cool Runnings*.

didn't even like it . . . the Jamaican power brokers thought, How dare these four men try to wreck a great thing that Jamaica has going on.' He thought the 'biggest hurdle was the Jamaican mindset. In Jamaica, Jamaicans were convinced that what we had achieved at the world championships and Olympics was so amazing it was remarkable. What were you going to change?' (And indeed, why?)

In their first few years they trained on the dirt track at Wolmer's. But the club began to struggle financially. Francis sold his car to keep MVP afloat. 'My credit rating was so bad I could not get a credit card.' Then he had an idea. He went to Johnson at UTech with an offer: he would coach their athletes for free (he was by now an IAAF-accredited coach) if MVP could use their facilities. He thus became Johnson's unpaid assistant. And now, well over a decade later, the partnership between university and club is, says Francis, 'hugely symbiotic. Most athletes who come to UTech know they'll be in MVP. It's almost like it's one; we are known as UTech/MVP. We share everything.'

The founding principles of the club they discussed in James's flat in 1999 remain paramount, however. James, in his talk in 2011, called them the 'three philosophies' of MVP:

1. We no longer saw track and field as an individual sport. We saw it then and still see it today as a team sport.

2. The option to stay and train in Jamaica is just that: an option. But it is critical to have this option.

3. Confidence. A Jamaican national hero, Marcus Garvey, said: 'If you haven't confidence in self, you are twice defeated in the race of life. With confidence, you have won even before you have started.'[19]

---

19 Garvey (1887–1940) was a political leader, skilled orator and hero to the Rastafari movement, who consider him a prophet. Ironically, given MVP's mission to

When they were getting started, says Francis, 'we were just looking for people we could get. There were some who I coached at Wolmer's. They would be more likely to believe in me and say, "OK, we'll give Coach a chance." The majority of the time we had to look for people who the coaches in the States were not going to be pursuing.'

Francis was also setting out to coach adults rather than kids. This posed a new challenge and required a different approach. Schoolchildren would, he explains, 'finish training in May and come back in September taller, stronger, faster, without you doing anything. As long as the youngster grows you don't have to pay too much attention to technique or anything like that because their body's natural progression . . . is ensuring that some kind of improvement occurs.

'When, at eighteen, nineteen, the growth slows – or for females when they're sixteen, seventeen – then it becomes a lot more difficult for them to improve. You no longer get the physical help from their bodies. For them to [improve] you need to ensure they do the right kind of work. So it's vastly more difficult – it's part of the reason why there is such a very low transfer rate in terms of talent as juniors to success as seniors.'

Francis, in any case, was not looking for the best high school athletes, mainly because he didn't think they'd be interested. 'At first we didn't dare approach anybody who people thought was good. With Asafa we directly picked him out because he came last. He looked OK but we knew there'd be little or no competition to get him.'

Asafa Powell was eighteen when he joined MVP. He had grown up in Linstead, in St Catherine Parish, twelve miles inland from Spanish

---

encourage Jamaican athletes to stay in Jamaica, Garvey was the founder of the Black Star Line, which promoted the return of the African diaspora to their ancestral lands. 'A people without the knowledge of their past history, origin and culture is like a tree without roots,' he said.

Town. He went to Charlemont High, not a leading force at Champs –
often they didn't even qualify.[20]

At Champs in 2000, Powell was third in the first round of the
100 metres in 11.45 and fourth in his 200 metres in 23.07; he didn't
progress beyond the heats. A year later he reached the 100 metres
final, after running 10.77 in the semi, but false-started. The race was
won by Marvin Anderson of St Jago in 10.40, ahead of another red-
hot talent, Steve Mullings.

Francis didn't see Powell's talent (nobody did), but he did see his
potential. His technique was so ragged – 'I used to lean way back,'
Powell has said. 'My arms weren't going up; my knees were going too
high; everything was wrong' – that Francis believed improvements
were possible in every department. To be fair, few would have disputed
that.

Something that counted in Powell's favour, perhaps, was that he
hadn't been through the kind of regime that athletes at schools such
as Calabar and Kingston College were exposed to. Francis might also
have imagined there was something in his genes. He was the youngest
of six boys (of course) born to William and Cislyn Powell, both pastors
in the Redemption National Church of God. His parents had been
decent sprinters in their youth, his father running 10.2 seconds for the
100 yards, his mother 11.4, but the talent seemed to have passed to
another of their sons, Donovan, who was eleven years Asafa's senior.
Donovan's personal best for 100 metres was 10.07, in 1995, but he
is even better known in Jamaica for inflicting the only defeat in four
years on Calabar's Daniel England at Champs, in the 200 metres in
1990. Donovan Powell attended one of the sprinting powerhouses,
St Jago (where Yohan Blake went to school). He also had a positive

---

20 Powell might be one of Charlemont High's most famous alumni, and was for a
   while arguably the most popular man in Jamaica, but his popularity had its limits.
   A proposal in 2010 to change the name of his former school to the Asafa Powell
   High School, which seemed to be led by the Asafa Powell Foundation, was opposed
   by other ex-pupils, and over 800 objections were reportedly posted on Facebook.

drugs test against his name, for ephedrine (a stimulant common in cold treatments) in 1995.

Asafa began working with Francis a week after Champs in 2001. The improvement was immediate. Three months later, on 22 June, he won the national under-20 100 metres in a personal best, 10.50 seconds. The next year he represented Jamaica at the Commonwealth Games in Manchester. He didn't make the final but did record another personal best, 10.26, in finishing fifth in the semi-final. In the relay, with Powell running the anchor leg, Jamaica took a silver medal behind England.

In the same year, the Powell family suffered the first of two tragedies. Asafa's brother Michael was shot dead by a mugger as he sat in a New York taxi. The next year, another of his brothers, Vaughn, dropped dead while playing American football. A heart attack was the verdict. Powell suffered a loss of confidence. 'I started to wonder,' he said, ' "Who's next?" '

But he carried on running, and training with Francis, and improving, becoming Jamaican national senior champion in 2003. A year later, he went below 10 seconds for the first time, running 9.99 seconds on G. C. Foster's threadbare track. Then he defended his national title with a sparkling 9.91 at the National Stadium: one of nine sub-10-second runs he recorded that season.

He was on his way.

Francis and MVP were on their way too. With Brigitte Foster winning a silver medal at the 2003 world championships, their reputation was burgeoning, even if some local resistance remained. At least now they didn't have to chase second-tier athletes. 'Eventually it became an option for athletes who people thought were good,' Francis says.

And people were paying attention, because Francis was asked to coach one of the island's brightest young prospects. He was from rural Trelawny, on the other side of the island, and his name was Usain Bolt.

'I was asked to coach Usain in 2003. But, well, I was told he was an extremely hard worker and I felt that most of his success at the time was due to the fact that he was training hard.'

In something of a mumble, Francis adds: 'Which was inaccurate.'

So he is the coach who turned down Bolt – though he insists he has no regrets. 'I wasn't put off by this,' he adds, referring to his belief that Bolt could be one of those athletes who peaked in his teens. 'What I was put off about, really, was the amount of people who were trying to claim a piece of him.' There was a growing entourage – Bolt's sponsors, Puma; his manager, Norman Peart; a European agent, Ricky Simms. 'I told the Puma people, "Look, if I'm going to coach Usain, most of these people are not going to have any influence, so it might not be a good thing,"' Francis says. He told them who he did and didn't want to be involved. But it was the constellation forming around him that he really found off-putting. 'I have never been a person who gravitates to an athlete because he is the best. It's more of a challenge to me to look at those people who others are ambivalent about, or who they don't think are any good.'

As per one of the MVP philosophies, he also believes in the idea of creating a team without major stars who stand head and shoulders above the others. It is all part, he says, of fostering a culture in which people are motivated – indeed, compelled – to improve. Almost any-body who commits to his programme will improve, he states, 'unless they are really, really, really, really bad'. Moreover, he adds, 'It is hard not to commit, because right now we have almost like a treadmill going downhill. Once you get on it, it's hard to stop because the whole environment, the whole culture, forces you to fit in.'

What he looks for, says Francis, 'are people who, based on their trend so far, look like they have some sort of upside. They've not been killed in high school; there's still something there to be got out. We try to work with them. To me it's a much better feeling taking an also-ran to the top.'

On the eve of the 2004 Olympic Games – the second of MVP's

existence – that is where the club's flag-bearer was. Asafa Powell ran in a star-studded 100 metres at the Weltklasse in Zurich, part of the IAAF's Golden League and traditionally the most prestigious meeting on the circuit. Olympic champion Maurice Greene was there, as was world champion Kim Collins and a young American prospect, Justin Gatlin. The tall figure of Powell (he is six foot three) was in the lane alongside Greene, and these two emerged at the front, Greene drifting towards Powell, emphasising that they were locked in battle. Their arms brushed but Powell didn't flinch; he remained focused on the line to win in 9.93, a hundredth of a second ahead of Greene, with Gatlin a distant third.

It was no longer a surprise. Powell was now being talked about in the same breath as Greene, Gatlin and Collins. With every passing race, Francis and MVP were demonstrating that they could produce world-class athletes at home in Jamaica. In Powell, they had the favourite for the blue riband event at the Olympic Games in Athens, the men's 100 metres. They were close to reaching their Everest; they could look up and see the summit.

9

JETS AND SHARKS

Well, we don't really have a relationship.
Stephen Francis on Glen Mills

It was October 2003 when Usain Bolt moved to Kingston, sharing a house with Jermaine Gonzales, a 400 metre specialist from the St Catherine Parish. A few months later, in January 2004, both runners moved in with Norman Peart, into a house in the Red Hills part of the city – at the salubrious end of a street that had Calabar High School at the other end.

Peart, the mentor appointed by Bolt's old school, had moved back to Kingston from Montego Bay at the same time. Now he wasn't just tutoring Bolt, but living with and looking after this kid just out of school, plucked from rural, sleepy Trelawny and parachuted into vibrant, violent Kingston.

'It was like becoming a dad for the first time,' he tells me. 'A parent entrusted with the golden treasure of Jamaica.'

Peart headed the rapidly expanding Team Bolt: the seventeen-year-old was sponsored by Puma, he attended the newly opened IAAF High Performance Training Centre in Kingston, where he was coached by Fitz Coleman, and he had a European-based agent, the Irishman

Ricky Simms. Another member of his entourage, then and now, was his best friend from school, Nugent 'NJ' Walker.

The headquarters of Team Bolt is a nondescript building from the outside, round the back of an auto insurance assessor's office, but with a cool interior, upholstered in dark green and yellow, a bit like the VIP area of a nightclub. When I was there, NJ was hovering in reception. His rather grand title is 'executive manager', but the impression is that his job description might more accurately read 'Usain's mate'.

As for Bolt himself, he was absent from HQ, though I could feel his presence, as I did elsewhere: at the track named after him at the University of the West Indies; the sports bar he owns in New Kingston, Tracks and Records; his favourite nightclub, the Quad; his parents' house in Trelawny; the Spartan gym where he trains.

When I asked Simms about doing an interview with Bolt in Jamaica, I was told: 'Usain hasn't done an interview in Jamaica since 2008.' So what about now? 'Usain hasn't done an interview in Jamaica since 2008.' No chance, then? 'Usain hasn't done an interview in Jamaica since 2008.' (Not actually true: Donald McRae of the *Guardian* did one in March 2010, organised by Puma, and Bolt spoke to a French documentary crew in 2011. But in 2014, when a crew making a film about Bob Marley asked for a short interview, they were told he would only do it for a price: £30,000.)

My contact with Bolt came in Europe rather than Jamaica, but in Jamaica I did feel close to him. It's a small place, so perhaps it was impossible not to. But it could be a bit freaky. One day, I had a call from Michelle, whose Stony Hill guest house I was staying in. 'I'm in the bank and Usain is here with me – shall I ask for an interview for you?' (I'm not sure if she did ask for an interview or just a selfie. She came home with a photograph, but Jamaicans tend to be laid-back even in the presence of their most famous countrymen and women. Which is partly why Bolt enjoys living there so much. Although he usually spends part of the summer in London, life is less stressful in Kingston because fewer people hassle him, which chimes with something Ziggy Marley said, that 'in Jamaica, you just someone, not nobody big'. Or as Bolt told McRae in one of his favourite nightclubs, Fiction: 'Most people know I'm there. But they also know I go to the clubs a lot, so they're relaxed. They're used to me in Kingston.' McRae is deservedly known as one of Britain's best sports writers, with a knack for prising open his interview subjects. He trailed Bolt for a few days, but the most revealing bits of his story are his own observations. In conversation, McRae found Bolt obliging but unreflective.)

I loitered in the vicinity of the Usain Bolt Track at the University of the West Indies, but although the campus is open, the track has a perimeter fence, with security staff at the entrance. Even if you drive towards it and look like you know what you're doing, they still stop you and turn you back.

Another day I visited the Spartan gym – I had just missed Bolt, said Steve Ming, a personal trainer there. He had been for an hour of free weights; the previous day he'd taken part in Ming's kick-boxing class, lurking at the back of the room. 'Sometimes a new person will say, "Is that Mr Bolt? Can I take a picture?" ' Ming says. 'But most are accustomed to seeing him, Yohan Blake, Warren Weir and the others on a daily basis. We don't have a policy for members. We don't need one.'

Does Ming sometimes sneak a look at what weights Bolt is squatting? 'I don't have to sneak a look. At the moment he's squatting a lot – 345 pounds on each side.' (That's 156 kilograms, or 312 kilograms in total, though these are partial, not full, squats.)

When Bolt first moved to Kingston, the entourage that today forms a protective cocoon around him was pretty much as it is now – the key people are the same. Simms first became aware of him during the 2002 world junior championships in Kingston, though the Irishman wasn't actually there. 'He was the one everyone was talking about,' he recalls. 'You could see his technique was ragged, but everyone was very excited about this big Jamaican guy.

'I was asked if I wanted to have a meeting with his people in 2003. He didn't want to go to the US – he wanted to stay close to his mum. He wanted to turn professional right away.'

By 'his people', Simms means his parents, plus Norman Peart, and Pascal Rolling at Puma. Peart tells me that he approached Simms after 'checking with people in the business'. It was necessary to have someone based in Europe because Peart didn't want to spend his life travelling, and Simms, a former middle-distance runner who took over Kim McDonald's athletes' agency when McDonald died suddenly in 2001, seemed like the ideal candidate. Simms, still only in his mid-thirties, is calm and understated, the antithesis of the flash sports agent (even if he does now live in Monaco). 'Ricky had an established business, a place to stay in London,' Peart explains. 'He wasn't operating out of a suitcase.'

It was a period of transition, says Peart, for him and for Bolt. He doesn't sugar-coat it, admitting it wasn't easy. Even before Bolt moved to Kingston, there was some controversy back in Trelawny, at his old school in particular. They considered that he was leaving a year early. 'The teachers didn't want him to leave,' says his father, Wellesley. 'They wanted the school name to be on top, but he'd outgrown all those so it was necessary for him to go. With Norman Peart, we decided it was best for him to go to Kingston.

'We went to Kingston to see where he would stay,' Wellesley continues. 'Gonzales stayed in the same house and every week I would go to see if things were OK. Well, he probably wasn't happy to go, to leave the house here. But after a few weeks, with the excitement in Kingston – he found what he did not have here.'

Bolt's move to Kingston seems preordained. It was certainly orchestrated at the very highest levels of Jamaican government, which goes to show how central athletics is to the country, and how central Bolt was to their future ambitions. P. J. Patterson, the prime minister, had sprung into action after the world junior championships, when he instructed Donald Quarrie to take Bolt under his wing. That wasn't realistic; Quarrie spent most of his time in Florida. Getting Bolt to Kingston became the priority. 'Obviously he had nothing to gain by staying at William Knibb,' says Patterson, sitting in his plush office on the twelfth floor of the Sagicor building in New Kingston, with views all the way down to the waterfront. 'He had to be moved.

'I met him,' Patterson continues. 'He was brimming with confidence, obviously a super-talent. We have a word in Jamaica, "brought-upsy". He was brought up properly; has two very good parents. He was disciplined, easy, humble.' Patterson confirms that he helped as 'arrangements were made for Bolt to move in with Gonzalez'.

Aside from his living arrangements, Bolt was installed in the High Performance Training Centre – one of several centres set up by the IAAF in developing countries, and the only one to focus on sprinting. His coach there was the well-respected and highly éxperienced Fitz Coleman. But within weeks it became clear that coach and athlete did not see eye to eye. Bolt wanted to focus on the 200 metres but felt Coleman's training was weighted towards the 400: 'Coach Coleman had me running 700, 600 and 500 metres all the time,' Bolt wrote in his autobiography. 'I hated waking up in the morning because that's when I reacted to the work the most. I was in agony; everything felt wrong.' For the first time, he was also doing weight training – a development that began to add muscle to his skinny frame. (By 2008 he had added 18 kilograms to his recorded weight in 2003, bulking up from 75 to 93 kilos.)

Jermaine Gonzalez, his housemate and sometime training partner, says that the impression of Bolt as laid-back, even lackadaisical, was never accurate. 'Not true. Not true. A lot of people think that he doesn't work hard. If you think he doesn't work hard, go and train with him. You cannot do what Usain do. He's not the most disciplined guy, I can tell you that, but when he comes to work, he's working and he's working really hard. Because he's jovial people think he's just doing what he does because he's talented. Not true.'

Wellesley Bolt backs up his son's claim that the training under Coleman was brutal. During one of his weekly visits to Kingston, he attended a session. It harked back to his unannounced journeys to Falmouth, the difference now being that instead of beating Usain for skipping training, he was concerned that he might be training too hard.

'Oh my God, it was rough,' Wellesley tells me on the porch of his house. 'I said, "Son, I didn't know it was that hard." I said, "You seems to be lazy, not training hard." But when I watched him train, I realised it was hard, hard work. When you see him race, you don't realise.' What kinds of things was he doing? 'They have those big [medicine] balls, carrying it up and down. It's rough. He vomit one time when I was there. He would say, "Dad, you see? You thought I had it easy." '

It wasn't all hard work. The lively Kingston club scene was a distraction. 'Movies, dance: in Kingston it was all there,' says Wellesley. 'Then Norman had to put his foot down, to keep him focused from the distractions.'

'He was a party guy,' says Peart, who was not exactly Mr Popular when it was time to curb Bolt's nightlife. 'He was not amused with me, because, you know, he got to the magical eighteen years. At that age they're trying to find themselves.'

Bolt has never been a big drinker – a pint or two of Guinness at most – but he liked a late night. He still does. 'The thing is, he's a single man,' says Simms. 'He's not doing anything wrong, it's something everyone else does.' On nights out these days, Simms adds, 'we normally have someone with him, and he often goes out the back door straight into a car. You try to make life as easy as possible for him. Though sometimes he likes to go out the front door . . .'

Before he moved to Kingston, the highlight of Bolt's 2003 season, his last as a schoolboy, was his 200 metres title at the world youth championships in Canada in a championship record 20.40 seconds. A close second was his final Champs, where he did the 200/400 double, setting records in both, with his 20.25 in the 200 still surviving.

In August, he went to Paris for the world senior championships. He was sixteen – turning seventeen while he was there – and thought he might be capable of making the 200 metres final, maybe even challenging for a medal. In the build-up to the championships, however, he was laid low by conjunctivitis (at least this was the official reason; I was told that he was not in good enough shape) and it was decided that he shouldn't race. But in an example of the forward thinking being applied to the 'golden treasure of Jamaica', he travelled with the team to gain experience of a major championship.

In Paris, *Trans World Sport*, the eclectic magazine-style TV programme, did a mini-feature on the prodigy. This shows a Jamaican party by the Seine, complete with a band that launches into a birthday tribute. Bolt, a gangly teenager looking like he's on a school trip, rucksack on his back, shuffles on to the stage; he seems uncomfortable being the centre of attention and mumbles along self-consciously to 'Happy Birthday'.

Patrick Anderson, part of the Jamaican delegation, was interviewed for the feature. 'He is one of those beautiful young men that is so talented it's unbelievable,' he said. 'Now, in a crowd, he's so modest and humble, he doesn't stand out, like some of these pretenders. That made me really warm to him. The kind of talent he has, you really have to nurse him.' Although Bolt wouldn't be competing in Paris, the experience would be useful, added Anderson, 'because we're expecting wonders at the Olympics next year, that's the big one'.

So enamoured by Bolt were the *Trans World Sport* team that they followed him to Jamaica a month later, turning up at his home in Trelawny. 'I really am proud of myself for doing so well and making Jamaica proud,' Bolt tells them, adding that Michael Johnson is his hero for 'always staying relaxed, no matter what kind of pressure he is under'. He confirms that his sights are firmly fixed on becoming a 200 and 400 metres runner; there is no mention of the 100 metres.

Perhaps the most revealing titbit in the footage from Trelawny has nothing to do with Bolt-the-athlete – or not directly. We see Bolt in his track gear standing by the side of a small road near Sherwood Content. When the camera pans out, a very different scene is revealed: there are cameras, vehicles and a large film crew. It looks like the set of a movie with a decent budget. They are shooting a Puma commercial. Bolt has just turned seventeen, yet he is somebody in whom, evidently, much is invested.

Simms, whose first visit to Jamaica wasn't until the winter of 2004, was not opposed to Bolt remaining on the island. 'The timing was good for him. There were good structures in place, with the IAAF High Performance Training Centre in Kingston. The problem at the start was that he was injured a lot, which meant he didn't train a lot. And his appetite for training wasn't that great, especially when he was getting hurt a lot. But he was such a huge talent he was able to get by on talent and a bit of work.'

This created something of a problem for Bolt in early 2004, when, at the CARIFTA Games in Bermuda, he ran 19.93 seconds to break the world junior record for 200 metres. It was a sensational time: he was the first teenager ever to go under 20 seconds. The race is extraordinary to watch: Bolt's winning margin is most of the finishing straight. Or as Robert Johnson, writing on the LetsRun website some years later, put it: 'Watching that made me feel like it was just unfair to make the other competitors even try to race Bolt. It's what you'd get if you filmed a horse racing humans.'

'The young Goliath of 200-metre running has installed himself as the gold-medal favourite for the Athens Olympics this summer,' said the *Bermuda Gazette*, which praised Bolt's 'ruthless demonstration of power and speed'.

For Bolt, however, it was a double-edged sword. The fact that it came on the back of Fitz Coleman's diet of endurance training seemed to validate the veteran coach's methods. 'You see?' Peart told Bolt, who had been complaining all winter about Coleman's training. 'You should believe in Coach's programme.' It only made Bolt more frustrated. He was annoyed that he had inadvertently endorsed Coleman's approach with his fast time.

Two weeks later, he broke down in training with a pulled hamstring. 'I was in agony, I could barely walk off the track and as I waved out for help the anger bubbled up inside. I felt pissed at the schedule, pissed at Mr Peart for telling me I had to suffer the pain, pissed at everybody for not listening to my complaints.'

Blink and you might have missed Bolt in Athens. His Olympic debut passed almost unnoticed: in the fourth first-round heat he was fifth in 21.05 – considerably slower than the 19.93 he recorded earlier in the season, which would have been good enough for a silver medal in Athens. Bolt knew he was in no fit state to challenge – in addition to his problems with his back and hamstring, he sprained his ankle a few days before the Games got under way – though the expectations on him in Jamaica were huge, which, he said, 'messed with my head'. In the heat itself, he felt capable of fourth, which would have meant qualifying for the next round, but he eased up, knowing he would go no further. Among the criticisms made following his Greek failure was that the crucifix he wore around his neck – a gift from his mother – and clamped in his teeth while he was sprinting was a distraction: how could he concentrate?

As the Jamaican press and public turned on Bolt when he returned home, the crucifix became a symbol of his failure. It seemed to many that he was following the path of Daniel England, Ali Watson and other prodigies who had shone as schoolboys then faded into obscurity. 'We keep hearing that Usain is young and we should give him a chance to improve,' one correspondent wrote to the *Gleaner*. 'The trouble is Usain Bolt has not been improving. He needs to get his act together and start achieving the results that his talent so desperately demands.'

There were also questions at Puma, Bolt's main sponsor, about the athlete in whom they had invested so much, both financially and as the figurehead of their association with the country. Apart from his poor performances, there were doubts about the wisdom of backing an athlete who many struggled to understand when he was speaking. 'I mean, in a big company you always have people who question stuff,' says Pascal Rolling, the marketing man who had a major stake in Bolt, since he had signed him. 'But I think from the sports marketing and the chairman's point of view we wanted to continue with Usain because we knew the potential he had.'

There was work to do, though – and not only on the track. 'At the time he was, like many Jamaicans, talking more in patois,' Rolling says. 'He was very difficult to understand. He needed to improve his English.' This is confirmed by Simon Lewis, an English communications executive whose job it was, in the run-up to the 2004 Olympics, to give Bolt media training at the Jamaican training camp in Germany. Of the Jamaicans 'Bolt had the broadest accent,' says Lewis. 'He was also extremely shy. When it was time for our sessions he would hide from me. He would eventually emerge laughing and joking – he was very playful, very likeable – but media training wasn't something he particularly wanted to do.'

Rolling and Puma planned more English and communication lessons for Bolt. But they never happened. 'We realised after a while that he was doing so many interviews and getting better so quickly that there wasn't any need for training.'

As soon as he returned to Jamaica, it was reported that Bolt would change coach. Out would go Fitz Coleman, in would come Glen Mills, who for seventeen years had been national coach. Mills had also coached Raymond Stewart, Jamaica's top sprinter of the eighties, and, more recently, Kim Collins of St Kitts, the 2003 world 100 metres champion.

Mills had wanted to be a sprinter himself but at the age of thirteen had realised it wasn't meant to be. 'I was disappointed that I wasn't able to measure up to the others,' he said. He would go and watch training instead, under Henry McDonald, the coach at his school, Camperdown. Eventually McDonald called him over: 'Come here, little man. I see you here every evening and you are not training any more. Why?' Mills told him he was interested in coaching, and McDonald appointed him his assistant. He started by taking the register, but by the age of sixteen he was coaching thirteen-year-olds. He soon had success with his sprinters, but his star was Stewart, who went straight from school to the Los Angeles Olympics, where he made the 100 metres final, then anchored the Jamaicans to a silver medal in the relay.

In early October 2004, with his partnership with Bolt confirmed, Mills told the *Gleaner* about his hopes for the eighteen-year-old. One of his first decisions was to restrict media access. 'While I can understand that Jamaica is interested in his well-being and development, he's constantly in the press and I think he needs less press attention,' he said. 'I've noticed over the last two years that every detail of his life is news and this puts pressure on him. While I've no intention to hide him from the media, I'll definitely be making an effort to reduce press attention. He needs a break to settle down and train in a serious way.'

Mills confirmed that the 200 metres would remain Bolt's priority, 'but I can see in the future the 400m could become his most dominant event,' he explained. 'He's 6ft 6ins and growing.'

In another interview Mills said, 'There are a number of challenges which have to be given equal importance, the first of which is to restore his confidence. This is the first time in his young career that he has experienced disappointment.' As for the two of them, 'We have to develop a coach/athlete relationship and understanding as early as possible. I have to learn about him as a person and he has to adjust to my coaching methods and demands because each coach has his own signature. I have to get a greater understanding of him because that's important in any relationship.'

Mills, who was fifty-five when he began coaching Bolt, spoke of his 'immense potential', but stressed that that was all it was – potential. And he made the point that Bolt's height (six-five, despite Mills thinking he was an inch taller) had perhaps tricked some into believing that he must be closer to reaching his potential. Just because he was tall didn't mean he was the finished article – he still had to fill out, to develop physically. This was happening, he was changing shape, but it meant 'his whole skeletal structure is fragile. Once the growth process slows down he will start to experience greater muscular density and significant increase of the muscular structure and will have less injuries related to the growth process.

'My experience working with athletes doesn't follow an upward graph from season to season,' added Mills, 'but there's no doubt he'll fulfil the expectations.'

There were also technical issues that Mills felt he had to address. Bolt had been a teenage phenomenon, and yet, Mills said later, 'one of the things that stood out like a sore thumb was his poor mechanics'. He was off-balance, which put pressure on his lower back, his hips and hamstrings. Mills videoed his training and analysed the angle of his back; he wanted 'a forward lean of somewhere around five to ten degrees'. He was not able to hold that optimum position at top speed, so Mills got him doing core strength work. He also got him to shorten his stride. He was over-reaching – a legacy, perhaps, of his 400 metres running, where the stride pattern is different. Mills thought it would take him up to two years to learn how to change the pattern and take shorter strides.

Wellesley Bolt had no say in his son's switch from Coleman to Mills. But he supported his decision. 'He said he doesn't like how Mr Coleman train him. I didn't see it that way, I was just seeing that he didn't want to train. He made up his mind himself, to leave Mr Coleman and go to Mr Mills. So I said, "He's the one doing the training, let's go along with it."

'He has some problems with Mr Mills in the early days,' Wellesley continues, 'because he was lazy. Mr Mills had to get under his skin.'

Mills told Bolt they would be working to a three-year plan, aiming to peak at the Beijing Olympics. He arranged for a masseur, Everald Edwards, to work with him; each training session would begin with a session on the table, having his muscles kneaded and manipulated, getting his body ready for the punishment. Most importantly, Mills got to know him and would visit him at home if he saw that he was down or distracted in training. When that happened, 'I'd go quiet,' Bolt said, and a visit from Mills would follow. Over a game of dominoes they would discuss what was on his mind and agree on a course of action; usually the course of action advised by the coach. 'I like to help them develop into total human beings,' Mills said. 'You try to be involved in the rest of their lives as much as they let you.'

Mills was keen to impress upon Bolt the importance of committing to a long-term plan: 'To educate him about the journey, not so much the destination . . . because if you're on the wrong road, you're going to end up in the wrong destination.'

Norman Peart says that one of Mills's great talents is the art of gentle persuasion. 'He says: "It's your choice. This is my advice. But it's up to you." Glen has an ability to deal with teenagers, youngsters.' Despite not being a father himself, 'he's like a father figure', Peart says. 'He tries to help them. There are some who have different problems: could be family matters or problems with a girlfriend or financial problems. He reaches out to them. He's more than a coach. But he tells them it as it is: "You wise up or you drown."

'Sure, he's strict,' Peart adds. 'But they're not afraid of him like he's a monster.'

At the Athens Olympics, Stephen Francis's rough diamond, Asafa Powell, who had been discussed as the favourite for the 100 metres, went below 10 seconds again, but his 9.94 was only good enough for fifth behind Justin Gatlin. It was a disappointment. In his breakthrough season, it was also an early indication of his fatal flaw: his failure to produce his best performances on the big stage, when it truly mattered. As if to emphasise the point, less than two weeks after the Olympic final, Powell won the Golden League in Brussels in 9.87, a personal best.

How Bolt might have fared under the other top coach, working a little over a mile away at the UTech campus, is a fascinating question. Francis and Mills are quite different. While Mills is a sprint specialist, Francis says he most enjoys coaching jumpers. Mills has had his greatest successes with male athletes, Francis with both men and women, though especially women.

Mills gets close to his athletes; Francis likes to maintain a distance, saying he avoids being 'too pally-pally because there has to be a level of authority'. He is not the father figure that Mills appears to be. 'It operates best,' he says, 'if there is at least a certain gulf. I am not in the European mode of coach as best friend.' The challenge comes, he adds, when athletes do well. 'Obviously you have difficulties when people are successful, because as they get more successful they start to look more to themselves and doubt what you tell them.'

One of the most intriguing, compelling aspects of the two camps of sprinters in Kingston is the antipathy between them, which seems to have its roots around the time of Powell's emergence and Bolt hooking up with Mills, which put his Racers Track Club on the map. Since then, MVP and Racers have kept up a rivalry that is always fierce and at times acrimonious. They resemble two gangs, like the Jets and the Sharks of *West Side Story*.

Perhaps it is because there just isn't room for two world-class clubs in the same city. But it also seems to have something to do with the relationship between Francis and Mills – despite once being good friends, these days they do not get on. Dennis Johnson told me about their friendship but couldn't shed much light on their falling-out. 'Mills and Francis are both from the ghetto,' he said. 'Mills is from Waterford, Francis from Mountain View Road: that's where they're from and you can't take that out of them. They used to be very good friends.'

What does Francis have to say about his relationship with Mills? 'Well, we don't really have a relationship,' he tells me. Then he concedes that 'We used to be good friends at one point in time.' How does he explain the fact that they don't speak to each other any more? 'I guess he's a bit busy and I'm busy.'

Francis and I are talking by the side of the grass track at UTech following another MVP training session. Francis continues explaining that he doesn't mix with many other coaches: 'I tend not to spend a lot of time at the local meets early on. I work away from the track at home, analysing data . . . I tend to be extremely busy.' But he and Mills didn't fall out because they are both busy, of course they didn't. Eventually Francis says it was because of 'leakage' – the alleged passing of MVP secrets to the Racers camp. There were 'transfers of personnel and systems and so on', he claims, 'which I think we, over here, were not happy with. So we decided, I think, that we had to act to stem the leakage. Put it that way.'

He insists it didn't go the other way; that he has never tried to find out Mills's secrets. He wouldn't be interested, he says. 'I don't have any curiosity at all.' But the alleged leakage upset him, and offended a code of honour. 'You know, I am still a believer in the old coaching creed. I don't believe in recruiting people who leak. I don't believe in bad-mouthing a coach.'

Is the rivalry with Racers healthy? I wonder. It is tempting to conclude that it must be, for all that Francis says MVP are 'kind of like an island over here'. There are parallels with the music scene in Jamaica from the late 1950s into the 1960s, which was built on and fuelled by intense rivalry between the 'sound men', each competing to be louder, to play the latest ska, rocksteady or reggae to the biggest audiences.

Francis's main issue, he says, comes when he has to persuade his own assistant coaches not to worry about Racers' recruitment of the latest teenage stars. 'All my assistant coaches believe that we must try and get the kind of high school talent which Racers acquires. They are upset that Racers cream off that talent, and they don't understand why it doesn't faze me. But, so, you do have tension in terms of that.'

But as his lack of regret over his decision not to work with Bolt illustrates, Francis prefers to polish rough diamonds. His favourite coach is Bill Belichick of the New England Patriots, who is famous for his gruff demeanour. ('Yes, it's true,' read a *Sports Illustrated* headline, 'Bill Belichick actually smiled.' This, the magazine went on to say, 'is akin to seeing Halley's Comet'.)

'I love Bill Belichick, I'm a big fan of his,' Francis tells me. He explains that he likes coaches 'like Jose Mourinho, who overcome the bias of not being good players'. These are the coaches who have to use their brains. Alex Ferguson is another, because of his knack of building and renewing teams. 'I'm inspired by coaches like those,' says Francis.

I put it to him that if MVP and Racers were football teams, they would be Barcelona and Real Madrid: one rearing home-grown talent, the other importing expensive Galácticos. He smiles (which he does a little more often than Belichick). 'As I said, I love to see somebody become great who nobody knew about. That's why Bill Belichick is my favourite coach. I mean, he can make good of people who nobody had a clue could be good. He does it year after year after year. He does it through preparation, through imagination, through all those intangibles which I think is essential for good coaching.'

I was keen to speak to Mills, of course. But I was familiar with his reputation and his reluctance to speak to journalists. He seemed something of an enigma. I was told that he is a deeply religious man, who attends Swallowfield Chapel in Kingston every Sunday, and who is not interested in material wealth; when he receives gifts from sponsors, he gives them away (including cars, apparently). He is also a confirmed bachelor. 'I've had my admirers,' he said in 2011, 'but marriage for me now, at 62? Well, I'll finish my life in serving my God and coaching my athletes.'

When I asked Bolt's manager, Norman Peart, about an interview with the coach, he laughed. 'Good luck,' he said. Ricky Simms, Bolt's agent, was no more encouraging. I asked if Mills's reticence stemmed from the fact that he was a man of few words. 'No, he has a lot of words,' said Simms. 'He's the heart and soul of training sessions.

'For Glen coaching is an art,' he continued. 'It's not magic. He looks at an athlete and sees what they need to do. There's no messing about, no big words. I sometimes laugh when you see American high school coaches come in with a load of big words and phrases.'

I paid a visit to Racers Track Club, at the University of the West Indies. They have an office in a hut by a grass running track, a short distance from the Usain Bolt Track, a gift from Puma and German firm BSW Regupol. The well-appointed campus seems to be surrounded on all sides by the Blue Mountains. It is a lush green paradise.

At Racers HQ, the door was opened by Cynthia Cooke, who helps run the club (and is a former head teacher at Mills's old school, Camperdown). Mills was not in, she said. She told me to email my interview request. She said she would ask Mills, but explained that 'he hates interviews'.

To try and convince Cooke – and by extension Mills – to give me my interview, I attached a newspaper story I had recently written about one of Mills's younger athletes, Zharnel Hughes, the 100 metres winner at Champs. Hughes, based at the IAAF high performance on the same university campus in Kingston, was eloquent and engaging and clearly a great prospect. Cooke emailed back that she had enjoyed it. I felt a warm glow. 'However,' read the final line of the first paragraph, 'it was offensive in parts.'

Offensive? I read on.

'You may wonder what on earth could be offensive,' Cooke continued. 'I am one of the many passionate, loyal, patriotic Jamaican track and field fans, or maybe fanatics. We find that the British media consistently seek to promote a negative image about our country, in every story they write about us.

'During your trip to Jamaica, I am sure you did not experience any violence except in the media' – this was actually true. 'Why was it necessary to mention that it was the most violent city in the Caribbean? What does that have to do with Zharnel's exploits on the track? Mentioning the scantily furnished apartment is redundant if the objective was to place Jamaica's significance in the grand world of wealth.

'Yes, I have said a lot! I guess you now understand our view of British journalists. (You are free to accuse me of doing the same. Finding one little negative in a slew of positives.)'

There goes my interview with Glen Mills, I thought. (Though in further emails, relations improved with Cynthia Cooke, especially when I told her that my wife had agreed with parts of her email: 'Thank God for women,' she wrote. 'It is instances such as these that make us understand why God saw it fit to complement man with woman. It took myself and your wife to "enlighten your darkness" on this topic, while having no ill feeling towards you . . . Again, in spite of my "touchiness", it was a good article.' Great, so how about that interview with Mills? She replied again: 'Having Coach Mills agree to any interview is very difficult. He hates interviews.')

Then, out of the blue, I got an email from Mills. It followed a question to Cooke about Francis's allegations of 'leakage': of the passing of secrets from MVP to Racers. 'Laughable,' Cooke replied. Indeed, she was so incensed that she said she would ask Mills for a full response. And a full response is what followed. Mills wasn't just angry; he was deeply offended:

Hi Mr Moore, please accept my best wishes. Thanks for your attempt to be balanced in writing your book and I wish you success.

I have read the allegations which Coach Francis is making that his training secrets have been leaked to Racers Track Club by former members of his club. This is one of the most absurd allegations to be made by him and his organisation. It is a fact that members from his club were accepted into Racers Track Club but it is totally false that they divulge secret methods that Mr Francis may have developed. Let the record show that I have never questioned nor interviewed any of these individuals which entered Racers from MVP about any aspect of their training programmes while they were being trained at MVP.

I have my own philosophy and methodology of training which I am willing to share with anyone. Before MVP was formed I had already acquired over thirty years of coaching knowledge and experience at the local and international levels.

I started coaching in 1964 at my alma mater Camperdown High School where I developed my philosophy and methodology while attending many international courses and seminars. My tenure at Camperdown developing programmes and methods of coaching sprinting was marked by extraordinary success that earned the school the title 'Sprint Factory'.

By 1983 I was appointed assistant national coach to the incomparable Herb McKenley and the following year [as] one of the coaches to the 1984 Olympic team of Jamaica. In that year I coached nineteen-year-old Raymond Stewart to be the fastest Jamaican and the fastest junior in the world. Stewart went on to place sixth in the 100 metres final at the Olympics in Los Angeles, [and] incidentally he was unbeaten at the Olympics up to the final of the 100 metres. I coached Kim Collins to Commonwealth and world champion titles long before any transfer of personnel from MVP. I could enumerate so many other achievements in coaching sprinters before the advent of MVP that makes Mr Francis's allegations utter rubbish.

I am mystified what are his reasons for such mischief or his desire to try to discredit Racers and my achievements but whatever they are it is not possible to remove the imprints I have made in sprinting history.

Best regards, Coach Mills

10

HEALING HANS

A Frankenstein-type experiment.
Travis Tygart, United States Anti-Doping Agency

One of the first things Glen Mills did when he began working with
Usain Bolt was to try and understand the injuries that had afflicted
him in the run-up to Athens. Bolt had been troubled by hamstring and
back problems, and not long before the Games got under way, he was
diagnosed with scoliosis – curvature of the spine.

Mills studied Bolt's medical notes. They were detailed and made a
big deal of the scoliosis, as though this was the root of all his problems.
There were suggested exercises and stretches to get his body ready
for training and alleviate the symptoms. It was perhaps unusual for
a doctor to offer such detailed advice – this was encroaching on the
coach's territory.

But the doctor was not just any doctor. Bolt's meeting with
him had been arranged after he broke down in training, when his
participation at the Athens Olympics seemed in the balance. He and
his entourage had been desperate. It was time for an addition to
Team Bolt.

*

Dr Hans-Wilhelm Müller-Wohlfahrt is one of the most important men in world sport. That is the only conclusion to draw from scrolling through his list of patients. Boris Becker, Paula Radcliffe, too many footballers to mention, including Diego Maradona, Cristiano Ronaldo, Steven Gerrard and half the English Premier League, as well as those of the club and national team to which he is official doctor: Bayern Munich and Germany. Other patients include 1987 Tour de France winner Stephen Roche and golfer José María Olazábal. The sprinters Linford Christie, Donovan Bailey, Maurice Greene, Tyson Gay and Asafa Powell have all been treated by him. And, since the summer of 2004, so has Usain Bolt.

'It was arranged for me to visit Dr Hans Müller-Wohlfahrt,' Bolt writes in his autobiography, without elaborating on who organised, or paid, for a seventeen-year-old wunderkind to travel to Germany and see the world's most renowned sports doctor. The connection was made through his German-based sponsor, Puma. 'I mean, Dr Müller-Wohlfahrt is one of the best sports medicine doctors in the world,' Pascal Rolling, the marketing man who signed Bolt, tells me, 'so when Usain had his recurrent problem, we said we need to bring him there to evaluate exactly how serious it was, and what could be done to stop the injury coming up all the time.'

When he arrived at Müller-Wohlfahrt's clinic, Bolt 'was laid out flat on a bed, as his fingers felt along the bumps and grooves of my spine, and he pushed against my hamstrings. When I glanced up, I noticed his eyes were closed. The man was feeling, sensing my injuries . . .' When Müller-Wohlfahrt was interrupted by a nurse, he reacted angrily, as though a spell had been broken. He started again. Thus the impression immediately formed is that of somebody with special, mystical powers, which can only be summoned by deep concentration. And yet in this instance the diagnosis came from an old-fashioned X-ray. Bolt was informed that he had scoliosis; quite a serious case of curvature of the spine. Müller-Wohlfahrt told him that it need not prevent him fulfilling his potential, but his training should be adapted accordingly.

For Bolt the diagnosis was the start of his journey back to fitness. It was also the first of dozens of trips to Munich and Müller-Wohlfahrt's clinic on the second floor of the Century Alte Hof building, originally built in the twelfth century and once Germany's imperial residence.

Müller-Wohlfahrt is not just a doctor to celebrities: he is a celebrity doctor. His high profile is due mainly to his work with sports stars – though his patients have also included Bono and Luciano Pavarotti – but he is also one half of a famous couple. His wife, Karin, is a well-known artist in Germany. His daughter, Maren, used to date Germany's most capped footballer, Lothar Matthäus. Those who have met Müller-Wohlfahrt in his lair tend to all emerge with the same breathless reaction. He is incredibly charismatic, they say; relentlessly positive and upbeat, and quite brilliant at breaking down the normal barriers that stand between doctor and patient, establishing an instant connection, a powerful bond. Typically he greets patients with either a bear hug or the kind of handshake preferred by teenagers: hand up, thumb out, while his other hand grasps your elbow. With dark shoulder-length hair, smooth caramel skin and lively eyes, he looks at least two decades younger than his seventy-plus years. And he is dapper, often sporting a black suit, white shirt and black tie. His all-female staff, meanwhile, wear immaculate white outfits. 'They look like angels,' says one sports doctor who has visited him. 'They're all absolutely beautiful.

'And he has a chef. You eat downstairs in a private dining room.'

Müller-Wohlfahrt qualified as a doctor in 1971, completing his training at the orthopaedic clinic of the Rudolf Virchow Hospital in Berlin. His entry to the world of professional sport came when he was appointed team doctor at Bundesliga side Hertha Berlin in 1975. He switched to Germany's biggest club, Bayern Munich, two years later and began working with the national team in 1996.

For forty years, then, he has worked at the highest level of sport, in which time there has been intrigue and mystery, scepticism and suspicion – even, or especially, within the medical profession – over his methods. Partly it is due to his reluctance to write scientific papers about his methods, or subject his work to peer review. Partly it might stem from the fervour of his patients, who can seem like disciples. But there is also envy. Plenty are jealous of the dashing doctor known as 'Healing Hans'.

Müller-Wohlfahrt describes his treatments as homeopathic. Consciously or not, there appears to be an Eastern influence to his practice of medicine. He relies heavily on injections of products that for some raise ethical questions, and for others provoke a squeamish reaction. For muscle injuries he swears by Actovegin, a calf-blood extract that is not banned under the World Anti-Doping Code, but is also not approved for sale in some countries, including the US and France. He uses products containing blood from goats,[21] and prescribes Hyalart (made by crushing the fleshy pink comb on a cockerel's head) for knee injuries, preferring these treatments to surgery wherever possible.

---

21 'St Johnstone star Peter MacDonald gets goat blood injections to cure hamstring problem,' was the unlikely headline in the *Daily Record* in early September 2009. 'At times it was uncomfortable because I had an epidural and more than 50 jags over four days,' said MacDonald, who reported that Arjen Robben, the Dutch star, had been in the next room having the same treatment.

According to one sports doctor familiar with his work, he has also used X-rays to treat ligament damage, killing the nerves with radiation. I asked this doctor his view of such treatment, and he said it wouldn't be allowed where he works, in the UK – the levels of radiation would be over safe limits.

'Nearly every one' of his injections contains Actovegin, Müller-Wohlfahrt has said, estimating that he has administered the calf-blood extract over a million times. But many in the medical and sporting community are unconvinced of its supposed healing properties. Patrick Arnold, the chemist at the centre of the infamous Balco drugs scandal of the early 2000s, has tried Actovegin and considers it a placebo, no more. Arnold describes Müller-Wohlfahrt's methods as 'pseudoscience', while Travis Tygart, head of the US Anti-Doping Agency, has claimed that those who subject themselves to such treatments are taking part in a 'Frankenstein-type experiment'.

This might be a little extreme. Others take a more nuanced view. Mike Davison, who manages Isokinetic Medical Group, a specialist sports injuries centre on Harley Street in London, is an admirer of Müller-Wohlfahrt, though he concedes that he is 'provocative', an 'agitator'. Says Davison: 'He's an outlier in the artistry of medicine. He's not accepting of conventional wisdom and science because he believes that is looking in the past rather than the future.'

Davison talks about Müller-Wohlfahrt as a genius who has pushed back the boundaries of sports medicine through a combination of 'instinct and infiltration'. 'My sense is that in Europe if not the world there's no individual in the last twenty-five years who has made a greater contribution to sports medicine for elite athletes.' Nobody gets athletes back training or competing quicker, stresses Davison. 'Yes, he will take risks. He doesn't admit to always having a 100 per cent success rate. But he binds athletes closer to him than any other doctor I've come across.'

It is his use of Actovegin that raises a red flag for many. I ask a sports doctor friend about Actovegin. He explains that it is 'the whole blood, spun down to remove the white blood cells and the red blood cells, so you're left with serum. It has all the tissue factors, the growth factors that circulate in the blood. They de-nature it to remove the large proteins, which can have transfusion reactions, particularly cross-species.'

The serum is a clear, sterile liquid. But what does it do exactly? What are its magic properties? 'That is complicated,' says the sports doctor. 'I believe it has a whole variety of activation factors, interlukins, growth factors, and when used in torn muscle it might accelerate the biological process [of healing]. Which I believe it will do, to some extent.'

There is a grey area in discussing doping: where does performance-enabling end and performance-enhancement begin? Tyson Gay came out with a fascinating, hugely revealing line when he explained why he consulted Müller-Wohlfahrt: 'I run too fast for my body.' Could Actovegin be described as a performance-enhancer, or is it simply used to repair damage? 'I personally think it's used in body repair,' says my doctor friend. 'I know people have given it intravenously, thinking it's helping recovery, but there's no science there and no scientific logic to think that would help.'

Would he use Actovegin? 'I wouldn't use Actovegin. I would use the person's own blood and spin it down.'

But this is banned under the anti-doping rules. 'Correct. But if you're a non-athlete, and you need treatment, it's fine. In hospitals, this plasma-rich distillate is used in mainstream medicine.'

Where many seem to agree, including Travis Tygart and Mike Davison, is on the notion that Müller-Wohlfahrt's personality goes a long way to explaining his appeal. His charisma is part of the treatment. 'He has an aura about him,' Davison says. 'I think he fundamentally loves his patients. No one should confuse their personal experience of health care with what he offers. In some ways we should encourage, in general health care, the warmth, love and care he shows towards his patients.' There is usually a boundary between doctor and patient.

'But in elite sport that boundary gets blurred because of the emotions involved,' Davison says. 'As is proved a lot in science, the placebo effect provides comfort and security for individuals who are vulnerable.' You don't often hear of world-class athletes being described as vulnerable. But an athlete with an injury, or who thinks he has an injury, is very vulnerable indeed, Davison says.

Tygart takes a less benign view. 'These sorts of gurus get a reputation within athlete populations,' he told ESPN. 'And these high-dollar athletes who are desperate to do anything and everything to win, even at the jeopardy of their own health, go to these guys. That is the culture. It is not right, but that is the culture.'

Yet in over four decades, even as some of his patients have fallen foul of the anti-doping authorities, Müller-Wohlfahrt's reputation has remained intact and unsullied. 'No one has ever pinned anything bad on him,' says Davison. 'I think he may have taken some risks early on.' But sports medicine – into which there is so little research – almost requires this, he argues. I can see Davison wrestling with this, in the way that medical people sometimes do when trying to describe something that is hugely resistant to simple, black-and-white interpretation – and sports medicine evidently comes into this category. 'Medicine is the application of scientific principles in a world of values,' he says. 'It's not just science, there's an artistry to it, and within muscle and tendon injuries Müller-Wohlfahrt has some of the greatest artistry skills in the world.'

He offers an example. 'A lot of people will send a patient for an MRI and then interpret the results. Dr Müller-Wohlfahrt will put someone in a functional position – maybe Bolt in a starting blocks position – and he will feel the tension of the muscle himself, and match that with the commentary from the individual, remembering that athletes probably know their body better than anyone else.'

Linford Christie, when he won the 100 metres at the 1992 Olympics, suggested that Müller-Wohlfahrt was more ethical than other doctors he'd consulted, who all recommended cortisone. Noted anti-doping crusaders, like Paula Radcliffe, have also endorsed Müller-Wohlfahrt's methods. The marathon world record holder was in Müller-Wohlfahrt's Munich clinic when Mike Fish, an ESPN reporter allowed a rare interview in 2011, paid a visit. Fish described the scene:

'... the doctor spent an hour listening patiently while tending to Radcliffe. As she lay on a treatment table, the sinewy, muscled distance runner gradually morphed into a human voodoo doll. The doctor went about sticking her with a bevy of needles, injecting a numbing agent and then leaving the needles in place. Into the needles' plastic base or hub that remained above the skin, he followed with injections of natural lubricants and hyaluronic acid.

'Radcliffe sighed as the initial injections penetrated deep beneath the skin, with some needles 2 to 3 inches long. Müller-Wohlfahrt used his right hand to deliver 14 injections into her lower back. Another two were directed into the front of her right hip, followed by four into the top of her left foot. He then manipulated her legs wildly – left and right, up and down.'

Radcliffe told Fish that she visited Müller-Wohlfahrt every two or three months for similar treatments. 'I call it coming for a tune-up or checkup,' she said. 'He is someone [athletes] trust.'

Despite his reluctance to give interviews – which he blames on a full diary; also the reason, he says, for not writing scientific papers or subjecting his work to peer review[22] – Müller-Wohlfahrt is hardly a shadowy, reclusive figure. He could hardly be more visible, because he often sat on the bench for Bayern Munich's matches; even as managers came and went, he remained. [23]

---

22 In 2012 Müller-Wohlfahrt did produce a book, *Muskelverletzungen im Sport* (*Muscle Injuries in Sports*). In it he acknowledges the lack of studies of muscle injuries, and that much of his information 'is thus admittedly based more on empirical knowledge than scientific data. But isn't it also true that other medical classifications are evidence-based only to a limited degree, due to a lack of scientific research?'

23 Until April 2015 when he abruptly quit after falling out with manager Pep Guardiola. Guardiola had been publicly critical of Bayern Munich's medical team.

In 2012, the club threw a lavish party for his seventieth birthday, with 190 guests, including German football legends Karl-Heinz Rummenigge, Franz Beckenbauer and Gerd Müller. In his toast, Rummenigge described Müller-Wohlfahrt as 'one of the most important people at the club for thirty-five years, exactly half his life so far. He may never have scored a goal for us, but he's made countless goals and triumphs possible in the first place.'

Nor does Müller-Wohlfahrt, unlike some sports doctors, appear reticent when it comes to his work with some of the world's leading sportsmen and -women – on the contrary. 'It's curious how many sports people talk about him,' says Daniel Drepper, a German investigative reporter who has written extensively about doping in football. 'I suspect he asks them to mention him.

'Some view him as a bit controversial,' Drepper continues, 'but in general the media reporting is really positive. He's seen as a genius. And he's a seventy-year-old guy who looks fifty-five.'

Despite his work investigating doping in football, Drepper has turned up nothing on Müller-Wohlfahrt. Not that he isn't sceptical, or doesn't have questions. But the doctor has been reluctant to engage.[24] 'We asked Müller-Wohlfahrt normal questions but also included questions about doping,' Drepper says. 'He directly responded through his lawyer, Christian Schertz, the most famous and expensive media attorney in Germany.'

Drepper continues: 'We are not sure if he does anything illegal, or whether he operates on the edge of illegality. People tell us that he talks to the anti-doping authority every year.' In the ESPN article, Fish said that Müller-Wohlfahrt 'routinely communicates with WADA about his treatment methods, including his use of Actovegin'. Fish also said

---

24 I emailed Müller-Wohlfahrt's clinic requesting an interview. Next morning a German number appeared on my mobile phone. 'Hello,' said the female voice, 'this is Dr Müller-Wohlfahrt's clinic.' 'Hello!' I said, impressed by their efficiency. 'Yes, well, I am calling to tell you that I am afraid Dr Müller-Wohlfahrt is too busy to give you an interview.'

that WADA's science director, Dr Olivier Rabin, 'vouches for Müller-Wohlfahrt's operating a clean practice, but he isn't ready to speak to the purported healing qualities of Actovegin'. Müller-Wohlfahrt told Fish he doesn't have any secrets, or use unknown, undetectable products: 'You risk your career. They [keep] the urine sample for years. So if they have technique to detect it later, then it will be found.'

The worst Drepper can say is that Müller-Wohlfahrt's methods are 'voodoo' and that his success could rest heavily on his charisma. It chimes with Davison's mention of his aura ('Medicine is an industry of the cult,' Davison says. 'There are no kite marks of quality') and Tygart's talk of gurus and the importance in elite sporting circles of reputation. It becomes a self-fulfilling prophecy, or a virtuous circle, whereby the very act of being on the books of the world's most famous sports doctor can imbue confidence; where little more than his personal attention can leave an athlete feeling restored, walking out of the clinic a little taller and stronger. Perhaps that is as potent as anything found in a bottle or syringe.

In 2013, Müller-Wohlfahrt spoke about medical strategies for muscle injuries in football at Isokinetic's Football Medicine Strategies Conference in London. In his trademark smart black suit, white shirt and black tie, he was hesitant and halting. The charismatic healer described by those who have visited him in his clinic was not discernible in the handsome but almost diffident figure who read in heavily accented English from his script, only occasionally glancing up.

It was one of the rare occasions when he has discussed, in some detail, his work – and he was candid about his use of Actovegin. 'I have changed my therapeutic approach only marginally since the seventies,' he told his audience, 'since it has been proved highly effective.'

He continued: 'Since the seventies I use Actovegin together with Traumeel [a homeopathic painkiller] in the treatment of muscle injuries. Actovegin is a deep-proteinised hemoderivative obtained by ultra-filtration of calf blood. It is constituted mostly of electrolytes, essential trace elements, a mixture of amino acids and intermediary products of carbohydrates.

'I know that there is still controversy about its biologic actions, especially in muscle tissue. But I'm still convinced that Actovegin is the most helpful and highly effective medicine in our treatment. The daily experiences of athletes, some [of whom] were treated not successfully elsewhere, support this. In over thirty-six years I have never experienced any side effects. No complication has occurred.'

He went on to argue for the 'conservative treatment' of injuries, explaining that surgery can be avoided with injections – or 'infiltrations', as he prefers to call them. Some of his critics object to this, saying that his treatments address the symptom, not the cause. Indeed, some of those critics were in the audience in London, judging by the tuts and shaking heads. Müller-Wohlfahrt explained that his priority is minimising the disruption to an athlete's training; the treatment itself is active. Rest may sometimes be necessary, but it seems to Müller-Wohlfahrt – like it does to every elite athlete – anathema. In this, he is squarely on the athlete's side. Perhaps that is why they get along so well.

As Müller-Wohlfahrt admitted in London, Actovegin is controversial. During the 2000 Tour de France, it was found in waste dumped by staff members of Lance Armstrong's US Postal team, prompting an investigation by the French authorities, and in 2009 the Canadian Anthony Galea, another sports doctor with a stable of stars – including Tiger Woods, Alex Rodriguez and Mark McCoy – was charged by Canadian authorities with selling an unapproved drug: Actovegin.

However, it is incorrect to say that Actovegin is illegal for sportspeople. It was briefly placed on the WADA banned list in 2000, then taken off; a WADA official compared it to a 'super vitamin for the blood'. It is not banned in the US, either; it has simply never been approved for sale by the Food and Drug Administration.

*

As Paula Radcliffe says, athletes trust Müller-Wohlfahrt – and given his track record, why wouldn't they?

Perhaps Radcliffe knows exactly how she is being treated, and what with. You could argue that her trust is implicit but well placed. Others might not be so well informed – or even interested. In talking about his visits to Müller-Wohlfahrt, the former footballer Jamie Redknapp recalled being told only that he was being given 'high-quality oil for the engine of a car'. Another footballer, Michael Johnson of Manchester City, said in an interview that he too had been treated by Müller-Wohlfahrt: 'I stayed a week in Germany and had a course of injections into my back and spine. I don't know what he put in there, but it worked.'

Asked by Mike Fish in 2011 whether he told his athletes what was in his needles, Müller-Wohlfahrt said: 'I try to explain to them, but they don't understand.'

One of the more inquisitive of his athlete patients was Stephen Roche, the 1987 Tour de France winner who began seeing Müller-Wohlfahrt in 1988 after three operations failed to clear up a knee injury. The loquacious Roche and the charismatic, attentive Müller-Wohlfahrt (who once took a private plane and helicopter to the Pyrenees to treat Roche at the Tour, staying for less than an hour) got on well. But they almost fell out early in their relationship when, as Roche explains it, 'I wanted to know what exactly he was injecting into my knee.'

After one injection, Roche observed the doctor putting the empty ampoule in the bin. He fished it out when Müller-Wohlfahrt was out of the room, slipped it in his pocket and took it back to his home in Paris, where he gave it to a doctor to analyse it. 'And it turned out it was extracted from calves' livers.' When Roche told Müller-Wohlfahrt what he'd done, the doctor 'froze and stood back'. 'Stephen,' he said, 'I'm very disappointed. I've been a doctor for twenty-five years and no athlete I've ever worked with has been involved with doping or even suspected of doping. My office has never had a hint of scandal. Everything we use is a natural product. I don't know how you could have thought that we might have used anything suspicious. No one has ever questioned me before. No one has ever taken anything from my office.'

In September 2013, Usain Bolt was asked by the French newspaper *Le Monde* about his relationship with Müller-Wohlfahrt. There had been controversy in France during the 2006 World Cup when a French player, Patrick Vieira, was prevented by the national team doctor from consulting with Müller-Wohlfahrt because Actovegin is banned in France.

'I do not know what it is,' said Bolt when asked by *Le Monde* whether Müller-Wohlfahrt had given him Actovegin. 'But let me tell you this: if he had given me something illegal, I know.' (In his book, Bolt writes: 'I'd heard through other athletes that calves' blood injections were a common prescription for his patients, and that sounded freaky to me. Still, everything that was used on my back was carefully administered within all the legal guidelines – nothing sketchy was injected – and Dr Müller-Wohlfahrt's syringes took away the pressure and pain from my spine.')

There are few athletes with whom Müller-Wohlfahrt has had such a long and fulfilling relationship as Bolt. The doctor has even said that his remit extends beyond treating Bolt's injuries, and giving him specific exercises to prevent problems with his fragile back, to 'analysing his sprint mechanics during track workouts when he's in town'.

It wasn't just scoliosis that was diagnosed in Müller-Wohlfahrt's Munich clinic in early summer 2004. In his examination, Müller-Wohlfahrt also observed the discrepancy in Bolt's legs: his right one is 1.5 centimetres shorter than the left. Not ideal for running round the bend of a track. It also makes his stride pattern asymmetrical – hardly unusual, but in Bolt's case it can be quite extreme, leading to extra stress on what is the most vulnerable part of a sprinter's body: his hamstring. In Bolt's case, his left hamstring.

Ever since that first visit when he was seventeen, Bolt has been a regular. He has said that he typically visits Müller-Wohlfahrt three or four times a year. 'He gives me the impression that he loves me,' he says. 'He's not just a doctor, he is a friend, almost family.'

The feeling is mutual. Of all the names in the visitors' book that sits in the reception of the Munich clinic, Bolt is Müller-Wohlfahrt's favourite, the star who shines brightest. It is Bolt's name that he invokes most frequently in conversation (taking huge delight in introducing him to the footballer Joe Cole, who on his first visit was kept waiting three hours. 'Joe!' said Müller-Wohlfahrt as he wrapped his arms around him. 'There's somebody I want you to meet . . . Usain?')

'The first time he came, nobody knew him,' Müller-Wohlfahrt told ESPN in 2011, 'but his coach sent him here to ask me whether it was worth it to train him. He was not sure whether he was able to train very, very hard. I said, "If he does this and this exercises – yes, then he can." So he started to do exercises and then the success grew more and more. For example, yesterday he phoned and he does his exercises. We have a very good connection, very good correspondence.'

In his office, a pair of Bolt's spikes have pride of place, displayed in a glass case. 'I have many trophies and items, but I don't display,' Müller-Wohlfahrt said. 'These are special.'

11

REAL AS IT GETS

The majority of them come from the same housing projects and were
singing in large part to get out of them. Partly it's this yearning,
a brilliant hungriness, that you hear.
John Jeremiah Sullivan on Jamaica's musicians

Shelly-Ann Fraser grew up in Waterhouse, a suburb of Kingston, one of Jamaica's poorest and most violent garrisons. A ghetto so notorious that it was name-checked in Jay Z's 'Real As It Gets'.

Shelly-Ann's mother, Maxine Simpson, who was one of fourteen children, worked as a street vendor, or 'higgler'. The family – Shelly-Ann, her mother and two brothers – lived in one of the zinc-roofed dwellings known as tenement yards.

It was a tough place to live. Two gangs had been engaged in a battle for control of Waterhouse since the 1970s: the Buckers, affiliated to the PNP, and the Yap Sam gang, claiming to represent the JLP. It was where Vybz Kartel, dancehall star and convicted murderer, grew up. Violence was an everyday reality (which, presumably, is what Jay Z means by 'real'). One day while Shelly-Ann was at school, her cousin Dwayne was shot dead; three days later his baby was born. Another day, her uncle Corey was gunned down.

At the age of ten, running for George Headley Primary School, Shelly-Ann was second in the 100 metres at Jamaica's primary schools Champs. She competed in bare feet. She had honed her sprinting in Waterhouse by running past the gangs of men, as her mother told her to do. They called her 'Merlene', after Merlene Ottey.

Speed was in her genes, thinks Shelly-Ann. Her mother was a good runner but 'she went to a mixed school and she got pregnant with my older brother when she was sixteen. That was it for her when it comes to athletics. But she was very fast; I would try to outrun her. I spoke to her coach: she was very good. So I knew I got the talent from her. And my mother tried to spark that interest in me. She was always the one person to tell me that if I was good at what I did I should be focused on it.'

Her mother's work was erratic and irregular. 'She would sell whatever was "in", so if it was Valentine's Day she was selling roses; if it was Christmas she was selling toys and firecrackers; it just depended what season it was.' It meant Maxine was rarely around for family occasions, and she missed most of Shelly-Ann's races once she started competing. Athletics meetings were on Saturdays, when 'she'd be in the country selling, and come back very late. At Christmas she'd be away all night so it would be me and my two brothers would have to look after ourselves.'

Shelly-Ann paints a vivid picture of a childhood that is all the more striking because of where she is sitting as she describes it. We are in an expensively equipped hair salon in a gated business park in New Kingston. The salon, Chic Hair Ja, belongs to her. It opened two months earlier. 'I get very bored with my hair,' says the woman famous for her colourful, adventurous hairstyles. 'I want to do so many things with it. This business was born from that love.'

The smart reception area is roughly the size of the house she shared with her mother and two brothers. It is decorated in pink and black, with floor-to-ceiling mirrors and leather sofas. Positive messages abound (a bit like her Twitter feed. Typical example: 'When no one celebrates you, learn to celebrate yourself. When no one compliments you, learn to compliment yourself! Good morning #Pryceless'). A sign in reception reads: 'It's all fun and games until someone breaks a nail.'

The salon is a symbol of how far she has come, of course. In the house that was the same size as the reception area, Shelly-Ann, her brothers and mother all shared one bed. She recalls that 'We had a small TV, a small fan, a couch, and a desk for the plates and stuff. And one bed. Four of us sleeping on the bed; we had to turn different ways so we could all fit. Sometimes I had my brother's feet in my mouth, or in my head.

'But I think it was still fun,' she adds. 'We had good times.'

There must have been . . . safety issues. 'Yeah, there were lots of safety issues,' she nods. 'I had to go to school early. I was coming out once, there was police in the yard because there was a lot of violence and a lot of shootings at that time. We had a curfew imposed on the community: nobody could come out until a certain time. But I had to get to school, so they let me pass.'

There were other unscheduled interruptions. 'We didn't have a wall structure to separate the houses, we had a fence, so men could come over. You had men coming over, walking through; sometimes we would hear them, I would say to my mum, "There's someone there," and she would say, "Sssshhhhh." But we survived.'

She is, as should now be clear, a survivor and a natural optimist. Waterhouse has improved, she thinks. 'I still go home every Sunday. I go to church there. It has gotten a lot better. There are a lot of times I would not dream to go down there at night; nine or ten o'clock at night you would not catch me there. But there's more peace now. I don't know if it's because a lot of the men who so-called ran the area have passed away . . .'

Fraser, who became Fraser-Pryce in 2011 when she married her boyfriend, Jason Pryce, attended Wolmer's High School for Girls. 'It was a very good school,' she says. For her it was also a way out of Waterhouse. 'You had persons say, "Oh, you'll never make it, you'll end up pregnant."[25] I felt I had something to prove.'

Where did it come from, her drive? 'I saw the struggles my mother had,' she says. 'And I had persons who believed in me.

'When I started high school, I went to the Penn Relays for the first time in 2000 and I met a lady who was part of the old girls' association. And she just started to take a liking to me. She paid my school fee for the following year, she bought my books and my uniforms. I asked her why, and she said, "You're going to be very good one day, I believe in you."' The woman's name was Jeanne Coke, then president of the Wolmer's Alumni Association, New York chapter.

At Champs in 2004, Shelly-Ann won the Class 2 girls' 100 metres in 11.73 seconds. A year later, she was second in Class 1; the winner, Anneisha McLaughlin, was the big star, the sprinter who seemed destined for great things. There was little to suggest that Fraser was

---

25 Nearly a quarter of babies in Jamaica are born to teenage mothers. Although many are unplanned, in the ghettos there can be an expectation of childbirth in young women; a childless girl may be stigmatised – called a 'mule' – when she is barely out of her teens.

even an Anneisha McLaughlin, never mind a Usain Bolt, the schoolboy who was four months older than her and already a household name in Jamaica. 'I wasn't a super-athlete, or a superstar at high school, I was just a normal athlete. I won once at Champs, when I'd almost finished school. I came second and third as well. You had a lot of talented athletes. Anneisha McLaughlin was so talented. It was fierce competition.'

When Fraser-Pryce left school, she thought about going to the US, as McLaughlin did. She was good enough to get an athletics scholarship to one of the smaller colleges. 'I had a few options.' Iowa was one of them. 'I knew the coach very well, he was a Jamaican.

'But one night I went to KFC here in Kingston and met Paul Francis.' He was running MVP with his brother, Stephen. 'When I saw Paul, he was saying, "What's happened, we're expecting you to be at UTech."'

Fraser replied: 'Oh, I don't know.'

'Come,' said Paul Francis, 'because Stephen wants you at UTech.'

'I went, sat down, had a conversation with Stephen Francis, and then I went home and said to my grandmother, "I'm going to UTech." I had made up my mind. I thought I would try it. If it didn't work out, I could go overseas.'

What convinced her? 'I don't think Stephen Francis convinced me, though I knew he could take me far if I listened. I think what sold it was that he had other athletes in his camp who were doing very well: he had Sherone Simpson, Asafa Powell, Bridget Foster, Michael Frater. I saw the progress they were making and decided, "I'm going to give this a chance."

'But I knew I had to be 100 per cent in; I couldn't have just one foot in.'

Francis had missed out on coaching Bolt two years earlier. But in Shelly-Ann Fraser he got the kind of athlete he loved, and the sort of challenge he relished. She was somebody few people rated and the opposite of Bolt in many ways: diminutive – five foot in bare feet – and shy, but with a big, infectious smile, and from the inner city rather than the country.

Francis discerned other strengths: her gritty determination to escape Waterhouse; her bubbly optimism; her independence; and the intelligence to realise an opportunity and seize it. Not that Shelly-Ann believed everything Francis told her. Early on he said that he thought she could make the team for the 2008 Olympics in Beijing. 'But I wasn't listening to that, I wasn't buying that kind of thing. The Olympics? Oh yeah?!'

In her first year with Francis, her personal best dropped from 11.7 to 11.3 between October and June. What changed in those months? 'I did a lot of technique training. If I didn't do something correct, I would be the one left on the track doing a hundred knees-up or arm swings; technique work until I was crying. He spent a lot of time on that.'

As a coach, Francis was strict. Fraser didn't always appreciate his gruff manner. 'I would say sometimes he's a dictator. He says he needs to be a dictator because athletes think they know best. He says if I know best I should coach myself, and I can't coach myself. But sometimes he is very harsh.'

And unlike Mills, he kept a distance. There was no 'pally-wally'-ness. Yet he and Shelly-Ann did establish a rapport, she says. They 'connect well', but only perhaps because she cedes total responsibility to him. 'For it to work for me, I have to be submissive in a sense,' she explains. 'If he says to do something, I do it, because he is in control.

'You can talk to him and he'll listen,' she adds. 'He understands . . . He might look very aggressive and unapproachable from the outside, but once you get close to him and talk to him one-to-one, you realise it's a shell.'

In 2007, her second full season with Francis and MVP, Fraser was selected for the Jamaican team for the world championships in Osaka.

Osaka was a prelude to Beijing: Powell took bronze in the 100 metres; Veronica Campbell won the women's 100 metres and took silver in the 200. And finally Jamaica got what it had been waiting for: twenty-year-old Usain Bolt won a senior medal – silver behind Tyson Gay in the 200 metres, in 19.91 seconds. Bolt was also part of the 4x100 metres relay team that was second to the USA. The American men remained dominant. Meanwhile, the Jamaican women won silver in both relays.

Fraser went to the Osaka world championships as a member of the sprint relay team. She didn't run, but 'seeing everybody competing and winning medals, that was my inspiration. The glory, the energy they felt when they won medals, that was my inspiration. I came back to Jamaica, I got my body fat down, I went to Juliet Cuthbert's fitness club. I went there and I worked out. I would be on break but I would be working. I worked very hard.'

She made more dramatic improvements over the winter before Beijing. And at the Jamaican trials in June she sprung a huge upset, beating the golden girl, the world 100 metres champion, Veronica Campbell-Brown (who had married Omar Brown, a fellow Jamaican sprinter, in November 2007). The top three in the trials qualified: Fraser was second, Campbell-Brown fourth. The backlash began immediately – who was this Shelly-Ann Fraser to be taking the place of the world champion? She was advised to give up her place for the good of Jamaica.

Francis weighed in on his athlete's behalf. 'They can't take you out,' he told her. 'You earned your spot.' It was the media and public campaign to oust her that really bothered Shelly-Ann. 'I was upset at my country. Here am I, a young athlete, making my first Olympic team, and you're telling me I should pull out because I don't have experience? Now, how do one get experience if you don't get the chance? It was very hurtful that they said the things they said.' As well as the media coverage, the selectors seemed to be prevaricating, waiting to see if one of the top three sustained an injury – as though they were trying to leave the door ajar for Campbell-Brown.

'In Jamaica we have diehard track fans,' says Fraser-Pryce. 'They take it very serious and personal. You can't have a bad race. If you run horribly they will slaughter you.'

There were no last-minute reprieves for Campbell-Brown. In only her second full season with MVP, Shelly-Ann Fraser was – as Stephen Francis had forecast – going to the Olympics as part of a fifty-one-strong Jamaican team (of whom thirty-nine were sprinters).[26]

When the team arrived at Beijing airport for the Games, on 1 August, they were met by Jamaica's ambassador to China, Wayne McCook. With his diplomatic status, McCook was able to enter the airport to give the athletes their official accreditations, which acted as a visa for the duration of the Games. But Francis refused to accept his accreditation. He wanted nothing to do with Team Jamaica. The bad blood hadn't just been caused by the controversy over Fraser's selection. A row had been simmering between MVP and the JAAA over the governing body's insistence that all Jamaican athletes attend a pre-Olympic training camp in Tianjin. 'The way that the JAAA is forcing us to prepare for the Olympics is not what we had in mind,' said Francis. 'We don't believe this is the ideal preparation.'

Pouring oil on the flames, he continued: 'I guess because they want to ensure that the athletes who I coach don't do well, they decided to come up with this camp and this mandatory thing. I guess they know that the preparation I have in mind doesn't involve a camp. So I guess there's a debate.'

At the heart of Francis's complaint was his fear that he would be prevented from coaching his own athletes in the build-up to the Games. Moreover, he believed that the JAAA organised their camp in Tianjin 'only after hearing in February that we were planning to have our own'. The governing body denied this, claiming that arrangements had been

---

26 It was reduced by one shortly before the Games when Julien Dunkley, a US-based sprinter who made the 4x100 metres relay squad, tested positive for an anabolic steroid at the Jamaican national championships.

made over a year previously. They also pointed out that they had held
a pre-Olympic camp for every Games since 1984. 'The suggestion that
our training camp was belatedly undertaken to "obstruct" Mr Stephen
Francis's own camp cannot be substantiated,' the JAAA responded.
The problem, they suggested, was Francis's general hostility towards
the governing body.

The head coach to the national team was Glen Mills, and it is
impossible to avoid the suspicion that the feud had something to do
with the underlying rivalry between the Racers and MVP. It also
reinforced the notion of Mills and Racers as establishment, Francis
and MVP as outsiders.

I asked the JAAA vice president, Vilma Charlton – herself a former
Olympian – for her take on the relationship between Francis and the
governing body. She was inclined to a charitable view. 'I understand
him,' she said. 'He wants the best for his athletes. He's a bright fella,
very brilliant; it's just his personality and we have to work with it.' She
looked thoughtful. 'He is very, very different. A peculiar person, but
that's because he's bright.' .

Francis backed down after a few days when he said he would accept
his accreditation after all. But he wouldn't pick it up himself, instead
sending an athlete (unnamed). The message relayed to the athlete was
that Francis should collect it in person. Which, eventually, he did.

Thus did the Jamaican athletics team's Beijing Olympic campaign
get under way.

On the night of Sunday 17 August, Shelly-Ann Fraser was one of
three Jamaicans who lined up for the final of the women's 100 metres
in Beijing; Kerron Stewart and Sherone Simpson, her MVP clubmate,
were the others. There was no clear favourite. Although Shelly-Ann
had won all three of her qualifying rounds, she was still a rank outsider.
Few had heard of her before the Jamaican trials two months earlier. But
the heats had shown that she was a tremendous starter. Her height – or
lack of it – meant that she seemed to spring out of the blocks.

As they were called to the start, Fraser wore an expression of wide-eyed surprise – perhaps she was as shocked as everybody else that she, little Shelly-Ann Fraser from the Waterhouse ghetto, was in an Olympic final. She was in lane four. As they waited for the gun, Torri Edwards, the 2003 world champion, twitched; but no false start. Fraser, in any case, was entirely focused on her race: her eyes, opening gradually wider over the 10.78 seconds it took her to cover the distance, locked on to the track ahead of her; her cheeks puffed out and mouth open in a small 'O'.

She was fastest out of the blocks, but seemed to find another gear in the second half of the race and the gap opened to two metres by the line. Fraser smiled her way to victory: it crept gradually across her face as she homed in on the line and punched the air. There was no stopping her then. She bounced up and down. And she kept smiling. 'I can't stop smiling,' she said once she made it around the track. 'My braces are hurting me.'

Behind her, Stewart and Simpson emerged from the pack and could not be separated by the photo finish: they were both awarded silver medals. A Jamaican clean sweep, a one-two-two. 'The Jamaicans showed up, and we totally didn't,' said Lauryn Williams, the American who was fourth. 'It's very humbling.' And this with Veronica Campbell-Brown, the world champion, missing.

Six years later, in her hair salon in Kingston, Shelly-Ann beams as she recalls the night she became the first Jamaican woman to win the Olympic 100 metres. 'Yeah, yeah! I felt so good because I said before that if I won I'd be jumping and screaming because I wouldn't know what to do with myself. It was awesome.'

What was going through her mind? She was thinking about how far she had come, where she had come from, and the hard work she had put in over the previous two years. 'I remembered the struggles, I remembered growing up, the fact no one wanted me to run, telling my coach I was too tired, that I couldn't do it. I remembered all that.'

Winning the Olympic 100 metres title didn't change Shelly-Ann Fraser, says Stephen Francis.

There were no invitations from David Letterman, no multimillion-pound sponsorship deals. It raises the question of whether she has the profile and recognition she deserves. 'Deserves, yes,' Francis says. 'But most people don't realise how good she could be if she got opportunities. She's a very good speaker, a teller of stories; a natural chatterbox who likes to perform, even more than Bolt.'

The upside was that after Beijing she remained hungry for more; her appetite for training was certainly undiminished. 'Yeah,' says Francis, 'because the difference is that Bolt has always thought he is getting what he deserves. Shelly-Ann always questions whether she deserves what she has.'

12

SHOCK AND AWE

When I saw the time, I knew I had to go out and catch him.
But even after the finish I couldn't catch him.
Asafa Powell

'I wanted to run the 100, not just the 200,' Usain Bolt said. 'My coach told me if I broke the national record for the 200, I could run a 100.'

At the Jamaican national championships in June 2007, he ran 19.75 to beat Donald Quarrie's thirty-six-year-old Jamaican record. 'After the race he didn't even say thank you,' said Mills. 'He just said, "When is the 100?"'

In his first professional 100 metres, a month later, in Rethymno, Greece, Bolt recorded 10.03. It was hardly earth-shattering, but his head had been turned; over the winter he worked at his start and explosiveness. Mills was fine with that; he believed that to win the 200 metres he had to be faster anyway. 'We mapped out a programme to improve his speed in the first part of the season,' he said, 'and then we would switch over to improving his 200 metres for the Olympics.'

When Mills began working with Bolt, everybody in Jamaica had an opinion about why he wasn't delivering on the promise he showed as a fifteen-year-old. He was too tall, he couldn't run the bend; or he suffered the curse of the sprinter: his body wasn't robust enough and was prone to breaking down. And he was lazy. 'I took it all on,' Mills said in a rare public speaking appearance at the IMD business school in Switzerland in 2009. 'But I like to do my own analysis, too. I did my own assessment and came up with something different.'

Sitting alongside his star athlete, wearing a white Adidas polo shirt and his usual jeans and trainers, shaven headed and rotund, Mills spoke slowly, deliberately, seeming not so much laid-back as verging on horizontal. Such a state lends itself to deadpan humour. 'I think the problem', he continued, 'was that he was not fast enough.'

In the first part of the 2008 season, they worked together on his 100 metres, to hone his speed. But Mills was clear on the reason why: to improve his chances in his main event, the 200 metres.

Then everything changed. On 3 May, Bolt entered the 100 metres at the Jamaican Invitational at the National Stadium in Kingston. With a just-legal tailwind of 1.8 metres a second, and after two false starts, he ran 9.76: the second fastest in history, behind Asafa Powell's world record 9.74 in Rieti eight months previously. Bolt's time caught everybody by surprise. 'Usain said he was shocked,' said Michael Johnson, the US's 200 and 400 metre world record holder. 'I'm shocked too. I never would have predicted he could run that fast over 100 metres.'

Twenty-eight days later, the sense of shock was even greater. With another tailwind – 1.7 metres a second this time – Bolt sprinted in New York's Icahn Stadium to a world record 9.72 seconds. He had become the fastest man in history in only his fifth attempt at the distance. Gay, the world champion, was second. He was stunned not only by the time but by Bolt's ability to overcome what was considered his disadvantage – his height – to move so fast. 'It looked like his knees were going past my face,' he said.

Now, said Bolt, he would go for the double in Beijing: the 100 and 200. Mills, speaking in New York after the world record, reflected: 'Over the past three years we've had our differences and we've had our ups and downs. But I can say for him he never lost sight of what the big picture is and although we differ in what is hard work, we are always able to get things done.'

Powell was one of the first to phone Bolt. 'You've made things rough on me now,' said the now former world record holder.

Back in Falmouth, Bolt's first coach, Devere Nugent, watched the world record in New York on television. 'I always knew, and probably outside of Glen Mills, I might've been the only one who knew that he could run a 100 metres. And what Glen did was what I did with him as a child: he bet him; he challenged him.' Nugent was not surprised that Bolt was so fast. 'If you keep a horse that wants to run locked up for fifteen years, once you release that horse, it's going to run.'

Early on the morning of the men's 100 metres final in Beijing – 9.30 a.m. Jamaican time – Nugent drove the thirty minutes from Falmouth to his and Bolt's home village of Sherwood Content, where he joined Wellesley Bolt and others – Bolt's mother Jennifer was in the 90,000 crowd at the Bird's Nest stadium in Beijing.

Inside the stadium, away from the camera lenses, the finalists waited in the call room. It is half-sanctuary, half-purgatory in there. 'I love the call room, the pressure that you feel,' said the British sprinter Dwain Chambers. 'You want to vomit. You think to yourself, why am I here? Why do I put myself through this stress? . . . It's like your driving test and wedding combined.'

It is here that races are won and lost, say athletes. Carl Lewis would shake opponents' hands and get in their faces, killing them with kindness. Maurice Greene would flex his muscles. Some athletes snarl and pout, sometimes to disguise the fact that they are shaking with nerves. Asafa Powell, crippled by self-doubt and fear, can't seem to act the part of the macho sprinter; he disappears into his own world.

In the call room in Beijing, Bolt did what he always does: laughing, joking, chatting to his rivals. 'They don't always talk back to me. Just stare back. I try not to focus too much on the race. I may sing a song.

My method is to stay relaxed. And not think about the race until the starter says, "On your marks." Then I take a deep breath, refocus, think, Let's get it done. It's all about staying relaxed.

'But some are really tense,' Bolt told an IMD business school seminar in 2009. 'Like, they're going to strangle you. Crazy, are some of them in the call room.' Describing the scene, he mimicked his rivals, leaning forward, narrowing his eyes, staring intently. 'They're ready,' he said. 'Ready to take you apart.'

Bolt was one of three Jamaicans in the final in Beijing, along with two of Francis's MVP athletes, Powell and Michael Frater. 'He's got a bit of a swagger,' said the BBC commentator, Steve Cram, as Bolt ran through his routine, smoothing his hair (what little there was: he was shorn, looking as youthful as his twenty-one years), smiling, then pointing to his face with a mock-serious expression. 'He's enjoying himself.' While the others looked as though they were on their way to their own execution, Bolt 'looked like he was heading to the beach', said Cram.

On an airless Beijing night – the wind gauge read '0.00 m/s' – they settled into the blocks and the stadium hushed, the only sound that of anticipation – echoey bangs and clatters, nervous giggles. In the set position, Bolt, in lane four but with only two runners on his inside, remained bigger and taller than the others, his backside sticking up.

Richard Thompson alongside him gets off to a flyer. As he drives out of the blocks, Bolt's left foot gently scuffs the track; the laces are loose on the same shoe and will gradually come undone over the next nine seconds. He drives for ten metres, head down, gradually unfolding. Then, once he's fully extended, comes the acceleration. Only there is no acceleration. Of course there is no acceleration. Dennis Johnson drilled this into me.

'Have you ever seen 100 metres run?' DJ asked.

'Yes,' I replied.

'Sure?'

'Is this a trick question?'

'No.'

'Yes, I have seen 100 metres run.'

'OK, we've established you've seen 100 metres run. OK. Have you ever seen one guy come from the back, speed up and win?'

'I think so, yes. Yes, Bolt in Beijing.'

'Bolt, yes.' Johnson allowed a long pause to hang between us. 'Are you sure you've seen that?'

'Erm, well . . .'

'You didn't see that,' DJ said. 'What you saw was some tiring before others. You can't speed up after six seconds. That's a physiological impossibility. So it's the guy who tires least who is going to win. What you see is the guys who finish second, third, fourth tiring and slowing down at a faster speed.'

At forty metres in the Bird's Nest they are just about level: Thompson, Bolt, Frater, with Powell a fraction behind. Bolt, having worked through the gears, doesn't speed up; he hits cruise control. It's his height, his long legs; they seem to give him an unfair advantage. He gobbles up the track while the others fall away.

At sixty metres, Bolt glances right. 'He's looking for Asafa,' says the commentator. 'Asafa isn't there.' Then he glances right again. 'He's looking for Thompson. Thompson isn't there.' Still looking to his right, he begins to ease up a full fifteen metres from the line, stretching his long arms like an enormous bird of prey coming in for landing. Then he thumps his chest and yells. The winning time, 9.69 seconds, is astonishing, not that Bolt notices that he has broken his own world record as he carries on sprinting, cavorting, around the track. The winning margin – several metres – is immediately declared the biggest ever: it wasn't necessary to check.

Watch Bolt's Beijing 100 metres final and his world junior 200 metres race in Kingston, six years apart, and it is as though you are watching a different athlete; the twenty-one-year-old Bolt had added muscle and technique: what they call 'form'. He had added one or two inches in height and eighteen kilos in weight. He was smoother; the

lolling head had gone. He was graceful but at the same time powerful and strong. Watching it brings to mind DJ's poetic description of Mills's sprinters' ability to dance across the surface of the track, their feet kissing the ground, all the more surprising in someone of Bolt's size, as though he defied the laws of physics.

'You couldn't hear, it was deafening,' Devere Nugent recalls of watching the 100 metres final in Sherwood Content. 'The noise in the room was absolutely deafening. Everybody came out to watch because I think we recognised that we were witnessing a moment in history that as long as we live probably will never happen again: that out of the belly of a small, rural village comes one that has stamped his mark on the world.'

Wellesley Bolt was watching at home because he was scared of flying. He recalls, 'It was tense moments for me. To be honest, I don't like flights. The mother enjoys. So I wasn't there for the 100. I said, "I'm not going." But after the 100, Digicel were Bolt's sponsor, they insist I have to go. I said, "OK, let's go."'

So Wellesley set off from Trelawny, bound for Beijing. 'I didn't think I'd catch the 200. Because the 200 was run while I was in the air.' Of course Bolt was unbeatable in the 200 metres. 'You're Usain's dad?'

said the security official to Wellesley in Beijing, when he landed. 'Oh God, he broke Michael Johnson's record.'

The 100 and 200 metres in Beijing were the last major races of his son's that Wellesley Bolt missed.

Asafa Powell cut a forlorn figure as Bolt carried on around the track, milking the acclaim, launching his 'To Di World' routine, dancing, establishing himself not only as a great athlete but also a showman.

While Bolt celebrated, Powell, fifth in his second successive Olympic final, stood dejected, hands on hips as he stared up at the replay on the big screen, the folds in the back of his neck making him look like a defeated boxer. Interviewed after the race, he couldn't bring himself to look at the camera; he stood with his back to it. 'Well, um, I messed up big time,' he said. 'My legs died on me. Usain ran an awesome race and I'm very happy for him.'

What went wrong? he was asked by the trackside interviewer, Phil Jones, who had his arm around Powell as though comforting him. 'I'm not sure what happened. I just have to live with it. I'm happy for Usain.'

Did it prove that he couldn't handle the big stage? 'Well, you know, it's really for myself I wanted to get the gold medal,' he said. 'It's quite obvious that I wasn't ready for the big stage.'

Powell left Jones and the media area to congratulate Bolt, and found himself swept up in his celebrations; it was irresistible, even for someone as defeated and deflated as Powell. Bolt performed a couple of Jamaican dancehall moves, the Gully Creepa and Nuh Linga – typical of the expressive, suggestive routines made popular by dancehall culture – and Powell joined in. Watching back home, Powell's parents were unimpressed. 'God gave [Asafa] those feet to bring joy to the world, but not in that form of dancing,' said his mother, Cislyn. 'We don't want Nuh Linga, we just want Jesus.'

She wasn't the only one who disapproved. Jacques Rogge, the IOC president, said that he thought Bolt's celebrations were unbecoming of an Olympic champion and showed a lack of respect for his opponents. 'That's not the way we perceive being a champion,' he said. Bolt, he added, should 'show more respect for his competitors and shake hands, give a tap on the shoulder to the other ones immediately after the finish and not make gestures like the one he made in the 100 metres'. On the US channel NBC, Bob Costas echoed Rogge, saying Bolt was 'disrespectful to his competitors, to the Olympic Games and to the fans'.

It was a baffling reaction to an outpouring of what looked like spontaneous joy from a twenty-one-year-old. Bolt wasn't making a political statement. Not that he was aware of, anyway. But perhaps that is exactly what he was doing – a cultural if not a political statement, at least. His very Jamaican celebration and the reaction to it intrigued and concerned some commentators, who detected a whiff of resentment that Bolt, the first Jamaican-born and Jamaican-trained gold medallist, was so brazenly flaunting his culture on such a hallowed stage. It was a clash of cultures between Bolt's exuberance and the conservatism of the Olympic movement. 'Bolt's display is an affront to both the imperial conquests the Olympics are supposed to honour and the colonial ethos and discipline that sport is supposed to instil into "natives",' a trio of academics, James McBean (a Jamaican), Michael Friedman and Callie Batts, would later assert in a book, *Beyond C. L. R. James*.

There was even some negative reaction in Jamaica, as Cislyn Powell's comments illustrated. But perhaps it is more accurate to describe it as shame, or a sense of embarrassment, owing less to the extrovert display – the showing off – than to the dancehall origins of the Gully Creepa and Nuh Linga, and their associations with the Kingston ghettos. And for the IOC establishment, perhaps Bolt, with his 'creolised display of exuberance', was getting above himself, offending Olympic ideals 'steeped in the ethos of the elite British boarding schools', as the academics put it, 'which [Olympic founder Pierre] de Coubertin believed were at the foundation of the British Empire's global domination'.

Bolt's lap of honour in Beijing was an expression of individuality and cultural identity. But it was only the start. Before too long, the victory laps would be accompanied by a prolonged blast of Bob Marley in stadiums from London to Moscow, Rome to Zurich. Puma, the German sportswear manufacturer so keen to align themselves to Jamaican culture when they signed Bolt, would later use the dancehall moves in an advert.

As for Bolt, he seemed to be doing what came naturally, though perhaps he was not completely oblivious to the significance of showcasing some of the moves he'd learned in the Quad nightclub. 'I love taking dances from Jamaica and putting it out to the world,' he said.

Bolt's win came twenty-four hours before Shelly-Ann Fraser became the second Jamaican 100 metres champion. Her motivation, she said, was not Bolt, it was her clubmate, Powell. She wanted to make up for his disappointment. As Stephen Francis puts it: 'Well, there is no reason for her to be overly elated at Usain Bolt, because after all she hardly sees Usain Bolt. Usain Bolt may as well live in England for all the time she sees him.'

There was more, much more: Bolt's golds and two more world records in the 200 metres and the 4x100 relay; Veronica Campbell-Brown's successful defence of her title and Kerron Stewart's bronze in the 200 metres; Shericka Williams's silver in the 400; Melaine Walker's gold in the 400 hurdles; bronze in the women's 4x400.

It was too much. It didn't merely invite suspicion. It opened the door and ushered it in.

The men's 100 metres was the show-stopper: the most sensational since Ben Johnson shot to a world record 9.79 seconds in Seoul in 1988. That fact alone was enough to give pause, to temper the euphoria. Johnson's run was seared into the consciousness, but so was news of his failed test for steroids a few days later. Since then, it was difficult to know how to react to incredible performances. If the heart rejoiced, the head urged caution.

Bolt's brilliance could be explained: he had been brilliant at fifteen, then held back by injury. His height advantage – his ability to move his long legs as fast as the shorter guys – helped rationalise his performance; after all, he required fewer steps, only forty-one compared to forty-five for most others.

With Fraser, the Pocket Rocket, it was more difficult to find a reason, or to accept that she had apparently come from nowhere. Watch and listen to the footage of the women's 100 metres in Beijing and you can hear the stunned reactions of the commentators: their failure to reach for the same superlatives they had used twenty-four hours earlier is striking. Her win was the kind of upset that keeps sport interesting. Unpredictability is supposed to be part of the appeal. But athletics, the 100 metres in particular, has had a habit of throwing up nasty surprises. Fraser's improvement in a year, from June 2007 to June 2008, was almost half a second: 11.31 to 10.85. And in Beijing she shaved off another seven-hundredths. It added a question mark to that Jay Z lyric. Real as it gets?

Carl Lewis, the US's nine-times Olympic gold medallist, said he had questions about the effectiveness and integrity of the anti-doping programme in Jamaica. More accurately, he wondered if there *was* an anti-doping programme in Jamaica. Although the IAAF insisted they were regularly testing the top Jamaicans (they said only four countries had been subject to more out-of-competition tests),[27] locally it was a different story, alleged Lewis. 'No one is accusing anyone,' said the sprinter who inherited Ben Johnson's gold medal in 1988. 'But don't live by a different rule and expect the same kind of respect. They say, "Oh, we've been great for the sport." No, you have not. No country has had that kind of dominance. I'm not saying they've done anything for certain. I don't know. But how dare anybody feel that there shouldn't be scrutiny, especially in our sport?'

---

27 According to Herb Elliott of the JAAA, in 2008, prior to the Olympics, Bolt was tested out of competition by the IAAF on four occasions, Powell six and Fraser three.

Lewis went on to say that if he were still competing, he would expect questions. He conceded that Bolt 'could be the greatest athlete of all time . . . But for someone to run 10.03 one year and 9.69 the next, if you don't question that in a sport that has the reputation it has right now, you're a fool. Period.'

It was true that Bolt had made a huge leap, but then again, he had only run one 100 metres the previous year. It was more useful to study his progression over 200 metres. He was somebody who had run a sub-20-second 200 metres as a teenager, and following the Beijing Olympics, *Athletics Weekly* charted his progress over five years in the longer event. Tracking his times from the age of sixteen, his improvement, culminating in Beijing with his world record 19.30, was 1.28 seconds, or 6.22 per cent. Of seven of his peers selected for the study, Bolt's improvement was, in percentage terms, ranked only sixth. The British runner Christian Malcolm had made the most dramatic gain: 1.50 seconds (6.95 per cent). John Regis, the retired British sprinter, had made a 7.50 per cent improvement over a similar period, while Michael Johnson made a bigger gain – 6.81 per cent – in a shorter period between eighteen and twenty-one. The magazine's conclusion: there was nothing exceptional about Bolt's improvement over 200 metres from the age of sixteen to twenty-one. The implication: he shouldn't be judged guilty on performance alone.

But apart from his credulity-stretching speed, the other problem for Bolt was that so many of his predecessors had associations with doping. 'Let's be real,' Lewis continued. 'Let me go through the list: Ben Johnson, Justin Gatlin, Tim Montgomery, Tyson Gay and the two Jamaicans [Bolt and Powell]. Six people have run under 9.80 legally, three have tested positive, and one had a year out.[28] Not to say [Bolt] is doing anything, but he's not going to have me saying he's great and

---

28 Lewis was speaking in 2008: since then, Tyson Gay has also tested positive. Now, of the nine who have gone under 9.80, only Bolt, Maurice Greene and another Jamaican, Nesta Carter, have never tested positive.

then two years later he gets popped. If I don't trust it, what does the public think?'

Lewis praised the drug-testing in the US, which he said gave him confidence in Veronica Campbell-Brown. 'Veronica Campbell-Brown lives in the United States and has been transparent and consistent. She won the worlds last year in the 100 metres and this year can't even make the team. Are you going to tell me that shouldn't be questioned?'

Bolt returned to Jamaica and to a party in the grounds of the William Knibb Memorial High School in Falmouth. Twenty thousand people turned up: three times the population of the town. Bolt appeared on the stage at 10 p.m., introduced by the dancehall reggae star Tony Matterhorn. 'One Carl Lewis wonders why we so fast,' Matterhorn addressed the crowd. 'I guess maybe he'll come to the islands and meet and greet the Jamaican mothers who make the greatest food in the world.'

Taking the microphone, Bolt struck a different note. An interesting one, before a captive audience. 'If you guys in the country don't act better, then people will still look down on the country,' he said. 'You guys try to do better. Start to look at yourself. Think before you act. Because Jamaica is a great place. People love coming here, but you have to stop the crime to let them want to come back. A lot of people say, "I'm coming to Jamaica, but I'm wondering about the crime." I say, "Don't worry about it. Jamaica is wonderful. It's nice. The vibe is . . . look at me: I enjoy myself every day." '

Shelly-Ann had a similar homecoming, with murals painted on the crumbling walls of Waterhouse in her honour. As the crowd waited for her, her mother, Maxine, in front of banks of speakers, with a thousand people gathered around her, picked up the microphone and sang, 'God is gooooood, God is good to me,' before launching into a prayer. When her girl finally arrived, there was pandemonium. The only sadness for Shelly-Ann was that Jeanne Coke, the Wolmer's 'old girl' who had supported her financially at school, couldn't be there.

Coke passed away in March, five months before the Olympics. 'It hurt,' says Shelly-Ann now, 'a lot of hurt – but I'm glad she saw me . . . she knew what was coming.'

Fraser was joined at her homecoming by a journalist from *Sports Illustrated*, who asked her about Lewis's comments and the scepticism that had greeted her win. 'I would want Mr Dope-Man to come test me every day,' said Fraser. 'I want him to test me in the morning, before I train, after I train, because I'm not hiding one thing and I'm not taking anything. I'm a nervous type of person. Whenever I do something bad I'm just going to tell you, because my conscience is going to hurt.

'I can tell you one thing about my teammates,' she continued. 'I know we are 100 per cent clean. Hard training— we are vomiting. I mean, US athletes are so privileged, they get everything they want. And when it doesn't work their way, they cry. They don't understand. We have to do good with what we have here. They have to come here to live it, to see it.'

Her words seemed heartfelt. But surely Carl Lewis was right to be sceptical. He wasn't the only one; we were all more inclined to ask questions than to acclaim unreservedly. I remember the atmosphere in the press room in Beijing as Bolt's time flashed up. Incredulous.

How credible was it that this tiny island had turned up in Beijing with their home-trained athletes and dominated the Olympic Games? They had wiped the floor with the Americans. No wonder Lewis was searching for answers. He claimed no country had ever dominated to the extent that Jamaica did in Beijing. One had. His very own USA, who routinely dominated (including in Lewis's day) and in 2004 won gold and bronze in the 100 metres, and gold, silver and bronze in both the 200 and the 400, as well as silver in the 4x100 and gold in the 4x400. But the USA had a population of over 300 million. Jamaica had fewer than three million.

Yet Beijing was only the start. Next was Berlin.

*

Bolt began 2009 with a dreadful car crash. At 1 p.m. on Wednesday 29 April, he was driving his black BMW M3 – a twenty-second birthday gift from Puma delivered to Jamaica only seventy-six days earlier – along Highway 2000, which cuts through the middle of the island, from Ocho Rios in the north to Spanish Town in the south.

Most of the roads in Jamaica are terrible: narrow, potholed, twisting. One of the few decent stretches of dual carriageway is Highway 2000, on the approach to Spanish Town. It was here, as he accelerated in torrential rain, that Bolt skidded, left the road and smashed through a barrier. The car rolled three times before ending on its roof.

Somehow Bolt and his two female passengers – nineteen-year-old Venecia Crew and twenty-year-old Latoya Taylor – were able to clamber from the car. They had only minor injuries – Bolt sustained his, thorns in his feet, thanks to his shoeless state. He believed a higher power had intervened to save him. But he had God in mind, not a German automotive manufacturer. As images of the squashed BMW flashed around the world – it looked as though a heavy object had landed on the roof – the company was keen to point out that the accident had highlighted the car's safety features.

Bolt hobbled painfully out of hospital two hours later, his still bare feet heavily strapped. Local reporters were there, and Bolt, speaking in the patois we don't usually hear, reassured them. 'Mi good, man, mi good,' he said, affecting a casual tone, though he must still have been in shock. From the passenger seat of the waiting car he continued: 'Am a good, man. A'm all right. A few talks, a'm good, man.'

He seemed anxious to get away, telling the reporters: 'We talk, man, we talk, we talk, we talk, all right? A'm all right man.' He was due to compete the following weekend at the National Stadium – would he still be able to run? 'Mi talk to mi coach about that. We talk, we talk.'

Fifty-nine days after his crash, Bolt ran 9.86 seconds at the National Stadium to win the Jamaican trials ahead of Powell. In Paris, twenty days after that, he won in 9.79. And at the world championships in

Berlin, 108 days after the car crash, he did what he hadn't done in Beijing, running all the way to the finish.

He stood at the start of his first world 100 metres final with a twinkle in his eye, a smile playing on his lips. He launched his arm up straight like an aeroplane taking off. Taking a few steps forward and shaking out his shoulders, he caught Powell's eye and invited him to join him in a bout of shadow boxing. As they swayed and threw mock punches at each other, it looked as though Bolt was consciously trying to get his uptight, nervous countryman to relax. It came naturally to Bolt, less so to Powell, but he joined in.

There were five Caribbean men in the final. Two of them were Jamaicans; the others included Daniel Bailey of Antigua and Barbuda, also coached by Glen Mills. It was telling that several of the finalists indulged in horseplay, as though Bolt, in Beijing, had established a new trend. The menacing, pumped-up machismo of Maurice Greene or Justin Gatlin now looked outdated, comical. Only Tyson Gay, the defending champion, looked serious, but not for show; in the lane next to Bolt, he appeared to be talking to himself. Beside him, Bolt was an overgrown child as he once again launched his long arm down the runway. He smoothed his hair and eyebrows, pursed his lips.

Berlin was a slow track, they reckoned. But there was a tailwind: 0.9 metres per second, compared to the perfectly still conditions of Beijing. Bolt reacted to the gun in 0.146 seconds (as opposed to 0.165 in Beijing). Only 0.89 seconds into his run he reached maximum power: 2,619.5 watts. From zero to twenty metres he was 0.02 seconds slower than he had been in Beijing; from twenty to forty metres, faster by 0.03.

In Beijing, he reached sixty metres in 6.32 seconds; in Berlin, 6.31. It was between sixty and eighty metres that he began to pull away (from his Beijing shadow), reaching his maximum speed, 27.44 miles per hour.

From eighty to a hundred metres he pulled away from the others as

well as the Beijing Bolt, going 0.11 seconds faster than in the Olympic
final. Did that help settle the debate over how much time he had lost
by thumping his chest and coasting the last ten metres in Beijing? In
Berlin, as Bolt ran all the way through the tape, Gay was closer than
anybody had been in Beijing. Gay's 9.71 seconds was a personal best
and would have been a world record had the man in front of him
never existed.

Bolt's time seemed fantastical; it pushed the boundaries of what
was thought possible: 9.58 seconds. A demolition of his own world
record, and all the world records that came before it – when, for the
best part of twenty years, a time of around 9.80 seemed to be at the
threshold of human performance. 'I knew it was going to be a great
race,' he told the BBC, 'and I executed it. It's a great time, a great
feeling, I feel good in myself and I knew I could do it. There was a big
build-up, great atmosphere. It wasn't going to be an easy race, but I
had a perfect start and just went from there. I came out here to do my
best and I did what I had to do.'

'When I saw the time,' said Asafa Powell, 'I knew I had to go out
and catch him. But even after the finish I couldn't catch him.'

Looking at Bolt's ten-metre splits in Berlin with Dennis Johnson's
words in mind – they all slow down, the one who slows least wins –
confirms the wisdom of his mantra. Bolt accelerates all the way to
seventy metres: his fastest ten-metre split is from sixty to seventy metres
(0.81 seconds), then he hardly slows at all, recording 0.82, 0.83 and
0.83 for the final three ten-metre splits. Slowing down, maybe, but not
so the naked eye would see.

His ability to minimise his deceleration over the final thirty metres
sets him apart. But it is not the only thing. Tom Tellez, who coached
Carl Lewis throughout his career, identified five phases of sprinting
and what each phase is worth as a percentage of a 100 metres race.
Reaction time, he reckoned, accounts for only 1 per cent – which
seems to make a mockery of the emphasis put on the start (though it

is impossible to look at each phase as a disparate part: one affects the other).

Block clearance is the next phase: 5 per cent. The third, the 'speed of efficient acceleration', is believed by Tellez to be the most important: 64 per cent. It is also the longest, taking top sprinters to, in most cases, sixty metres. Maintaining top speed is worth 18 per cent. Finally, the deceleration phase is 12 per cent.

In terms of top speed, there might be little difference between Bolt and the others. But he reaches his top speed later than most. According to Jimson Lee, a coach and physiologist, Bolt and Tyson Gay are the only sprinters in history who have been able to accelerate all the way to seventy metres.

The received wisdom is that sprinters accelerate up to sixty metres then slow, with the final forty metres largely about damage limitation. 'You want to "delay" your top speed as long as possible,' Lee says. 'You want a smooth acceleration: the longer, the better.' Because of his longer training efforts (perhaps also his background as a 400 metres runner, as Devere Nugent suggested), Bolt is conceivably more accustomed to and better equipped for a smooth, gradual acceleration. Yet he also has explosive speed.

Lee has, along with many others, given a lot of thought to Bolt's training. Although they are cagey about their methods, it is understood that the Mills camp follows a 'short to long' programme, starting with short efforts and progressing to longer distances. In this context, short means pure speed – thirty to fifty metres – while long means speed endurance – 250 to 400 metres. Mills's thinking is that you are not going to be one of the fastest in the world if you are not one of the fastest in the world over thirty metres. As he has put it, 'We tend to train the speed then stretch it out.' Or: 'I believe in speed, from a yard to a mile, as my number one objective.' Interestingly, Stephen Francis prefers the opposite, 'long to short': 'High volume, short recovery' in the pre-season, 'leading on to low volume, long recovery, high intensity'.

*

Back in Jamaica, in the midst of the off season (pre-season, if you're an athlete), I ask Francis about the two philosophies, short to long and long to short, and the thinking that underpins each. He admits he prefers long to short. His athletes do the kind of training that Bolt so hated doing with Fitz Coleman – long efforts, up to 400 metres. 'Most sprinters wouldn't want to train with us because we do stuff that they don't do,' Francis says. 'I'm a big fan of sprinters running 300s, and they run them from the start of training until February or thereabouts. And then they go out and have to run a 400 at a meet.'

Francis's belief is that the benefits are mental as well as physical, building 'a certain commitment in my sprinters. When you have had to do that kind of work you become more committed because of the suffering that you've had to go through.' It is almost as though the 100 and 200 metres races that make up a sprinter's diet in the summer are a reward for the gruelling winter.

Mills places more of an emphasis on shorter intervals: honing his sprinters' speed, worrying less about endurance. His philosophy seems similar to that of the late Charlie Francis, Ben Johnson's coach. Charlie Francis's name may have been forever sullied by Johnson's positive test, and his subsequent admissions about his doping regime, but he was a visionary, whose book, *Speed Trap*, is still acknowledged as a bible of coaching and training.

Charlie Francis dismissed the accepted wisdom, which he said was prevalent in the US, that sprinters had to build an endurance base before working on their speed. He equated it to a pyramid, but added that 'If these people had designed the Great Pyramid, it would have covered 700 acres and topped off at 30 feet.'

For sprinters, reckoned Francis, it was the sharp point – representing pure speed – that mattered, not the endurance base. If the goal is to go as fast as possible in less than ten seconds, then why train over thirty, or forty? Why train to go longer, slower?

Stephen Francis understands this thinking, but says that it isn't an either/or question. 'We have a number of different things going on at any given time.' Mills would doubtless say the same. One of his athletes, the promising teenager Zharnel Hughes, told me of a typical session. 'I'm working right now on speed endurance,' he said – it was December. 'Like today, we had something called the diagonal. We run sixty metres across the field, walk forty-five metres, ten times. Tomorrow we do ten [intervals of] 300 metres at 44 seconds pace, with five minutes recovery. That's very rough. But Coach says this is the easy part: "Wait until the season starts!" We train six days, with Sunday off.'

As I watched MVP train at UTech in early December, Shelly-Ann Fraser-Pryce, Nesta Carter and the other sprinters were doing explosive thirty-metre intervals, with harnesses around their waists, dragging weights (each pulls about 20 per cent of their bodyweight, Francis told me). 'I don't think our methods hamper the results we get,' Francis explained. 'It means our athletes have to work a little bit harder, but as I said, until there is some research which tells me that [running longer intervals] is definitely hampering the athletes then I think it works well for us – it may not for somebody else.

'We pretty much believe that sprinters are athletes who need to get fit, to suffer a bit, rather than just go out there and run thirty metres day in, day out.'

At the Berlin world championships, as Bolt raced to his outrageous world record, Powell provided more evidence that Francis's methods were effective. He was third behind Bolt and Gay – his first individual medal in a major championship. Perhaps the shadow boxing with Bolt did help after all.

But most were preoccupied with Bolt and his 9.58 seconds. And the question: how did it compare to his run in Beijing? The following wind was worth a tenth of a second, it was estimated, so on a still night in Berlin he might have run 9.68 (while with a just-legal 2.0m/s tailwind he would have done 9.46). By this reckoning, there was only a hundredth of a second between Beijing and Berlin. Yet in Beijing he coasted the final ten metres. Had he not done so, claimed some, he would have stopped the clock at 9.64. So was Beijing a superior Bolt performance? Jimson Lee thinks not. When I ask him which was the better run, he doesn't hesitate: 'Berlin.'

Four nights later, in the 200 metres, Bolt's reaction time is even quicker than in the 100: 0.133 seconds. That makes the outcome inevitable. Emerging from the bend, the other Jamaican in the final, the US-based Steve Mullings, is second, while Bolt, running into a 0.3m/s headwind, pushes all the way to the line. He has the kind of lead – at least ten metres – he had in 2002 at the junior world championships, but here he isn't just racing for the win. His eyes are locked ahead – no looking right and left for opponents – until he crosses the line and glances to the left, to the clock. It reads 19.20 – before being adjusted to 19.19 – and Bolt's grimace cracks into a smile. Another world record, one that is, if anything, even more remarkable than his 100 metres mark.

Anything Bolt could do, Shelly-Ann Fraser could almost match. She won the 100 metres ahead of her MVP clubmate Kerron Stewart in a world championship record 10.73 seconds. She didn't emulate Bolt by going faster than any of her predecessors – that might be impossible. With a tailwind of just 0.1 m/s, Fraser's time in Berlin was over two-tenths slower than a twenty-one-year-old world record that is so out of reach it might as well be on the moon.

'Well now, I've heard things about that record,' says Shelly-Ann in her hair salon in Kingston. The record is infamous for more than one reason. It is held by the late Florence Griffith-Joyner, set at the 1988 US Olympic trials in Minneapolis. The wind blew hard that weekend, assisting Carl Lewis as he ran to a world-best 9.78 seconds in the men's 100 metres; but at 5.2 metres per second it was well over the legal limit so didn't count. Yet as Joyner lined up for the women's 100 metres, and the flags blew, the wind gauge read 0.0. Over by the long jump pit, meanwhile, another gauge read 4.3. Joyner blasted to the win in

10.49 seconds, quarter of a second faster than Evelyn Ashford's world record.

Most of the questions about Joyner – who went on to win the 100 metres at the Seoul Olympics – concerned how she had been transformed, at the relatively advanced age of twenty-eight, from decent 200 metres runner to fastest woman in history. The British athletics writer Pat Butcher wrote at the time about this transformation, which encompassed more than just her speed on the track. When Butcher first encountered her, in 1985, Flo-Jo was 'one of the most beautiful women I had ever seen, petite, oval-faced with unblemished skin. It would be three years before I would get as close to her again, in Seoul 1988, by which time she had metamorphosed. Apart from the overall muscular definition and diminution of breasts, her jaw had elongated, a condition called acromegaly, known to be an effect of human growth hormone. She wore thick pan-stick make-up, to cover the widespread acne, a side-effect of male hormones, and her voice had deepened substantially.'

Butcher also recalled a press conference in Tokyo, following the Seoul Olympics, when Flo-Jo's predecessor as Olympic champion, Evelyn Ashford, turned on the journalists, asking: 'Why don't you guys write the real story?'

Even more questions followed Flo-Jo's abrupt retirement after Seoul. Ten years later, she suffered an epileptic seizure in her sleep and died. She was thirty-eight.

Stephen Francis shakes his head at the legacy Flo-Jo left female sprinters. 'Shelly's unlucky,' he says. 'If circumstances had not allowed a wind-assisted record to be world record . . . She's also unlucky because almost all her 10.7 races have been in headwinds. You keep telling her, "Don't worry about it, you'll get the conditions." '

The lack of a world record is one reason why Fraser-Pryce doesn't have anything like the profile of Bolt. Does she resent the fact that while Bolt is one of the world's most famous athletes, she struggles for recognition outside Jamaica? Not to mention missing out on the multimillion-dollar deals, the American talk show appearances, the celebrity lifestyle. 'Well now, I'm a very down-to-earth person,' she insists. 'I'm OK with it. I'm fine.'

13

THE BEAST

We are humans, we are bound to make mistakes.
Yohan Blake

I have arranged to meet the man who calls himself 'the Beast' in Hope Gardens in Kingston, where – just as in Shelly-Ann Fraser-Pryce's hair salon – another side of the city is very much in evidence.

The botanical gardens are spread over 200 acres, with palm avenues, manicured lawns, a bandstand, lush green hills rising up in the distance, a zoo next door. It is a place that reeks of affluence, the tranquillity pierced only by the cries and screams of young children – a primary school sports day. Yohan Blake's agent, Timothy Spencer, whose son attends the school, tells me not to worry that his client is late: he is on his way. 'This is really unlike Yohan. He's not usually late.' Turns out Blake had taken the wrong road and got lost in the neighbouring zoo.

While we wait, I chat to Spencer, who, in his shades, designer jeans and white shirt, top two buttons undone, looks like he might have stepped out of a wine bar in Chelsea. He's chatty, friendly, and wonderfully indiscreet. When he hears that I write about cycling, he is particularly interested in talking about Lance Armstrong's doping, mouth opening and head shaking slowly as he hears about the extent and sophistication of Armstrong's cheating. Spencer is a member of the Jamaican middle class: a successful businessman in Kingston, who seems to help Blake as a favour. He tells me that he's more involved in running Blake's foundation than in acting as his agent on a day-to-day basis (Blake has a US-based agent, Cubie Seegobin). Spencer seems more like a big brother, an impression confirmed when, on a later visit to Jamaica, I met him in a hotel bar. On that occasion, Blake phoned him in a state of panic: he'd heard a noise outside his house and wanted Spencer to call the Ministry of National Security. Spencer shook his head, laughed, and told Blake not to worry.

This didn't seem very Beast-like. The nickname dated back to the autumn of 2008, when Blake began training with Glen Mills and Bolt said he was struck by the eighteen-year-old's work ethic: 'Watch out for Yohan Blake. He works like a beast. He's there with me step for step in training.' 'You know why Usain calls me the Beast?' Blake said. 'Because when you're sleeping, I'm working, I'm toiling through the night. It's what great men do.'

Finally Blake appears, ambling self-consciously towards the grass where the kids are holding their races. The MC excitedly introduces him: 'It's our Olympian – El Centro's favourite! Uncle Yohan "the Beast" Blake!' Children swarm around him, and Blake signs autographs and poses for some pictures with their mothers, all the time looking distinctly uncomfortable.

He is no more relaxed when he breaks off and saunters over towards Spencer and me. He wears baggy jeans and trainers, an oversized baseball cap covering his cornrow hair. He keeps a Bluetooth device in his ear, like a cab driver. As we sit on a bench, I tell him that I was in his home town, Montego Bay, a couple of days earlier. 'Montego Bay is where it all started for me,' Blake says intently. 'The wanting to get to the top, this drive for what your parents is going through, the suffering, and you want to take your parents out of that. I said I wanted to do something and God answered my prayer.'

Blake's shyness is apparent as his eyes flicker and then focus straight in front of him; he avoids eye contact. He seems more cat than beast; graceful and feline, with small, gentle features and dark, sparkling eyes.

Blake's parents, Veda and Shirley, are still together, though there have apparently been some rocky moments (and children with other people). 'My dad was a drinks mixer,' Blake says, 'my mum was a domestic worker: that was the jobs available at the time and that's what they did.'

It was cricket Blake loved when he was growing up – he still does. In fact, he gives the impression that he would rather be a cricketer than an athlete. When he was twelve, the family moved to Clarendon, on the same side of the island as Kingston, though his parents are back in Montego Bay now. 'In a nice home that I bought for them,' Blake says. 'That was the plan, you know? But they don't like the whole glamorous thing; they stay humble, quiet.'

They must be proud of him. 'Every day,' he says softly.

In Clarendon, Blake went to Green Park all-age school. 'I wasn't an athlete then, I was a cricketer. That was my focus. I didn't know anything about track and field. Then I was running up to bowl really fast, and my teacher said, "You know, man, this boy can really sprint."'

The principal told him he should go to one of Jamaica's top athletics schools – Calabar, Kingston College or St Jago. He recommended St Jago on the basis of the coach there, Danny Hawthorne. 'Mr Hawthorne is a very good coach,' Blake says. 'He took me under his wing and made me run a Champs record and a national junior record.'

Blake missed cricket, but seemed, at a very young age, to take a pragmatic view, seeing athletics as a means to an end. 'Track and field was what was presented to me at the time, and I was getting what I wanted really fast. I was running really fast, so I used that as a drive to help my family. They needed help and they needed it fast.'

So the motivation was to earn money to help them? 'Yeah, that was it. That was the drive: to get my mum out of poverty, to get myself out of poverty, to help poor people.' And running fast, even training hard, beats collecting empty beer bottles to sell, which is how he raised money as a kid. How big is his family? 'In all there's eleven of us kids,' he says, and giggles. 'Back in the day there was nothing to do but have fun.' Naturally, he is one of the youngest – with lots of older brothers. 'I'm seventh – somewhere in the middle.' Three are half-siblings. Shirley Blake is father to eleven children, Veda is mother to eight.

It was Asafa Powell who inspired Blake. The schoolboy was fifteen when Powell, still living and training in Jamaica, broke the world record. Around the same time, Blake ran 10.65 seconds in the final of the world youth championships in Marrakech as he trailed in seventh, three tenths behind the winner, Harry Aikines-Aryeetey of Great Britain. The next year saw a big improvement: Blake ran 10.33 to win the Central American and Caribbean junior championship, then he took a bronze medal in the world junior race in Beijing. But 2007 was the breakthrough, when he claimed Raymond Stewart's twenty-eight-year-old national junior 100 metres record by a hundredth of a second with 10.18 in the first heat at the Carifta Games. In the final he lowered it further, to 10.11. He was still only seventeen. 'My first time at the world juniors, when I came third, I thought: There's a future for me. You see Asafa Powell and all them running and I think, You know what, I can do something in track and field.' But the following year he returned to the world juniors and slipped down a place, finishing fourth. There was a silver lining to that disappointment, says Blake. 'It teach me how to lose.'

The programme and workload at school was intense and punishing for a seventeen-year-old. 'I was running the 4x100, the 200, the 100 and 4x400. That was a lot for my body to take.' In 2007, when he set a new record at 100 metres (10.21) and won the 200, Blake also helped St Jago to a record in the 4x100 – their time of 39.80 beat the Glen Mills-coached Camperdown, and was the first time any Jamaican school had gone below 40 seconds – and then he anchored the triumphant, record-breaking 4x400 squad. With his hair shorn, it was a youthful-looking Blake in the yellow vest and green shorts of St Jago, far less muscular than the powerful-looking senior athlete of a few years later.

In his final year at school, Blake was approached by Jamaica's national coach, Glen Mills. 'Coach Mills said to me, "There's a future for you but you need to know what you're going to do." He didn't say, "Come train with me." But I made a choice from there.' The choice was to join Mills's club, Racers. 'And up to today I don't regret it,' says Blake, 'because I'm the second-fastest man not only in the world but in the universe.'

Blake joined Mills in the summer of 2008 – just as Bolt was rewriting the record books in Beijing – but in doing so he walked out on Hawthorne, quite literally. He had been living with his high school coach for three years, and Hawthorne was planning a future for the pair of them: he wanted to look after his star sprinter as he entered the professional ranks – he was convinced Blake was going to be bigger than Powell, bigger than Bolt. But 2008 had not gone as well as 2007: Blake was beaten in the 200 metres at Champs by another St Jago sprinter, Nickel Ashmeade. This, perhaps, was why Mills was concerned, and also why Blake was receptive to his approach.

Hawthorne, still head coach at St Jago today, was devastated when Blake left him. 'I don't know anything,' he told the local press on being informed that Blake had teamed up with Mills. 'Nobody has said anything to me.' Hawthorne was called later by Blake's parents explaining their son's decision.

When Mills first cast his eye over Blake, he was not impressed. 'The first thing when we got him, he had a back and a hamstring problem that we had to attend to,' Mills said. Perhaps all the training and racing at St Jago was catching up with him. Then, in his first outing as a Racers Track Club athlete, Blake seemed to suffer stage fright. As Mills put it: 'When he started in his first meet, he froze. The gun fired and he didn't run. So we had to be patient with him and work on him both mentally and physically. We corrected his back, strengthened his hamstrings and then once that was in place, we started to work on him bio-mechanically.'

The effects were almost immediate. 'What I achieve in one year with Coach Mills,' Blake shakes his head, unable to find the words to describe his transformation. 'I was nineteen when I ran my first 9.94' – in May 2009 in Paris – 'the youngest man to go under 10 seconds. That proved the decision I made was right.'

What is Mills's secret? 'His secret is the love for the athletes,' Blake says. 'The time he puts in and the technical stuff he do. Every day he say: "Yohan, you need to eat this, you need to do that, you need to keep ahead of that." He draw a diagram of all you need to do; little things. It's twenty-four hours. He drives to every athlete's home and talks to them. That's the kind of person he is.'

Mills also suggested some changes to his technique. 'Yeah, because in high school I ran with my arms at my chest. I didn't move them. Technically now I'm getting really good.'

I spoke to Zharnel Hughes, the eighteen-year-old who is also coached by Mills and who broke Blake's 100 metres record at 2014 Champs. Hughes said that he can be training and unaware that his coach is watching him when, as if from nowhere, he will hear a voice:

Mills's. Blake smiles at that. 'Coach Mills is like a ghost. He appears when you don't expect him, or you hear him when you don't even know he's there. "Lift your knees!" That's all you hear, and you don't even see him.'

Blake says he enjoys training. 'I love it. If you don't love it, you won't do it. I try to enjoy it even when the programme is hard. We're human and I would tell a lie if I said I don't get moments of not wanting to do it. But every time I get that moment I have to remind myself why I do it.'

A month after his sub-10-second 100 metres in Paris, the Beast was derailed. At the national championships in June, which served as a trial for the 2009 world championships in Berlin, he tested positive for methylxanthine, a stimulant in the same family as caffeine, though also a drug that can dilate the airways to aid breathing. The substance wasn't on the banned list, but was closely related to one that was, and after some deliberation, it was considered a doping offence. Another four Jamaican athletes, including the sprinters Marvin Anderson, Allodin Fothergill and Lansford Spence, tested positive for the same substance. Fothergill and Spence were also members of Mills's Racers Track Club. They were initially cleared by Jamaica's anti-doping disciplinary panel. The Jamaica Anti-Doping Commission (JADCO, which had only come into existence on the eve of the Beijing Olympics) then appealed the decision of the disciplinary panel. In the end the athletes were suspended for three months. For Blake, it meant missing the world championships. It also left a blot against his name.

Even more worryingly, Blake was a member of Racers. He was coached by Mills. The bottom line: he trained with Bolt, the man single-handedly restoring the lustre to a sport tarnished by a succession of scandals, from Ben Johnson to Marion Jones and Justin Gatlin.

The headlines said it all: 'Usain Bolt's training partner linked to positive Jamaican drug tests' (*Guardian*), 'Bolt's friend Blake named as one of five athletes to have failed a drugs test' (*Daily Mail*). Patrick Collins in the *Mail* compared the news to a dark cloud appearing over athletics: 'And the entire sport of track and field shivered in apprehension.'

It was a red flag: others would follow.

It was September 2010. Shelly-Ann Fraser was at UTech, coming out of an advanced communication course, when her phone rang. She glanced at the screen: her coach, Stephen Francis. 'Where are you?' he asked. She told him she was at university. 'That painkiller you took in China,' said Francis. 'Did you write it down?'

'No, I didn't write it down because it was a painkiller.'

'You tested positive.'

'No, you're crazy.'

She hung up and nearly collapsed. 'I remember my legs went weak. I sat down and I called my husband: "Where are you, I need you to pick me up." I was crying, I was hysterical. No, this is impossible! At that time I questioned my faith, I questioned everything. I told myself, but I'm not cheating! It was unfair.'

What happened, she says, was that she delayed dental treatment before a Diamond League meeting in Shanghai in May. 'I had braces at that time and needed root canal [work]. But because I was flying to China the next week my dentist told me she couldn't do full root canal. I had semi root canal so I could travel.'

On the plane to China she began to suffer from severe toothache. She had some Aleve with her, but it did nothing. When she arrived at her hotel she turned the lights off, put a hot towel on her face, then went to see the doctor. By now her face was swollen. The doctor gave her antibiotics and painkillers. These didn't work either.

'I went to Coach,' she recalls, 'and said, "I'm in such pain."' Francis gave her a painkiller he was taking for kidney stones. That did alleviate the pain, though she ran poorly, finishing second to Carmelita Jeter in 11.29. But the painkiller contained oxycodone: a powerful opioid-based narcotic, sometimes used as an alternative to morphine, that isn't considered to be performance-enhancing but is on the banned list. When she was drug-tested after the race she was given a form on which to list any medications she was taking. She neglected to write the painkiller Francis had given her.

When the Jamaican athletics federation notified her that she had tested positive, they asked if she wanted her B-sample tested. She said no. 'There was no point; it wasn't a mistake, I remember vividly taking the painkiller. I just didn't think to write it down.'

The worst part of it, she says, was the coverage of her case. She published a statement, but few seemed prepared to believe the one about the athlete who took her coach's painkiller. 'I went on every media, I read every newspaper article, and I saw "Jamaican sprinter tests positive for doping". I was like, "doping"? That sounds like I test positive for steroids or something. No, they can't report that. My coach sat me down and said, "Shelly-Ann, you can't stop persons from saying what they want to say. Even before this painkiller thing came about, the fact you won the Olympics in 10.7, the fact you ran 10.8 and persons didn't know who you were . . . they were saying you were on drugs."

'But I was so hurt. This is not supposed to happen to me. I worried what persons would say about me, what my sponsors would think. I sat there in front of the federation and told them what happened. I didn't want them to feel sorry for me. I was young and I think I was very naive. I said to myself, There's no need to hide because I'm telling the truth. But it was hard.'

She was given a six-month suspension. She recognised she had made a mistake and knew that another one would cost her her career. 'For me, I tell you, when that thing happened, I didn't want anything to come near my mouth, I swear. If something happen to me, God forbid, that's it for me.'

As with Blake, a second doping offence would see her banned for life. 'So I can't be careless. The only thing that passes my mouth are vitamins and that's normal vitamins because I'm so scared about what's out there. You never know.' She says she doesn't take any supplements.

Her case was one of six in Jamaica in the space of a year. And since then there have been others, many of them, according to the athletes, because of 'mistakes': mainly, as in Blake's case, supplements that don't list any banned substance in their ingredients.

Some excuses seem as far-fetched as 'the dog ate my homework'. Yet the cases of Blake, Fraser and others in Jamaica have seemed less than clear-cut. The result of carelessness and cock-ups rather than part of some wider, more sinister conspiracy. Or is that too charitable? Or just plain naive? Blake explained at the time that he had taken energy-boosting tablets whose ingredients did not list methylxanthine (in any case, the stimulant was not banned – though it was later added to the WADA list).

He says that he had checked it out and believed it was a legal supplement. But he concedes it was a mistake. 'We are humans, we are bound to make mistakes. You can't kill yourself about it. But my mother say prevention is better than cure, if you know what I mean. Before you do anything, just be careful.' He says that since then he has been ultra careful about what he puts in his body.

'When you see these cases happen, it heightens your awareness,' Shelly-Ann tells me. 'You hear athletes taking supplements that are contaminated. I read a story about someone, not an athlete, taking a B12 vitamin and they got facial hair and everything; they found it was contaminated. Now, if an athlete took a contaminated B12 and that happened, would you say they were doping?'

14

THREADS

When you run a 9-second 100 metres or 19-second 200 metres
your body is gonna be ripped up.
Tyson Gay to Steve Mullings

'It's so obvious that they're up to something,' Victor Conte says of the Jamaican sprinters. But up to what? 'State-sponsored doping.'

You would assume that Conte would know what he is talking about. His name is synonymous with doping, since he was the man who ran the Balco operation: a doping ring that in the early 2000s included the world's fastest woman and man, Marion Jones and Tim Montgomery. He has been saying since 2008 that he thinks the secret behind the Jamaicans' success is doping. He gets exasperated that nobody seems to listen. I suppose this comes with the territory of being a convicted drugs cheat, though these days, in his new guise as boxing trainer, Conte insists he is committed to the cause of clean sport. He is certainly a vocal proponent of fair play, and a crusader against drugs cheats.

But state-sponsored doping? That is some claim.

According to the IAAF, drug-testing at the 2009 Berlin world championships represented a big step forward. A thousand urine and blood samples were collected. The IAAF president, Lamine Diack, said that the samples would be stored for future analysis, using new testing methods as they were developed.

According to others, the testing was – and always has been – ineffective. Around 2 per cent of tests turn out positive – year after year that figure is fairly stable – which is either a sign that not many athletes are doping, or that most cheats are not caught. It is widely understood that in-competition tests are unlikely to yield many positives. The reasons are obvious: athletes know they are likely to be tested; drugs are of most benefit in training, not in competition. Failing a test at a major event is akin to failing two tests, says Dick Pound, the former head of WADA: 'A drugs test and an IQ test.'

Pound estimates that 10 per cent of cheats are caught – which means he thinks that around one in five competitors are doping. The athletes themselves, when asked on the eve of the 2012 Olympics, said they thought it was around 10 per cent. Conte says it's more like 60 per cent.

The truth is this: nobody knows.

Into the vacuum of knowledge, speculation floods. In the absence of facts, guesswork is all we have. We grasp at anything – rumours or threads, however tenuous, connecting an athlete to a notorious coach, chemist or doctor. And of course performances. In an event with the history of the 100 metres, a great performance is enough to elicit suspicion.

There are some who contend that there is a natural threshold: that anyone running below a certain time must be doping. But this is hugely problematic. Can anybody claim to know the limits of natural human performance? Or quantify how much of a difference drugs can make – what they are worth in terms of times?

Conte believes he has a reasonable idea. When he was running the Bay Area Laboratory Co-operative (Balco) he gave his athletes 'the full enchilada' of doping products – the blood booster EPO, testosterone, human growth hormone, insulin, as well as a 'designer steroid', tetrahydrogestrinone (THG). This was his secret weapon, known as 'the Clear' because it was undetectable. And for years he got away with it.

He and his athletes, including Jones and Montgomery and Britain's Dwain Chambers, might never have been caught. They were rumbled not by conventional drug-testing, but because in June 2003 a rival coach, Trevor Graham, a US-based Jamaican, sent a syringe containing traces of THG to the US Anti-Doping Agency (USADA). With the syringe he included a note explaining that Conte's athletes were using this mystery substance. The agency sent the syringe to an anti-doping lab in Los Angeles, which analysed its contents, identified its anabolic properties and developed a test for it. Then they retested Conte's athletes, catching Chambers, among others, and setting in motion a chain of events that led eventually to the imprisonment of Conte and Jones.

Two days after Graham's package arrived at USADA, Jeff Novitsky, a federal agent who had been carrying out his own (separate) investigation into the activities of Conte and Balco, discovered a letter while going through Conte's rubbish. It was written by Conte, addressed to USADA and the IAAF, and accused Trevor Graham of systematically doping his own athletes with the help of a Mexican contact. Conte had obviously had second thoughts about sending it.

When Graham was outed as the anonymous syringe-sender – partly because he couldn't help boasting about it – he accepted the praise that followed with humility. 'I was just a coach doing the right thing,' he said. 'No regrets.'

But eventually he too was charged with doping his athletes (who included the 2004 Olympic 100 metres champion Justin Gatlin). Graham ended up with a year's house arrest and a lifetime coaching ban. Another Jamaican who became embroiled in the fallout from the Balco scandal was Raymond Stewart, the coach to another Jamaica-born athlete, Jerome Young, who ran for the US. Stewart also ended up with a lifetime coaching ban.

Of the two Jamaican-born coaches, Stewart is far better known than Graham as an athlete. He ran in four Olympic Games, making the 100 metres final a record three times in a row. In the most notorious final of all, in Seoul in 1988, he pulled up injured mid-race – something he blamed on the Jamaican team not having adequate medical or physio support (he was treated before the final by a member of Ben Johnson's entourage).

Stewart's personal best of 9.96 seconds makes him the fifth-fastest Jamaican of all time. He first emerged at Camperdown High School, which developed an enviable reputation for sprinting from the late 1970s under its coach, Glen Mills – it was the 'sprint factory' as Mills himself told me. It was Mills who coached Stewart before he left Jamaica for Texas Christian University in Fort Worth in 1985. In 1983, running for Camperdown, Stewart won the 100 and 200 metres at Champs, held at its temporary home of Sabina Park in Kingston, winning the 100 in a record-equalling 10.3 (on grass). In 1984, he repeated the sprint double at Champs and later that year helped Jamaica to one of their most significant results – a silver medal in the men's 4x100 metres at the Los Angeles Olympics.

Graham didn't have the same distinguished career (I could find no record of him even running at Champs), though he did represent Jamaica, alongside Stewart, at the Seoul Olympics. He was a member of the 4x400 relay squad that won a silver medal, though he didn't run in the final. He too left Jamaica for an American college – in Graham's case St Augustine College in North Carolina.

When the Balco case exploded, and then Graham was found to be as guilty as Conte of doping his athletes, it was a former discus thrower from Mexico (Graham's 'Mexican contact') who appeared to be the thread connecting many of the world's leading coaches and athletes. Ángel Guillermo Heredia Hernández, also known as 'Memo', the son of a chemical engineer from Mexico City, was part guru, part supplier. Although largely self-taught, what Heredia didn't know about drugs and how to pass drug tests didn't seem worth knowing.

Graham was the coach with whom he worked most closely, but Heredia's introduction to the world elite originally came through Stewart. The pair met when Heredia went to Texas A&M University-Kingsville to study kinesiology. Stewart was launching his coaching career, and Heredia told him he could help his athletes. He took Stewart to Mexico City to visit a laboratory where a member of his family worked; it was here that some of the world's top athletes would later have their blood and urine screened to ensure they would pass drug tests.

Heredia began working with other coaches, too. In 1996 he was contacted by Graham, who drove to his home in Laredo, Mexico, with two of his less well-known athletes during the Christmas holiday. They stayed, said Heredia, for four or five days.

Now Heredia had access to some of the fastest sprinters in the world, including Montgomery and Jones, who at the time were both coached by Graham (they would link up with Conte later). Later, Heredia claimed that he also worked with Graham's cousin, Winthrop Graham (another Jamaican), as well as John Smith (who coached Maurice Greene) and Dennis Mitchell. Thus did he spin a web connecting many of the world's top sprinters from the late 1990s into the early 2000s. Between them, Heredia's clients won twenty-six Olympic medals and twenty-one world championship medals. 'At one time, between Victor Conte and me, you could say we had the whole of US track and field in our pocket,' he told the journalist David Walsh in 2008.

It was inevitable, then, that Heredia's name would become familiar to the federal investigator Jeff Novitsky, a toweringly tall, bald figure. When Novitsky finally tracked him down and confronted him, he knew as much about Heredia as Heredia knew about performance-enhancing drugs. Novitsky presented him with a choice: turn informer or go to prison. Heredia took the first option, becoming the prosecution's star witness (Source A) and testifying against Raymond Stewart, Trevor Graham and the athletes he had helped to cheat. 'Even at the last moment, I felt I was betraying my oath, the underground oath among athletes,' he said later. 'What hurt me was that, deep down, I didn't want to put all this stuff on the table. I truly felt sad about it, but Trevor sent that syringe and in the end, I had no choice.'

In the end, Travis Tygart, the head of USADA, was less than impressed with Heredia. After the initial slew of information, he 'went quiet'. He disappeared back to Mexico for a while. Then he reappeared in the sport of boxing with a new name, or a variation on his actual name: he was now Ángel Hernández. The man who identified the trainer formerly known as Ángel Heredia was Victor Conte (on Twitter). When he was outed, Heredia explained that Hernández was simply easier to spell to reporters. But to Conte it looked like he was trying to hide his identity. He wanted to know why.

Since his re-emergence, Hernández/Heredia has worked with some top boxers, including his fellow Mexican Juan Manuel Marquez, insisting that his methods have changed, that he is in favour of clean sport and that his fighters are drug-free. But in a sport that has traditionally had something of a lax attitude to doping, some are reluctant to take him at his word – his old nemesis Victor Conte foremost among them.

There have also been rumours – many of them fuelled by Heredia himself, through a series of tantalising, provocative tweets – that he still works with track and field athletes. In August 2008, during the Beijing Olympics, he gave an interview to the German publication *Spiegel*. This was instantly notorious; and for athletics fans it made for grim, depressing reading. Asked if he would watch the 100 metres final in Beijing, Heredia replied: 'Of course. But the winner will not be clean. Not even any of the contestants will be clean.' There is no way to prove this, pressed the reporter. 'There is no doubt about it,' replied Heredia. 'The difference between 10.0 seconds and 9.7 seconds is the drugs.'

It was a long interview, 3,000 words, presented in its entirety as a

Q&A. In it, Heredia buried the myth that drugs can transform athletes: 'In reality you have to train inconceivably hard, be very talented and have a perfect team of trainers and support staff. And then it is the best drugs that make the difference. It is all a great composition, a symphony.'

He went on to explain why athletes take drugs: 'Athletes hear rumours and they become worried. That the competition has other tricks, that they might get caught when they travel.' He said when they take drugs: 'When the season ended in October, we waited for a couple of weeks for the body to cleanse itself. Then in November, we loaded growth hormone and EPO, and twice a week we examined the body to make sure that no lumps were forming in the blood. Then we gave testosterone shots. This first programme lasted eight to ten weeks, then we took a break.' He revealed how they circumvented the tests: 'I had to know my athletes well and have an overview of what federation tested with which methods'; he gathered information by using 'vigilance [and] informers'. And he explained what he used: 'I always combined several things. For example, I had one substance called actovison that increased blood circulation – not detectable. That was good from a health standpoint and even better from a competitive standpoint. Then we had the growth factors IGF-1 and IGF-2. And EPO. EPO increases the number of red blood cells and thus the transportation of oxygen, which is the key for every athlete: the athlete wants to recover quickly, keep the load at a constantly high level and achieve a constant performance.'

Asked why he seemed to lurk in the shadows, Heredia said: 'I rarely travelled to the big events, but that was because of jealousy: the Americans didn't want me to work with the Jamaicans and vice versa. But shadows? No. It was one big chain, from athletes to agents to sponsors, and I was part of it. But everyone knew how the game worked. Everyone wanted it to be this way, because everyone got rich off it.'

The only way drug-testers could win, he added, was if they invested all the money generated by the sport and tested every athlete twice a week – 'but only then. What's happening now is laughable. It's a token. They should save their money – or give it to me. I'll give it to the orphans of Mexico.'

He concluded: 'Peak performances are a fairytale, my friend.' Which might be the only thing on which he and Victor Conte agree.

I am speaking to Conte, or rather, Conte is speaking to me down the phone from California. You don't ask Conte many questions – you simply tee him up, and off he goes. The former rock guitarist, who looks a bit like a TV magician with his slicked-back dark hair and pencil moustache, lives up to his reputation as a larger-than-life figure. Or, as some have described him, a publicity-hungry big-mouth whose regular briefings of reporters during the Balco investigation infuriated his own lawyers and perhaps helped land him behind bars. Yet he is also engaging, curious – and deeply suspicious.

After spending four months in prison in 2007, he too re-emerged as a boxing trainer, also professing to have changed his ways – to be fair, Conte has continued to cooperate with anti-doping organisations – and as the owner of a nutrition company. Conte hates Heredia, or Memo, as he insists on calling him. The reason for his animosity, he explains, is simply that while he opted 'to accept the full consequences for my mistakes and not testify against anybody in the case, Memo chose to throw all his athletes under the bus . . . He was their leader and when caught, Memo ratted his athletes out.' (Their animosity plays out on Twitter, where Conte interrogates Heredia and Heredia goads Conte in response, sometimes, just to rub it in, adding #felon to his tweets.)

Conte claims that in 2009 he was told by a track and field insider (a former athlete turned agent) that Memo was working 'with twenty-five track athletes, most of them Jamaicans', including Usain Bolt. The allegation that Bolt was involved with Heredia was published by Deadspin, the sports website, in August 2011 ('What Do Usain Bolt

and Juan Manuel Marquez Have in Common?' read the headline. 'They Train With the Same Admitted Steroid Dealer'). This was flatly denied by Bolt's agent, Ricky Simms. 'I have no idea why Usain's name was brought up,' he said. 'Usain has no connection with any of these people. Nobody from Team Bolt has any connection or knows any of these people.'

'They would say that, wouldn't they?' says Conte. His conviction that the Jamaicans are up to no good is unwavering. He says he first became suspicious when he saw the results of the Olympic trials in 2008. 'First thing that caught my attention: the most decorated Jamaican athlete, Veronica Campbell-Brown, ran 10.88, got fourth and didn't even make the team. Then those three girls ahead of her got all three medals. I looked up Shelly-Ann Fraser. She ran 11.3 the previous year and I don't believe it's possible, based on what I know, to run five metres faster in the course of one year.'

But how can he know that? 'Look, here's the comparison I use. Kelli White [100 and 200 metres world champion in 2003] could run 11.19. With all the sophisticated drugs I was giving her, with some of the best coaching in the world – and she was a hyper responder – she went from 11.19 to 10.85 legit and 10.79 wind-aided. I mean, this is a really sophisticated doping programme with excellent coaching. Do I believe it's possible to make those types of gains in a period of one year without the use of performance-enhancing drugs? I personally don't believe that's possible.'

There is one significant difference between White and Fraser-Pryce. White was twenty-three when she ran 11.19 in 2000. She was twenty-six when she made the leap to 10.85: an unusual age at which to suddenly improve – and as we now know, it was drug-fuelled. When Fraser-Pryce made her big improvement, she was twenty-one: an age at which sudden gains are not so unusual, albeit hers was dramatic. Fraser-Pryce explains it by saying that the previous winter was the first she trained seriously, lost weight and added work at Juliet Cuthbert's gym to the technical training she was doing with Francis and MVP. (And despite Conte's example of White, it remains difficult to quantify the effect of drugs. Chambers, with 'the full enchilada', actually went slower.)[29]

Conte says that he watched events in Beijing and Berlin in a state of bewildered curiosity, partly because he didn't see the Jamaicans coming. For almost two decades he had been a fixture on the global athletics circuit: he was trackside as Ben Johnson blasted to the gold medal in Seoul in 1988, and subsequently he became a regular behind-the-scenes fixture at athletics meetings, with his little black bag full of pills and potions. He says that throughout his period at the top of athletics

---

29 In 2013, a paper by Aaron Herman and Maciej Henneberg of the University of Adelaide titled 'The Doping Myth: 100m sprint results are not improved by doping' was published in the *International Journal of Drug Policy*. After studying performances by top sprinters from 1980–2011, including known doped ones, they found that 'No significant differences ... between dopers and non-dopers were found in their average results,' and concluded that either '(1) "Doping" as used by athletes so detected does not improve results, or (2) "doping" is widespread and only sometimes detected. Since there was no improvement in overall results during the last quarter of the century, the first conclusion is more likely.' Victor Conte and others might argue nevertheless that (2) is more likely.

he was not really aware of the Jamaicans, apart from the individuals –
such as Raymond Stewart, Merlene Ottey and Bert Cameron – who
emerged from some US college or other.

He had never even heard of – far less met – the coaches behind
the Jamaican gold rush. 'My sources were telling me that what's so
strange about all this is that they were not all that high on Glen Mills
as a coach,' Conte says. 'They just don't think he's all that good as a
coach. They think Stephen Francis is a much more scientific and much
better coach.'

Conte wasn't the only sceptic. Immediately after the Berlin world
championships, Stephen Francis was also sounding a warning bell.
In a remarkable interview with a Jamaican journalist, Kayon Raynor,
Francis was spitting nails after his latest falling-out with the JAAA.

It was Beijing all over again: a dispute with the governing body
over the pre-competition training camp. Before the championships
it was reported that Francis's athletes – including Asafa Powell and
Shelly-Ann Fraser – would be sent home for missing the camp. They
eventually ran, won their medals then returned to Jamaica to the news
that they could face fines over the training camp fiasco. Francis was
livid, particularly, he told Raynor, when he believed the JAAA should
be focusing their attention on more important matters.

'The problem the JAAA have is that they are sitting on top of, in my
opinion, a serious drug problem,' he said. 'I think that is the problem
they should be addressing. They have three athletes, five athletes,
who have tested positive for a fairly serious substance which could be
covering up bigger substances.' He was talking about Yohan Blake
and the others who tested positive at the national championships.
Francis said that by selecting these athletes for Berlin, the Jamaican
federation 'made a fool of themselves', and then 'embarrassed
the country' when, on being sanctioned, the athletes were later
withdrawn.

Five years later, I am speaking to Francis after a training session at UTech. I mention this interview and ask if he still believes Jamaica is sitting on top of a big drugs problem. 'I don't think . . . I don't see the signs as much now as I saw then. I suspect that for there to be a continual drugs problem you have to have the science to keep up. Anything that you have has maybe a two-year window before they catch up with you and people move on to something else.'

He repeats a familiar refrain, one you hear all the time on the island: that serious doping is a problem in the US, not in Jamaica. Bert Cameron, the 1983 400 metres world champion who now coaches in Jamaica, told me that it has always been an American phenomenon: 'I am totally against anybody who takes an enhancing substance because of what I went through in the eighties and nineties. People who were not better than me, I see them running faster. But we couldn't say anything. If we do, we get blacklisted, and can't go to Europe. Now it's different, you can speak out now.'

Have things changed? Francis shrugs. 'I am no longer worried too much about the drugs, because guess what: most of the time someone gets a one-year boost then they have to back off because they're on the testing list.'

At MVP they are strict about drugs and supplements, insists Francis (though as we shall see, there are limits to how much they can control what athletes do of their own accord). But how, when drugs appear to be so prevalent, does Francis convince his athletes they can reach the top without doping? 'Because most of them see that the people who they train with, they see how the success comes about, right? The supplements we use here we have been using since 1999. We haven't had a change, mainly because I can't trust any other companies to not put stimulants and that kind of stuff in, to give you a buzz. So therefore we take the same thing as all the high schools are taking. So everybody here eventually sees "Oh, it has nothing really to do with what you take."'

'When Asafa was coming up he used to take nothing,' Francis continues. 'You had to fight him to take a little creatine. You had to follow him. The drug-testing form would come in and he'd have nothing on it.'

Francis admits that he does understand the temptation. 'Let's face it, if you're faced with something that you know is going to make you better, and you know the chance of being caught is very small, then you're probably going to take a chance. But we operate a closed shop. We don't let anyone in from outside. We don't go to gyms. We use our little ragged gym here to do our weight training. We are self-contained.'

Many of the more recent cases of doping seem to come about when athletes hook up with freelance 'gurus' – budget or low-rent Müller-Wohlfahrts who describe themselves as sports doctors, chiropractors or anti-ageing specialists, and who convince athletes they can help them with legal potions and treatments that often turn out not to be legal after all. Usually it is the athlete who faces the consequences alone, with the 'guru' free to carry on their business. Has Francis been approached by such outsiders with offers of help? 'Oh yeah, I mean, over the years people come to you and say, "Bwoy, I have this thing that can do this . . ." You tell them: "Send me an email." '

Are these people from Jamaica or overseas? 'Mostly overseas. You tell them, "Send me an email", and the email come in and you don't answer and it more or less stops.'

Victor Conte is convinced that one overseas 'guru' who has links to the Jamaican athletes is his old bête noire Ángel 'Memo' Heredia. He is not the only one who is suspicious. But Heredia is a perplexing, enigmatic figure. He regularly tweets that he is in, or on his way to, Jamaica. I was told that he lives these days in Florida – only a two-hour flight away. In November 2014 he tweeted: 'Thank you Jamaica!!! Nice training gear', and attached a picture of a Puma top.

Conte tweeted back: 'Interesting that Usain Bolt is a Puma athlete.'

Which is exactly the point. Why would Heredia send out tweets like this if he really was working with Bolt? 'Why tease people, you mean?' Conte replies. 'Because he really wants to be associated with the success of Usain Bolt. He wants that credit. That's the reason.'

That might be the reason – but it doesn't mean he is working with Bolt. It makes little sense. When he gave his interview to *Spiegel*, he claimed all the Olympic 100 metres finalists were on drugs. Does that suggest he was working with any of them? One theory is that he began working with Bolt between Beijing and Berlin. But why would the Olympic champion and world record holder – the fastest man in history – decide to hook up with a man intimately involved in the sport's biggest ever drugs scandal? (Moreover, a man who threw his athletes 'under the bus' when he was caught.)

I tried phoning Heredia, then emailed him, and eventually he responded: 'Congratulations on your upcoming book, can you brief me more about your project? Such as questions, topics, etc. Best regards, Heredia.' I replied to his email but didn't hear back. I tried calling again – he appeared to be in Puerto Rico.

Conte is desperate to expose Heredia, partly because they are rivals once more, in boxing now, partly because he thinks he's up to no good – mostly, I suspect, because he despises him. Interestingly, they have never met. 'People wonder why I'm out there doing this,' he says of his public feud with Heredia. 'It's because I'm trying to put a spotlight on the cockroaches so they gotta go back into hiding.'

Conte has little faith in the anti-doping agencies, including WADA, though he does concede that the game has changed. He echoes what Francis says, that testing has improved. It has become more difficult to dope; it requires more sophistication (which doesn't mean doping has been eliminated; it hasn't). He doesn't think there are new, undetectable steroids, like 'the Clear'. 'No,' he says. 'I'm convinced there isn't. Lemme tell you the reason why. All anabolic molecules, steroids and other molecules, have a very similar, what they call mass spectrogram fragmentation pattern. These sit on a graph like mountain tops going up, so they know where these peaks are in the graph.

'Therefore – and I'll explain exactly why I say this – if you have these peaks that are in a certain range as testosterone – and every single anabolic steroid is similar in structure to testosterone – well, it triggers an alert to go back and look closer at this sample.'

Under anti-doping rules introduced post-Balco, the labs no longer have to know what a substance is – all they have to show is that it is similar to testosterone, i.e. that it is an anabolic steroid. 'That sucked out the designers; it shut it down,' says Conte.

But there are still major loopholes, he says, such as the rule that says an athlete's ratio of testosterone to epitestosterone (its 'mirror') must be no higher than 4:1. 'A piece of cake to beat,' Conte claims. 'You get these fast-acting gels and creams and if you take this stuff after the tester has come, in a matter of hours you're back down below the 4:1 ratio.' Under the 'whereabouts' programme, whereby athletes nominate a one-hour daily window to be tested, they can be confident they will not be tested for another twenty-four hours, at least. 'So these guys can use testosterone on a daily basis and beat the test,' says Conte.

But not necessarily. Not with a more advanced (and costly) method – the carbon isotope ratio (CIR) test. 'We know, for example, that Lance Armstrong was using testosterone during the Tour de France,' Conte says. 'They'd have busted his ass if they'd used the carbon isotope test. But in all his career they never tested his urine using the CIR method. Why?'

Conte wants the samples collected in Beijing and Berlin tested using this method. The samples can be kept for up to ten years, then tested using the latest technology – so the IAAF and IOC have until 2018 and 2019. There seems to be no will to test before then, though Conte has tried. 'I gave Dick Pound lots of information about who I thought was using performance-enhancing drugs and who their coaches were. He presented this to WADA and specifically asked them to test the samples from the Olympic Games in 2008 and the world championships in 2009 and they absolutely refused to use carbon isotope ratio testing for synthetic testosterone on those samples. They didn't want anything to do with that.'

I checked this with Pound, the former WADA president, and he clarified and corrected Conte's claim in an email: 'The samples at the Olympic Games are "owned" by the IOC and the IAAF and they are the only organisations that can retest. WADA has no rights to retest such samples. I have no specific recollection of speaking to [WADA director] David Howman on that matter, but I expect that if I had, that is what he would have reminded me.'

Pound did add, though, that, 'WADA had tried to get more testing done on the samples from Athens, but the IOC refused to do so.'

Conte doesn't believe the samples will ever be tested. 'Because if they go back and do the tests, what does this do to the credibility of the Olympic Games? It would make everybody question everything. It would be bad for business.' But there is conflicting evidence for this. Appearing to support Conte's argument, a WADA-commissioned survey of athletes at the 2011 world championships claimed, staggeringly, that 29 per cent admitted doping in the past year. The findings were never published but were leaked in 2013 to the *New York Times* by three of the researchers, who said that when they presented their results to WADA, they were told that the IAAF would need to review the final draft. Nick Davies, the IAAF spokesman, told the paper that the study 'was not complete for publication' and was 'based only on a social science protocol, a kind of vox pop of athletes' opinions'. However, he 'indicated blood tests from the world championship [in August 2013] in Moscow would be combined with the previous research to produce what the IAAF believed would be a more comprehensive study'.[30]

But Conte's claim that the authorities will never do retrospective testing is not quite accurate: in 2013, the IAAF announced that after

---

30 When I asked the IAAF about this, I was told: 'The IAAF is working on another prevalence study based on the analytical data collected at the IAAF World Champs in Daegu 2011 and in Moscow 2013. The IAAF is the only sports federation to have conducted such a prevalence study.'

testing 100 samples from the Paris world championships in 2003, five medallists had been caught. 'We have an eight-year statute of limitations on anti-doping, so seven years past the event is really when you want to test, using the most up-to-date equipment,' Davies told the BBC. 'The message we're trying to give out is: "Don't even think about it, because even six or seven years down the road, something you think you got away with you won't." ' In the new WADA code, introduced in 2015, the statute of limitations has been increased to ten years.

The anti-doping fight has been stepped up considerably since Conte was up to his tricks with Jones, Montgomery and the rest. Back then it was easy to beat the system, mainly because there wasn't really à system. WADA was only established in 1999, and it was a couple more years before it became operational; the national agencies followed.

Now, for the top athletes at least, there is the 'whereabouts' programme of out-of-competition testing – if not by the athlete's own national anti-doping agency then by the international governing body. 'Well, even that's possible to circumvent,' Conte says. 'Here's the big loophole. You're allowed two missed tests in any eighteen-month period, right?' Three missed tests constitutes an anti-doping offence. 'So, for whereabouts, you say you'll be at training centre X, then go instead to training centre Y. They miss you: strike one.'

True, though the testers could return the next day, and the day after that, and if they miss you each time, that's three strikes, which means a doping offence. Conte counters that the athlete could have used the fast-acting, quick-clearing testosterone cream on day one, and have no concerns.

State-sponsored doping? Conte's allegation is extraordinary, but the fact of what he alleges is not, of course, unprecedented. The programmes in East Germany and the Soviet Union in the 1970s and '80s are well known, but there must be other countries in which sporting authorities covered up positives, or turned a blind eye, or actively helped their athletes to pass tests. The USA stand accused of doing exactly that before the 1984 Olympic Games.

What does 'sponsored' mean, exactly? I am not too sure. It's not quite state-organised, or state-sanctioned. But it suggests something more than turning a blind eye.

In Jamaica, the national anti-doping agency, JADCO, did find positive tests almost from the moment they came into being in 2008. There was a steady stream, in fact, mainly for relatively minor offences, including Yohan Blake and the others in 2009. Then, at the 2011 national championships, they caught Steve Mullings for a second time, which meant a life ban.

Mullings had been a Champs star – a contemporary of Asafa Powell but considerably better as a teenager – who lived and trained in the US with Tyson Gay and his coach, Lance Brauman. He was a member of the Jamaican team at the world championships in Berlin, part of the quartet that, with Bolt, Powell and Michael Frater, won gold in the 4x100 metres relay. He then struggled with injuries but in 2011 made a dramatic improvement, running 9.80 seconds in Eugene, Oregon, in early June. Previously his best was 10.03, but in 2011 he beat 10 seconds on no fewer than seven occasions. He was twenty-eight.

At the Jamaican national championships a few weeks after his 9.80-run in Eugene, he tested positive for furosemide, a diuretic suspected of being used as a masking agent. It was his second positive, after failing a test for testosterone in 2004 – also at the Jamaican national championships. News of his latest positive broke just days before the 2011 world championships in Daegu.

I spoke to Mullings thinking that, with nothing to lose, he would offer some insight into the world of athletics and doping. But he is more interested in clearing his name and remains furious with JADCO, who, he says, made a number of mistakes in his case, and showed a reluctance – suspicious, he claims – to allow him to submit to a DNA test. Despite all the apparent evidence against him, and the suspicion generated by his sudden improvement in 2011, Mullings could actually have a point, certainly in the case of his first positive test in 2004. On that occasion, he was tested twice, after the 100 and the 200 metres: only the 100 metres sample came back positive.

Another of Mullings's gripes is his claim that by 2011, a new orthodoxy existed in Jamaica. He says that US-based athletes, once the golden boys and girls, were now discriminated against. 'It's now not Jamaica versus the world; it's Jamaican athletes who train in Jamaica against those who train in the US,' he tells me. 'It wasn't a surprise to me when I tested positive. I had a feeling they were going to get me; I told Nickel Ashmeade [his Jamaican training partner] that.' He adds that there was resentment when he took a Jamaican-based athlete's place in the national team for major championships. 'The 200 metres was OK, but in 2011, when I got one of the spots in the 100 metres, they didn't want me taking that.'

When he was positive a second time, he says he had been tested in the US numerous times, including after his 9.80 run in Eugene. 'Why would I wait till I go to Jamaica to take some drug-blocker? You telling me the US [drug-testing] system isn't good, but the Jamaican system is the best?'

Mullings maintains he was clean and that he avoided drugs. 'I wanted to go to the Trevor Graham group and people said, "Man, they all take drugs over there." You go to the Brauman group and the only thing Coach Brauman recommends is coaching, protein and amino acids. That's it. I never had drugs around me, never, ever.' He says he was careful with supplements, sticking to 'vitamins'. 'The IAAF makes it clear you're responsible for what's in your body, so you have to have supplements tested.'

Besides, he says, drugs don't make you faster; it's all about recovery. 'Some athletes recover like they're superhuman. Everyone wants to recover; they want to have doctors who know what they're doing, who give you legal stuff to help you recover.'

His training partner and friend Tyson Gay told him: 'When you run a 9-second 100 metres or 19-second 200 metres your body is gonna be ripped up. I don't know how these people recover.'

'It's true,' Mullings continues. 'When I ran 9.80, my body was ripped up. I remember when Tyson ran 19.5, we were in New York, and he fell off the chair. In 2009, in a restaurant, he falls off the chair because he was so ripped up. But I've seen people run these times and walk away like nothing happened.'

When he tested positive a second time, Mullings says he was offered a deal by the Jamaica Athletic Administrative Association. 'They had a doctor contact me wanting me to confess. They said they could give me six months if I confessed. But how could I confess to something I didn't do?'

Instead, having taken a lie detector test (which he passed) and requested a DNA test, he appealed to the Court of Arbitration for Sport in Lausanne. 'No guilty man asks for a DNA test,' he says. 'Jamaica took six weeks to give them the paperwork, then wrote them a letter saying I shouldn't get a DNA test because no one else has had one, and if everyone asks for one, we can't afford it.'

Mullings is convinced dark forces were out to get him, 'to get me off the team' for Daegu so that his place could be filled by a Jamaica-based athlete instead. Ultimately, he says, 'I wasn't big enough. If you don't have money, you don't get no justice.'

So if he was set up, by whom? 'I don't really want to call anyone's name out,' he says. 'They know themselves. For my hearing, they said, "You have to come to Jamaica." I know Jamaica; people will tell you about Jamaica. If people want to get rid of you fast they give you a ticket to Jamaica. I feared for my life, but I went there. Then it took them ten minutes to give me a lifetime ban.'

I also wanted to speak to Raymond Stewart. His lifetime ban was based on Heredia's testimony, and money transfers that Heredia said were for steroids and EPO.

In the USADA arbitration hearing against Stewart, it was claimed that he acquired drugs for his wife, Beverly McDonald – a fellow Jamaican, also an athlete – and that he sent her to be blood-tested by Heredia in Mexico prior to the 2004 Olympic trials. McDonald was a member of the Jamaican 4x100 metres relay teams that won silver in Sydney in 2000 and a memorable gold in Athens in 2004; she was also a bronze medallist in the individual 200 metres in Sydney.

Stewart lives in Texas and works for a life assurance company. He doesn't return to Jamaica often. 'When I go I might go to the north coast [the opposite side to Kingston], in and out. My mum is still there, my dad passed away a while back, and I have one brother still there.'

But more than his doping ban, I wanted to speak to Stewart about the young coach who recruited him in the 1970s: Glen Mills. Stewart recalls interest from other schools – Jamaica College, Calabar. 'But I wasn't into all-boys stuff.' He also wanted a couple of friends to go with him, and Mills was willing to accommodate them.

Stewart says that Mills was 'more like a mentor, a dad'. He would only have been in his mid-thirties at the time, but as Stewart says, father figures were in short supply. 'You notice in Jamaica there are not too many kids around with a dad that can guide them on the right track. I have to admit I learned a lot from Mills discipline-wise. It helped when I left Camperdown and moved over to the States here. He was good at teaching me not to get too distracted; to take advantage of my scholarship and not waste it.'

Mills was not, says Stewart, a great technician – at least not when he worked with him. Before he went to Camperdown, Stewart worked with another coach who 'had me doing high knees, high knees, high knees, every day. I said, "Hey, man, when am I going to actually run?" It was all technique. That played a big role in how I ended up as a sprinter.' At Camperdown, 'Mills polished what I already had.'

Perhaps Mills also learned from Stewart, who was clearly a phenomenal talent. After Stewart left school and went to college in the US, their paths kept crossing when Stewart was selected for the national team. 'Mills was always travelling with the national team – he was one of the coaches on every national team I was on.' Stewart bursts out laughing. 'In Jamaica, nothing changes; every championship they think those are the only guys who can get the job done.'

You get the impression, talking to Stewart, that his respect for Mills is limited. When I ask him if he is surprised at what his old coach has achieved, that seems to be an overstatement. 'His success comes through not just Bolt, right,' Stewart says. 'If I hadn't come through track and field back then, there wouldn't be no Glen Mills.

'One of the reasons for him to be where he's at right now, it's my name that kept him floating. He will not admit that to a lot of people.' Not that Stewart bears a grudge. He says he and Mills are no longer in contact, but if he spoke to him now he'd say: 'Hey, great job, big respect to you and all that stuff.'

Stewart continues: 'He's at the point right now where he's got the fastest man in the world and he's producing a few behind him as well, so he's learned the game. He can actually keep continuing to repeat.' Like a production line at a factory? 'Right. That's what they used to call Camperdown: the sprint factory.'

On the case against him, Stewart can talk and talk. He feels he was stitched up by the US authorities, that it was political, anti-Jamaican ('They tend to go after foreigners; their own people got a slap on the wrist') and that in any case, the charges against him were false. 'I don't care about track and field any more. It has nothing to offer me, not a damn thing. Those guys can kiss my ass. I'm outta here.' Even if the accusations were true, Stewart says he was harshly treated. 'They paint you as if you blew up the Twin Towers!'

Then there's Heredia, his former friend. 'Man, that kid . . . that guy lies so much people just don't understand.' He can't believe that it was Heredia's testimony that led to his punishment. 'They take the guy who is a drug dealer, make him make phone calls, set people up on the phone.' Stewart claims – improbably, I feel – that when he was recorded asking Heredia questions about drugs, he was simply curious.

'If a guy is picking your brains, asking you questions, is there a crime to that? Does it mean I'm going to do what you tell me to do?'

Stewart is far from stupid ('Some people want to achieve something in life, and others think they want it' is one of several profound observations), and his perspective on the current state of Jamaican athletics is fascinating. He has watched from afar as they have risen to the top by staying at home – something that was never an option for him, because he wanted to gain an education, to earn money and have 'a better life'.

'We were drinking water out of a little pond,' he says. 'Now they have companies going in there – companies are going down, sponsoring athletes. Nutrition companies. These guys have nutrition – we didn't even know where the next meal was coming from.'

There are clearly advantages to the new orthodoxy. It has worked spectacularly for Bolt, Fraser-Pryce, Blake, Powell and others. But it isn't all milk and honey. Stewart thinks there are dangers in the new system, where every kid thinks they can be Bolt or Blake when, clearly, they can't. 'A lot of kids who are there can come here [to the US] and further their education and still perform on the track, but the coaches in Jamaica are telling them, "Don't go, stay home." But if they don't do anything within another two, three years their career goes sour; they go to the countryside where no one talks about them, you know what I mean?'

The coaches are to blame, he says. Not Mills and Stephen Francis, but those who aspire to be Mills or Francis. 'They figure, "OK, I've got a superstar, I can become the next Glen Mills coaching this guy." The kid is brainwashed and the coach doesn't think about what's best for the kid.

'They don't let him go and do something for himself, you know what I mean? That's the problem plaguing Jamaica now.'

15

THE TESTER

Everybody's against drugs, in every country, until one
of their heroes tests positive.
Paul Wright

'I put it this way,' Paul Wright tells me. 'In the medical profession you
have doctors who sign sick leave for people who are not sick. You have
bad doctors. And lawyers. And journalists! You have people who take
money from housing sales and don't turn it over. You have people who
murder children. You have people who behead women.

'But in athletics,' he adds, 'no bad people in athletics. Everybody in
athletics is related to Pope Francis!'

Just as people asked questions about the Jamaican athletes in Beijing
and Berlin, so questions were asked about the competence of the
Jamaican sports authorities, the athletics federation and, in particular,
the national anti-doping agency.

The Jamaican anti-doping agency? It conjured up images
of a hut on a beach with the testers lying in hammocks smoking
ganja, saying, 'Yeah, man.' A patronising stereotype? Of course. But
it was reinforced by Victor Conte, who told me of one story that
reached him. 'I heard that Herb Elliott, the guy in charge of Jamaican

anti-doping, was in Beijing chest-bumping the Jamaican athletes in the mixed zone!' So not just too laid-back, as the stereotype has it, but too close, too chummy, to the athletes, and in a country that is no stranger to corruption. It didn't exactly inspire confidence.

In fact, when the Jamaica Anti-Doping Commission (JADCO) was set up in 2008, the island did have one person who had been at the vanguard of drug-testing in sport.

Dr Paul Wright's interest in the subject went all the way back to the 1970s. But the sport was different then, and so were the drugs. As a student at the University of the West Indies in Kingston, Wright was a footballer, a goalkeeper. He finished his medical studies at the Royal Free Hospital in London, and on returning to Jamaica in 1976 was asked by his old coach to go with the national youth team to a tournament in Puerto Rico. They needed a doctor, so off went Wright, fresh out of medical school and not even fully qualified yet, as the official team physician.

These days Wright is a large, white-bearded, avuncular fellow who, in his cluttered office at the Nuttall Hospital in central Kingston, keeps half an eye on the small TV sitting on top of a filing cabinet, showing a football match involving Chelsea. His desk is covered in papers and other surfaces with trophies – he owns two racehorses. The phone rings incessantly – each time it's the media seeking comment on the cases involving Asafa Powell, Sherone Simpson and Veronica Campbell-Brown. Wright refuses each request. Yet he seems happy to sit chatting to me about the same subject.

'Where were we?' he says, returning his phone to the desk after the latest call. The late 1970s, I say – Puerto Rico. 'Yes! So I went as team physician – and realised that I knew absolutely nothing about sports medicine.'

It was a subject that interested him, so he did some research, discovering 'a thing called the American Academy of Orthopaedic Surgeons in Sports Medicine. And that's what I always wanted to do – orthopaedics.' He got in touch with this organisation and was invited to Virginia to a conference, where he learned that there was also an American College of Sports Medicine. 'So I promptly joined. They had courses, team physician courses, the works. So I did those things. As I did more and more, I realised, um, there's drugs here.'

With his growing experience – including a two-month stint studying sports medicine at Leipzig University in East Germany – Wright became the doctor to the Jamaican national football team. The Confederation of North, Central American and Caribbean Association Football (CONCACAF) then made him vice president of their medical committee. He also chaired the medical committee of the Caribbean Football Union. 'And there was no drug testing going on,' he says.

He felt that a few of the players were using drugs. Not performance-enhancing ones, but the drug that is as common as coffee in Jamaica: marijuana, or ganja. In other words, it wasn't performance-enhancing drugs that concerned Wright, but performance-inhibiting ones.

He contacted a company in the States that manufactured a kit that screened for three substances: amphetamines, cocaine and marijuana. 'Just a drop of urine would tell you if they were positive,' Wright says. 'I bought a set of kits with my own money and told them I was going to start this programme of drug-testing.' There was only one laboratory in Kingston equipped to test the urine: the police forensic lab. 'I told them I had absolutely no money. They said they couldn't do it for free, would I get sponsorship?'

Wright approached Carreras, the cigarette company who backed Dennis Johnson's athletics roadshow, and they said yes. Now Wright was up and running: a one-man WADA. It was the early 1980s, when the concept of drugs in sport was a vague, barely acknowledged scourge. Next, the Caribbean Football Union asked him to test all the islands' teams.

But as Wright says, his concern wasn't cheating. He was more worried about the 'corner culture' that existed in Jamaica. He explains: 'In a community, the group would gather under a streetlight. And the

kingpins were people that sell drugs, the murderers, the hit men and so on. And the kids would be drawn to these things, because these are really big guys. In those days the club football was communities versus communities. I believed that if I could get the community to have an interest in the young men who play for the team, not to use cocaine and marijuana, I would be winning a . . . a bigger picture: keeping the drugs out of the hands of the vulnerable kids, the marginalised kids in the community.'

One Sunday morning, Wright 'packed my little case and drove to Alligator Pond, out in Manchester' – a fishing village on the south-western coast of the island, where the Jamaican football team were training. He told the manager he was there to drug-test the whole team. The manager was 'uncomfortable' with this, 'but I stood my ground', says Wright, 'because I was in charge of the medical committee. So I tested the whole team and six people failed the test.' There wasn't a punishment, as such. For a first offence the player had to register in an anti-drug programme. A second offence meant they had to actually join the programme. 'But the third time,' says Wright, 'you were gone.'

This was the agreed protocol. But there was a problem: a severe backlog at the forensic lab in Kingston. It meant a six-month delay in confirming those six positives, by which time the football team was at a training camp in Brazil. This is where it got complicated, because the powers-that-be, a sponsor in particular, didn't want six of the players pulling out of the camp to check into drug rehab. Again Wright tried to stand his ground, but this time he met his match. 'I was fired publicly on television,' he says. The tests were ridiculed. 'They said, "These people have never used drugs in their life!"' Excuses included that 'One of them had drunk ganja tea which his grandmother gave him because he had fever.' Following Wright's dismissal, it was announced that a new drug-testing programme would start in two weeks. 'It never restarted and they had no intention of doing that,' he says.

He turned his attention to racehorses. Or rather the jockeys. Again he was looking for the holy herb, marijuana. 'I selected them randomly. Same rules: fail one test, you register; fail two, you join the programme; fail three times, you're out.

'The number one and number two jockeys tested positive.' Wright rolls his eyes. It was déjà vu. 'Big uproar! They have never used drugs in their life; I am the wickedest person that has ever lived; I must have done something to the urine; they don't know what I did to the urine when they leave it with me . . . and I was fired, boom!'

That wasn't the end of Wright's interest or involvement in sport. He is a Wolmer's old boy (like Stephen Francis) and has always helped out with the school's sports teams, including the athletics team. Unusually for a drug-tester, his is a prominent voice in Jamaican sport: he writes a regular column for *Sport Globe*, a weekly paper. It was here, after Champs, that he criticised Calabar for allowing Javon Francis to run the 200 metres a couple of hours after his record-breaking 400 metres. His verdict? 'Child abuse!'

Wright has also worked at the highest level, acting as doctor to Jamaican athletics teams in international competition. In 1998 he was doctor to the Americas team at the IAAF World Cup – an intercontinental championships now known as the IAAF Continental

Cup – in Johannesburg, South Africa. The experience gave him a revealing insight into the mindset of the elite athlete – or at least some of them.

Looking after the Americas team was a big responsibility, though it did not include the USA, who had their own team. 'I said I would be doctor on one condition – that the team has to go to similar elevation for three weeks before the games,' Wright says. Johannesburg is at 5,700-feet altitude. 'They never heard of this, but they agreed. So we went.' They stayed in a 'kind of safari place' for three weeks, during which time one of the Canadian athletes strained his hamstring. A replacement was called up: Obadele Thompson, the 100 and 200 metres specialist from Barbados. But when Thompson got there, he was exhausted. He had travelled to South Africa straight from Moscow, where he finished second in the IAAF Grand Prix final in 10.11 seconds. Wright met him at the airport on the Wednesday evening and could see how tired he was, which was a problem. His race was just forty-eight hours later. 'He was dead,' says Wright, 'so at dinner, everyone's there, and I say, "When you go upstairs, take this, right?" and I gave him a blue tablet.

'Next morning he comes down the stairs, I'm at the back of the line for breakfast. He says, "Dr Wright!" and jumps on my back. "What is wrong with you?" I say.

' "What did you do?" he says. "I have never felt this good in my life! Doc, I cannot wait to race!" '

When it came to the 100 metres, Thompson ran 9.87 seconds, a personal best, to win. Wright was in his hotel room that night. There was a knock at the door and he opened it to another athlete. 'Doctor, could I have a blue pill, please?' That was only the start. 'Everybody's coming for a blue pill!' Wright says. 'These people believed I drugged the guy – they thought I was doping him!'

What was the pill, then? 'Halcion,' says Wright. 'He needed to sleep. That is all this guy needed. I gave him two five-milligram halcion pills. He slept the whole night and he was a new man.' Halcion contains benzodiazepines, also found in valium. It's a relaxant and sedative with no performance-enhancing effects (if anything, the opposite).

'I tell people the best aphrodisiac in life is sleep, you know?' says Wright. Some remained convinced, however, that he had doped Thompson. Particularly, Wright adds, because 'Obadele never ran that fast again.'[31]

A year later, the Jamaican team was rocked on the eve of the world athletics championships in Seville when Merlene Ottey, thirty-nine years old but hoping to compete in her sixth Olympic Games in Sydney, tested positive for nandrolone after a meeting in Lucerne. Ottey was one of a spate of positives for this steroid at the time, along with fellow sprinters Linford Christie, Dennis Mitchell, Javier Sotomayor of Cuba and European 200 metres champion Dougie Walker, as well as dozens of footballers and tennis players. Ottey was outraged. 'I have lived my personal and athletic life with the utmost honesty and integrity,' she said. She denied ever using a banned substance.

Jamaica leapt to her defence. Herb Elliott, the chest-bumping doctor in Beijing who would later be at the helm of JADCO, described it as 'a travesty of justice'. Elliott's main gripe was that Ottey's name had been made public before her B sample had been tested. But he seemed in no doubt as to her innocence. 'This is a shock for all of us,' he said. 'I have known her since she was seven. I have never known her to be on any substance.'

Reading press reports from this time, it seemed that there was only one prominent Jamaican who was prepared to believe the worst. 'We've always held Merlene as an icon, a drug-free track queen,' said Dr Paul Wright. 'Now that's all crumbled to dust.'[32]

*

---

31 Obadele Thompson later married Marion Jones.

32 Ottey was initially cleared of a doping offence by the JAAA, though the IAAF appealed that decision. Eventually she was exonerated. The Court of Arbitration for Sport ruled that the retesting of her sample was not completed in time.

Before the 2008 Olympic Games, there was an ultimatum from the World Anti-Doping Agency. Jamaica was a signatory to the WADA code, introduced in 2004, but had done little to implement it. 'WADA told them, "If you don't implement the thing, nobody is going to the Olympics",' Wright recalls. 'So within two weeks the law was drafted and pushed through parliament. One parliamentarian, Ronald Thwaites, got up and said, "How am I asked today to write something into law that I haven't read? This is crazy!" The prime minister gets up and says, "We know what's good for you – sign it, because we're going to the Olympics."'

JADCO came into existence later that year.[33] They needed people with experience in drug-testing, and there was one obvious candidate: Dr Paul Wright. Despite having been fired twice from previous drug-testing roles, he was, like the 'eight or nine' other testers, employed on a freelance basis, paid a modest day rate (around £55, he says) to conduct tests on behalf of JADCO.

Among the new organisation's responsibilities was to run a 'whereabouts' programme. This meant that athletes had to nominate a daily one-hour window when they would be available for testing. They had to submit this information three months in advance, though changes were allowed if the athlete informed the agency. A lot of athletes nominate their home as the place and early in the morning as the time. Wright says that he tended to turn up early. 'If the athlete said 7–8 a.m. and I turned up at 5.30, it created panic. I thought, This is very suspicious. They would refuse to pass urine until seven o'clock.'

I am not sure that it is necessarily suspicious to react with alarm if somebody appears at your home at 5.30 a.m. But Wright says it would

---

33 Not only did Jamaica not have its own agency, it had also opted out of the WADA-approved Caribbean Regional Anti-Doping Organisation (RADO). RADO's head, Dr Adrian Lorde of Barbados, when asked if testing was sufficient in Jamaica, said: 'I don't get that impression. I would like to think they do that testing there but I really don't know . . . We really don't know what is going on in Jamaica.'

be the same in the evening: he thought one or two athletes' panic was
due to the fact that he appeared at all. 'Sometimes they would switch to
nine o'clock at night and I would turn up. One athlete couldn't believe
that I would really come at nine o'clock at night. I said, "But you put
nine on the programme." "Yes, but I never knew you would really
come!"' Wright shakes his head. 'They would be extremely angry if I
came, even though I would point out to them that "You said that this
is the time I could come."

'So I was an outcast, really. They just didn't like me.'

Wright says he tried hard in his testing role with JADCO, at least
initially, not to create an 'us and them' mentality. He didn't want to be
seen by the athletes as the enemy – and besides, why on earth would he
be? Surely a clean athlete would regard him as a friend. In a spirit of
solidarity, he tried to help with advice. When he turned up to test some
of the MVP athletes, he noticed that during training, their drinking
bottles, each with the athlete's name on it, would be left on a shelf out
of sight of the athletes and coaches. 'You can't leave these unattended,'
he told the club, 'because these are the biggest sprinters in the world,
and there are people can watch them train. What if it suits somebody
to come and put something in the bottle?'

Wright was enterprising and came up with a novel solution for
testing for EPO. To do that, he had to send the urine overseas, to a lab
with testing equipment for the blood-boosting drug, but the problem
came with storing the urine at a cold enough temperature. 'I would
take the urine to the local ice cream factory, pack it in dry ice and ship
it to the lab,' he says. 'I found ways to do these things.'

Another hurdle he had to overcome was an unexpected one – at
least to me. One of WADA's rules is that the tester must observe the
athlete giving the sample: in other words, watch him pee (for obvious
reasons, female testers collect samples from female athletes). This is
to prevent any sabotage or swapping of samples – it is not unknown
for athletes to have bulbs or condoms of 'clean' urine hidden on (or
even in) their person. (An apocryphal tale has a Belgian cyclist being

informed that he hadn't tested positive but that his sample indicated he was pregnant. He had used his wife's urine.)

'Some people thought I was helping but the athletes got the impression that, number one, I was a pervert,' says Wright. 'That I just wanted to look at men's penises, that was my biggest aim in life, I got a sexual kick out of that.'

Really? 'Yeah! I was a batty man, I was a pervert. They would say all these things but it don't bother me.'

Homophobia in Jamaica seems deeply ingrained, though I was told that virulent anti-gay attitudes are a fairly recent phenomenon. Dancehall music, which exploded in the early 1990s, has contributed to it. 'It's like boom bye bye/Inna batty boy head,' sang Buju Banton, urging that gay men be shot in the head. Casual homophobia can be found in mainstream media too. In a 2006 *Jamaica Observer* article about a male prostitute, the (female) reporter asserted: 'We are led to believe that people are born with gay tendencies . . . the subject will continue to aggravate many heterosexuals who think that it is downright nasty. And to be labelled as a "b . . . [batty] man" while in the wrong crowd may almost certainly lead to death.'

There are various theories about the roots of such attitudes, from the hold of religion to perceptions of masculinity. But any attempts to deconstruct homophobia would not have got Dr Wright very far with athletes reluctant to pee in front of him. 'They say that when they're tested abroad they turn their back and the guy doesn't stay and watch them pee,' Wright says. 'I say, "No, no, no, no. I have to see where that urine comes from."

'And they say, "Boss, you must be a pervert. All those children that you say are yours, they really yours?"'

How does he respond to that? 'I laugh. I laugh, because in Jamaica if you get upset it's because it's true.'

Although he encountered some obstacles, Wright does not subscribe to the view that the only explanation can be that Jamaica's athletes are all

part of a sophisticated, systematic doping programme. He is neither a
cynic nor a conspiracy theorist. But that doesn't mean he assumes they
are all clean. That would be foolish, he says, as he reels off his list of
doctors, lawyers and, yes, journalists, who give their colleagues a bad
name. Whereas 'everyone in athletics is related to Pope Francis!' 'You
got to be kidding me,' he adds.

Wright recognises the responsibility of Jamaicans themselves to
have an anti-doping programme that the rest of the world believes
in and trusts. 'Dick Pound [the former WADA president] has said,
publicly, that we make sure that when our athletes leave Jamaica they
are drug-free.' In other words, Pound has alleged that the athletes are
screened before they leave the island, to ensure they pass drugs tests
when they compete abroad. 'He has said it,' Wright continues. 'And
the chairman of JADCO, Herb Elliott, called him a racist. And I wrote
to him, I said, "You can't call the man a racist, because we're not doing
the job, Herb." If we don't do the job, these people are going to say
these things. All we have to do is do the job. Do the job. We have to
have people who understand drug testing and who cannot be bought
and don't worry about doing this for Jamaica – you're not doing it for
Jamaica, you're doing it for track and field.'

A claim that has often been made is that if a big-name athlete
tested positive in Jamaica, they would be ostracised, banished from the
island. Glen Mills said as much in 2008. He stated that Jamaicans were
proud of their clean record: 'It is something that we guard dearly, and
it is something that [if an athlete tested positive] the country would
turn on you. They would turn on you so strong. It's something they
would never forgive. And athletes are aware of that and try to walk
the tightrope.'

Does this claim stand up to scrutiny? I am not sure. When Yohan
Blake and the other four athletes tested positive at the national
championships, the athletes were not ostracised.

Wright dismisses the idea that Jamaica would turn on a drugs cheat
with a wave of his hand. He knows that in the event of a positive test,

the anger is often directed not at the athlete, but at the testers. There can be a sinister dimension to this, he claims. 'People test positive, right? Big people test positive. The phone rings. "I am such and such" – a big person – "how can we help?"'

Wright's response: 'We? We?! You're on your own, boss.'

He continues: 'I knew that the moment a prominent athlete tests positive – they coming for me. They're not coming for the athlete.'

He has first-hand experience of this? 'Yeah, twice.' The parallels with his experiences with football and horse racing are uncanny. Wearily he trots out the old lines: 'I was the one who put something in the urine; I was the one who did all these things; I was the one who gave them the drugs.'

In his years as a drug-tester Wright says he has received threatening phone calls, and worse. On one occasion he returned home, entered the living room, turned on the light switch – and nothing happened. 'They broke into my house and stole one light bulb. One light bulb.' It's a popular tactic of intimidation, he says. 'I got the message. I got the message.'

It isn't that people are against drug-testing, he adds. On the contrary: everybody with a stake in sport – fans, media, politicians, athletes, coaches – is anti-drugs and firmly in favour of robust testing. It isn't testing that people object to. It's positive tests. This is not unique to Jamaica.

As Wright puts it, 'Everybody's against drugs, in every country, until one of their heroes tests positive.'

16

GENES AND YAMS

Slavery runs through Jamaican life today like the black line in a lobster.
Ian Thomson, *The Dead Yard*

If the doubting world had questions about the Jamaicans' sprinting domination, the answers, believed Professor Errol Morrison, could be found in Jamaica: in the place, the people, and what was on their dinner plates.

Morrison is an eminent scientist, a former president of UTech and an expert on diabetes, which is a major health problem in Jamaica.[34] His sunny disposition belies his work in this field. I meet him at his clinic in the Diabetes Centre just off Old Hope Road in New Kingston; he smiles as I enter and doesn't stop smiling the whole time I am there. If his enthusiasm could be bottled and sold, it would be potent stuff.

Perhaps that is because what we are talking about is, for Morrison, an interesting sideline rather than the life-or-death stuff of his daily

---

34 Especially, it seems, among former athletes; of the island's retired Olympians, it has been estimated that around 30 per cent have type 2 diabetes. A high proportion of fast-twitch glycolytic fibres and a decreased number of slow-twitch oxidative fibres are associated with type 2 diabetes.

work. Nevertheless, the subject – why does Jamaica produce so many good sprinters – has appealed to his curiosity since a journalist, Patrick Cooper, approached him in the early 2000s with his theory about why people of West African descent seemed to be faster than non-West Africans. Cooper's research, over many years, had led him to the conclusion that the sickle cell trait – common in those of West African origin, where it offers protection against malaria – produced 'physiological adjustments' and 'compensatory mechanisms', including a higher proportion of fast-twitch muscle fibres.

Cooper turned his thesis into a book, *Black Superman*, published in 2003. Together, he and Morrison then contributed a paper expanding on some of these ideas for the *West Indian Medical Journal* in 2006. Cooper was battling cancer at the time: he died in 2009.

If it is the case that those with the sickle cell trait do have a higher proportion of fast-twitch muscles (and lower haemoglobin, making them less well suited to endurance events), the reasons why have proved elusive. But Morrison became more interested in the subject, especially when another eminent scientist, Professor Yannis Pitsiladis, began visiting Jamaica.

Pitsiladis first came around the same time as Morrison and Cooper's paper was published. Morrison was not the only one who welcomed him. Vilma Charlton, the Olympic sprinter turned academic, had wondered about the existence of a 'sprint gene'. She felt that Pitsiladis, of the biomedical and life sciences faculty at the University of Glasgow, could be just the man to identify it. 'We got so excited,' she says. 'We thought, Now we can find the answer!'

Dennis Johnson also welcomed Pitsiladis; they got on like a house on fire, and in 2011, Pitsiladis, Johnson and another Jamaican sprinter-turned-academic, Anthony Davis, published a paper together, 'The Science of Speed: Determinants of Performance in the 100m Sprint'. This appeared in the *International Journal of Sports Science & Coaching*.

I first met Pitsiladis when he was about to embark on his Jamaican odyssey. He had spent years studying the world's best endurance runners in Ethiopia and Kenya from his office in the West End of Glasgow, where he ran the International Centre for East African Running Science (ICEARS). It was March 2007, and Pitsiladis told me that he was preparing to expand his research, turning his attention to sprinters. Even then, a year before Beijing, Jamaica was the obvious place to go.

Pitsiladis, like Morrison, was a bundle of energy: fast-talking, fidgety and restless. Of Greek origin but with a gentle South African accent, he quickly – like Dennis Johnson – turned the tables, firing questions at me. 'Every sprinter who has run 100 metres in under 10 seconds is black,' he said. (Since then, one white man, Christophe Lemaitre, has accomplished this feat.) 'Why do you think that is?'

This was a difficult question to answer. The problem is that most answers run the risk of sounding, well, racist. Which was a problem acknowledged by Cooper, who wrote in *Black Superman* that the debate (or non-debate) around the subject was 'shaped by two powerful and related fears: those of racial biology and "the dark history of eugenics" '. David Epstein, in his book *The Sports Gene*, spoke to scientists who said they had researched the subject, and thought they could make a contribution to the (non-)debate, but chose not to. Their reticence, thought Epstein, stemmed from an essentially irrational idea: that 'any suggestion of a physical advantage among a group of people could be equated to a corresponding lack of intellect'. It was, he said, 'as if athleticism and intelligence were on some kind of biological teeter-totter'.

Which is balderdash. In fact, it is an idea that developed in the US only as black athletes began to excel at sport. 'The idea that athleticism was suddenly inversely proportional to intellect was never a cause of bigotry,' said Epstein, 'but rather a result of it.'

Yet the idea that black people are athletically superior has taken a firm hold, to the point where now there is an assumption that a white man cannot win the Olympic 100 metres. The last one was Allan Wells in 1980: he was also the last white man to make the final.

On one of his visits to Jamaica, Pitsiladis gave a lecture entitled 'White Men Can't Run' (subtitle: 'Where's the Scientific Evidence?'). In this, and in his paper with Johnson and Davis, he identified a problem that follows from the idea that black athletes have a genetic advantage. The stereotype might lead to a self-fulfilling prophecy. Black athletes believe they can win, white athletes believe they cannot and therefore exclude themselves, thereby reinforcing the stereotype 'to the extent that the unsubstantiated idea of the biological superiority of the African or "black" athlete in these athletic events becomes dogma'.

Unsubstantiated it may be, but the perceived superiority of black athletes in sprint (and endurance) running events remains, as Epstein's reluctant scientists seemed to confirm, a sensitive issue. And one that I, being quizzed by Pitsiladis in his office in Glasgow, felt ill-equipped to answer. He eventually broke the silence: 'You are thinking,' he said, 'that the black person has some kind of advantage over the white person?'

I nodded. 'Hmmm,' he said. 'I may disagree. I would say that you should speak to a sociologist. I could say that it has nothing to do with biology.'

Almost eight years after meeting Pitsiladis in Glasgow, I visit him in Eastbourne: in 2014, he became Professor of Sport and Exercise Science at the University of Brighton, taking with him the world's largest DNA 'biobank' from world-class athletes (containing genetic material from over 1,000 individuals).

He is more interested in Jamaican sprinting and East African endurance running than ever. When we meet, he has just launched a project to break two hours for the marathon (the world record is 2.02.57). Once he has overseen that, with an as-yet-unidentified (clean) athlete supported by experts in every imaginable field, he wants to set a similarly ambitious target for the 100 metres – but more on that later.

Pitsiladis had many years' experience of research in Africa before he travelled to the Caribbean, but he found Jamaica a far more challenging place to work. 'Ten times more difficult,' he tells me. There was, a huge amount of resistance and suspicion, and not just in the groups of athletes but among the wider population too. He was keen to collect genetic material from the Maroons – the descendants of escaped slaves renowned for their resilience and toughness, who still live in isolated hilltop villages in Trelawny – and other communities. But there was, from some, fierce opposition, hostility and myriad rumours about his real purpose. A story spread in one community that with his swabs he was infecting people with HIV.

Then there was Stephen Francis, who 'didn't want us walking round swabbing people'. Pitsiladis understood that. 'It's a pain in the butt having anyone hanging around, and what could we give back?' But he believed he did have something he could offer Francis: sports science support. He envisaged setting up an institute of sport in Jamaica with his own lab (an idea he hasn't given up on completely, and thinks could happen once the sub-two-hour marathon project is completed).

Then Pitsiladis met Dennis Johnson. 'A fantastic guy, we got on so well,' he enthuses. 'An evidence guy, and the person who is closest to the truth of the Jamaican sprinting phenomenon.' Johnson helped prise open the door to Francis's MVP club. These days, Pitsiladis and Francis are firm friends (Pitsiladis mentions a recent visit to a Kingston nightclub in the company of Francis, who I struggle to imagine in a club).

Then, through Anthony Davis, a Jamaican who came to study under Pitsiladis in Glasgow, Pitsiladis gained an introduction to Glen Mills's Racers Track Club. For reasons of medical confidentiality, he cannot say whose DNA he has collected. If he could, it might be quicker to say which top sprinters' DNA he has *not* studied.

Pitsiladis began his project in Jamaica at just the right time, months before the Beijing gold rush. He began to make regular visits, funding his research with help from journalists eager to learn about his work, and on one occasion thanks to the owner of his local curry house, whose son wanted to accompany him and meet Usain Bolt. It has afforded him a remarkable view inside the Jamaican sprint factory.

For Pitsiladis, it was never all about genetics, or finding a particular gene. As he explains, 'Genetics is one of the tools I use, and allows me to get evidence.' With his own eyes, and through talking to Johnson, Vilma Charlton, Mills, Francis, and many others, he gathered more evidence. He was interested in identifying all the different pieces that contributed to Jamaican success. He went to Champs, obviously. He visited Maroon communities. He collected biological material. When he came to study the athletes, he was interested in – but not obsessed by – the doping question. A keen athlete himself, he watched training sessions and studied Francis and Mills, noting that they had different approaches and methods. 'And they both work,' he tells me now. 'Which tells you they're probably both wrong.'

'When I say wrong,' he clarifies, 'it's probably wrong for some of the athletes and right for some others.'

Pitsiladis still likes to turn the tables. 'Did you see sophistication in Jamaica?' he asks me. 'In terms of the training?'

I tell him that I saw sprinters pulling weights, doing technical drills, doing two-legged jumps into a sandpit. 'No sophistication!' Pitsiladis says with such excitement that he is almost shouting. 'In athletics, in a lot of sports, I see total amateurism.' Yet it seems to work – for some. Which is his point – he thinks it's quite random; that the science is lacking. 'But even if there's no science in it, no scientific basis to what they do, and you're leaning on natural instincts, you will see people getting faster.'

Just think – he doesn't say, but is clearly wondering – how much faster they could go. Yet they go fast enough to win at the very highest level, which leads many to conclude that Jamaica is at the cutting edge in terms of training, preparation and, ultimately, performance. But what if they aren't? Pitsiladis makes a point about athletics that is often overlooked. It is *the* Olympic sport; the blue riband; the one people most closely associate with the Games. And from this comes the idea that track and field, as it is known in the US and increasingly in Jamaica, is a global sport, and that it attracts the crème de la crème.

But what if it doesn't? In their paper, Pitsiladis, Johnson and Davis remark upon the 'appreciable world-wide demise of elite sprinting' over the last couple of decades. It has something to do, they suggest, with the fact that so many fast white runners may be excluding themselves (based on the stereotype mentioned earlier), but even more to do with money. Specifically, the 'defection of the most talented sprinters to more lucrative sports such as football'. They identify talented sprinters who opted instead for American football. The system is changing, too, with the number of track scholarships on offer at US colleges declining markedly in recent times: in 2011 it was one for every eight or nine in American football. 'Sprinting', they write, 'is threatening to become simply a means of training for the football season rather than a sporting choice.' Pitsiladis and others speculate that there are football players, basketball players, soccer players, who might, with proper sprint training, be faster than Tyson Gay or Justin Gatlin . . . or Usain Bolt.

All of this has only pushed Pitsiladis further towards the conclusion that the Jamaican success has little to do with genes – or rather, with a specific gene. In this sense his mind hasn't altered since we sat in his office in Glasgow in 2007. But it is surprising to hear from somebody who, while not a geneticist himself, has devoted so many years to searching for a genetic explanation.

Originally Pitsiladis began his study of elite athletes because the existing research, especially concerning genes, 'was a little woolly'. That is being generous: 'Not a single African's genetics had been looked at from the point of view of performance. No black athlete had given DNA and had their genes looked at. So all the knowledge we thought we had about genetics and performance was based on an assumption.'

The assumption being that athletic ability must be down to genes.

'Then where are they?' Pitsiladis asks. 'It wouldn't be good enough for me, as a scientist, to repeat the myth – sorry, I mean the view: it's not a myth until it's been dismissed – that black athletes are simply naturally superior. I needed evidence. And if I found the "magic gene", I would patent it.'

He started looking in Ethiopia, where initially he encountered some resistance. But before too long, both there and in Kenya, he earned the trust and enjoyed the cooperation of most athletes, who let him collect 'biological material' – all it needed was a swab of saliva. Then he 'searched and searched and searched, and I haven't found' any magic gene. His conclusion: 'There is no compelling genetic evidence that there are race-related genes to explain this phenomenon.'

Through his visits to Africa, Pitsiladis began to believe that sociological or cultural factors were more decisive. He learned that there were around 3,000 Kenyans who made a living through running. It was seen not necessarily as a lucrative career, but it was a viable one. And for kids growing up in poor communities, there were thousands of role models. On his visits, children and parents would flock around Pitsiladis, assuming he was an agent.

Such experiences encouraged him to look beyond genes. The sheer complexity of the task is another reason to look further afield. If humans have somewhere between 20,000 and 30,000 genes, he explains, 'and 95 per cent of them are the same as a chimpanzee's, and between humans there is 99.9 per cent commonality, then we can isolate those genes that we suspect might be significant but there's a lot of work to do. We can spend one year studying a single gene . . . and I'm not going to live to 30,000.'

Then there is the fact that studying a single gene in isolation can be meaningless. Epstein compares the 23,000 genes in a human body to a 23,000-page recipe book, which in theory 'provides directions for the creation of the body . . . but if one page is moved, altered, or torn out, then some of the other 22,999 pages may suddenly contain new instructions'.

It seems that searching for a 'speed gene' isn't like looking for a needle in a haystack. It's like looking for a particular piece of hay in a haystack.

The antithesis of Cooper and Morrison's argument – that there are genetic characteristics unique to people of West African origin – is the 10,000-hour rule, made popular by Malcolm Gladwell. In his 2008 book *Outliers*, Gladwell argues that what separates Usain Bolt from his peers, or Tiger Woods or Bill Gates from theirs, is a combination of environment, opportunity and, crucially, lots and lots of practice: 10,000 hours, to be precise.

Pitsiladis has been coming to a not-dissimilar conclusion, but with a major caveat. Ten thousand hours' practice might be necessary (in fact, Pitsiladis thinks that a world-class athlete needs 'massively more than that'), but it is not sufficient. That is to say, not everybody can achieve greatness simply by doing a lot of training. First and foremost you need, as Pitsiladis says, the 'right parents'. Which, he concedes, means the 'right' genes.

For sprinters, there is a gene that does seem to be essential: a variant of the ACTN3 gene, which produces a protein, a-actinin-3, in the fast-twitch muscle fibres. In Jamaica, around 70 per cent of the population have this gene variant; in the US, the figure is 60 per cent. The only conclusion, however, is that without it you will probably not reach an Olympic 100-metre final. Even with it, there is no guarantee that you will. Billions have it. Most cannot run 100 metres in 9.9 seconds.

Errol Morrison clings on to the idea that one of the main explanations for the Jamaicans' success is genetic. Back in his office in Old Hope Road, he tells me, 'The specific genetic manifestation is still eluding us.' But he doesn't doubt that it is there.

In fact, he and Pitsiladis are not that far apart in some crucial respects (and they have considerable mutual admiration). Morrison insists that one manifestation of the genetic influence is staring them in the face: the runners' bodies. The narrow hips, long legs; even, he says, the shape of their backs. 'I've said to Yannis – but he's stubborn – I said, "Yannis, the performance is not genetically driven: the performance is facilitated by the anatomical structure."

'You look at all of our athletes, you will see them with what they call the scoliosis of the spine.' It is the condition that Bolt was diagnosed with in 2004. 'They all have that!' insists Morrison. 'Look at our Shelly-Ann: the spine has that curvature. But it helps with the knee lift.

'Then of course,' he adds, 'you have the environmental impacts: coaching, food and so on.

'Yannis would like to see something in the musculature that says, "Here is a fast runner, here is an endurance runner," and he's not picking that up. But I really don't think that is where you have to look.'

Where should you look, then? 'I don't think there's a gene for performance; genes make structure, they're proteins, but there's predisposition. And there's environment, and there's also our diet!' Morrison says.

The significance of the Jamaican diet has been frequently cited and often dismissed with a scornful laugh. Usain Bolt is a product of eating yams, you say? Why, yes, of course. Morrison urges me not to dismiss the idea completely. He says the staple diet in Jamaica – including yams, sweet potatoes, green bananas – is steroid-based. If youngsters are reared on this food, and pushed hard in training (as many are), they can develop into strong athletes. He goes into some detail about diosgenin, the steroid molecule in yams, and its anabolic (muscle-building) properties. Eating yams is not like pumping yourself full of testosterone, he makes clear – the effect is only relative to other foodstuffs. But, fascinatingly, the chemical structure of the yam is identical to human testosterone: yams were used to produce the first synthetic testosterone in the 1930s. And the yams in Trelawny, where Bolt and so many others are from, are said to have special properties. (P. J. Patterson, the former prime minister, also proposed the yams theory to me, then admitted rather sadly: 'I'm not sure Usain Bolt likes yams, though.')

I find myself agreeing with Morrison that there might be something in the diet theory: if not for performance-enhancement then simply because so much food is so particular and peculiar to Jamaica. Its distinctiveness took me by surprise: fruits I had never heard of, along with the daily staples of jerk chicken, dumplings, boiled green bananas, yams with the weight and density of cannonballs, breakfast of ackee and saltfish. There's a world of difference to the US, even though it's so close. It might be another reason why staying at home works for so many athletes.

'Slavery runs through Jamaican life today like the black line in a lobster,' wrote Ian Thomson in *The Dead Yard*. He was referring to slavery's violent legacy, but another one, according to a popular theory, gives the descendants of slaves a genetic advantage.

This was a theory explored by the US's four-time Olympic gold medallist Michael Johnson in a 2012 television programme, *Survival of the Fastest*. 'It's impossible to think that being descended from slaves hasn't left an imprint through the generations,' Johnson concluded. 'Difficult as it was to hear, slavery has benefited descendants like me – I believe there is a superior athletic gene in us.'

It is a seductive, if uncomfortable – not to mention grotesque – proposition: slavery as the ultimate Darwinian 'survival of the fittest' human experiment. So brutal was the Middle Passage from Africa to the Caribbean that all but the very strongest survived – boats were packed with more slaves than required, allowing for 'wastage' on the crossing; dead bodies were thrown into the sea, but so were people who were sick. One in four people transported across the Atlantic for slavery died before reaching their destination. Countless others, if they made it to the sugar plantations in Jamaica, perished in the terrible living and working conditions. One estimate is that between 1702 and 1808, around 840,000 Africans were shipped to Jamaica and into slavery.

There is another group reckoned to be significant in the Jamaican athletics story: the ex-slaves known as the Maroons, who escaped to Cockpit Country, in the same corner of the island as Trelawny, and survived in this hostile terrain, fighting off first the Spanish, then the British. If ordinary slaves were tough, Maroons were – are – super-tough. It ties into the theory promoted by Johnson's TV show: that the only African-Jamaicans remaining when slavery was abolished were the fittest, toughest, strongest. And of course their genes, to be passed down through the generations.

Pitsiladis was supposed to be involved with the television pro-gramme, but you will not find his name in the credits. The reason is obvious. As he keeps repeating, he is interested in evidence: 'I don't care about gut feeling.' And as seductive and sensational as the slave theory is – the TV programme attracted lots of press coverage and earnest discussion – Pitsiladis is not aware of any scientific evidence to support it. On the contrary, 'If the idea is that you have survival of the fittest through the slave trade and all that, Jamaicans are going to be similar genetically – and they're not.'

Most serious scientists seem to dismiss the idea that the Jamaicans' success can be traced back to slavery. Still, Pitsiladis does wonder if Africa provides some answers. He has analysed the genes of endurance runners from Ethiopia and Kenya and sprinters from Jamaica to try and establish just how 'African' they are. Are the 'purer' Africans better athletes?

When Pitsiladis looked at Ethiopian athletes, he discovered genes more frequently found in Europe, 'So that dispelled that myth.' In Kenya he found that athletes were 'more African' than the Ethiopians, but there was no difference between the athletes and the general population. So that seemed to dispel another myth.

'But when you look at the sprinters, it becomes more interesting,' he goes on. 'We looked at the Jamaicans. We found that slightly above 99 per cent of the Jamaican athletes are African. We did the same study looking at the US sprinters, and found roughly 10 per cent were non-African.'

The good Jamaican sprinters did appear to be 'more African'. Only there is a catch. As time goes on, they are becoming less African – they are being 'diluted down'. Yet they are also running faster. And there's another problem with the theory. If the explanation lies in Africa, why is sprinting a Jamaican phenomenon? Why not a Nigerian phenomenon? 'The Nigerians are still very good,' says Pitsiladis, 'but although they are more "African" on both [mother's and father's] sides, it's the Jamaicans who have the greater success.'

I have my own theory – that it isn't a specific gene, but rather the combination of genes that might explain the Jamaicans' athletic gifts. You don't need to do genetic profiling, you only need eyes to realise that Jamaica is a diverse place, and surely a diverse gene pool is a healthy gene pool. The country's motto is apt: 'Out of many, one people.' And as P. J. Patterson told me: 'Few Jamaicans are pure anything.' On this island of fewer than three million, there are large communities of African, Spanish, British, Indian, Chinese, Syrian and Lebanese extraction, among many others.

I put my theory to Pitsiladis. 'It is a very diverse place,' he agrees.

'If you speak to some people, they will say the mixed gene pool is an advantage. But I see no evidence for that.'

Oh well.

Environment, then. Pitsiladis stresses the importance of environment, and also of socio-economic conditions. The pockets of excellence in Ethiopia, Kenya and Jamaica all have one thing in common, he says: poverty. 'When I go out to Ethiopia, Kenya, Jamaica, it's so obvious. Wherever you look there are people running, and the African way of life.

'My children live less than a mile from school – we drive them there. In Kenya, a five-year-old will run to school. When we test them, they are fitter than some of our athletes. Is that genetics?'

Another environmental factor – one that Morrison and others highlight too – is the company of other elite performers. The virtuous circle effect. 'In science, if I want to become better, I'll go and work with the better scientists,' says Pitsiladis. 'If you want to become a top athlete, go and work with the best.'

There is, he concludes, no one simple explanation. 'All of it put together explains what we see. Not drugs, not finances . . . But what I would say in addition is that what appears to produce the quality guys, assuming they have the right genes, is how hungry they are. And often that is dictated by how hard their living conditions are. Usain Bolt is incredibly gifted, sure, but he trains incredibly hard.'

Perhaps it is a selfish gene he should be looking for, because Pitsiladis says that what the very best athletes have in common 'is how selfish they are. Every hour of the day is related to how they train harder, nothing else.' It's a part of the equation that cannot be ignored: 'If they aren't training hard like that and they have the right genes, it's irrelevant, it's not going to happen.'

Another common denominator in Jamaica, Ethiopia and Kenya is the extent to which athletics is ingrained in the sporting culture, and the age at which kids start running – and running seriously. 'We believe that starting to run from a young age – especially without shoes – lets them run pretty hard throughout their careers with fewer injuries than would normally happen,' Pitsiladis says. 'You're building a strong foundation.'

The big threat to these countries' culture of high performance could be money – an abundance of it. Pitsiladis reckons that if Kenya, Ethiopia or Jamaica became wealthy overnight, the medals would dry up. 'You may find other, hungrier countries, like Eritrea or Uganda, start excelling.

'And not,' Pitsiladis adds, 'because all of a sudden they have the right genes.'

17

THE G OF THE BANG

All I could hear was something said 'Go' in my head.
Usain Bolt

Yohan Blake is famous for training hard, like a beast. But what does he do when he's not working? How does he spend his downtime?

'Catch wild coyotes,' he says.

'What?'

'That's a joke, man. I play Ludi, I play dominoes, I play cricket with my boys, you know?'

His eyes flicker; he glances towards his agent and friend, Timothy Spencer, and quietly adds: 'Sometimes I read love novels, you know?'

'Love novels?'

'You know, you have *Romeo and Juliet*, you have *The Notebook*. I'm actually reading *The Notebook* every day. You know this love story; this guy and girl were seventeen, you know. Put it in your phone, look it up. I read motivational books, too. Ben Carson.' He shrugs. 'I don't like to sit down. I like to keep active.'

I have no idea if Blake is telling the truth or winding me up. I change the subject. What's the story with his nails? He wears them long. Not just a little bit long, but a good inch: like claws. I tell him that I haven't seen nails like that on an athlete since Flo-Jo.

'Yes, like a beast.' He glances admiringly at them. 'I will cut them at different intervals.'

Spencer interrupts. 'It's a superstitious thing.'

'It isn't,' says Blake.

'It is,' says Spencer. 'He won't cut them before a race. But he cut them for Lausanne and ran 9.69, so I said, "What do you think of that, Yohan?"'

In 2011, the world's fastest two men trained together every day. Blake, still only twenty-one, had progressed rapidly the previous season, whereas Bolt had barely raced and suffered only his second defeat over 100 metres, after his 2008 loss to Asafa Powell in Stockholm. This time he was beaten by Tyson Gay, again in Stockholm. Yet as the 2011 season got under way, it was Blake who seemed to pose the real threat. Bolt must have felt it; he must have been conscious of the younger man on his shoulder, gaining speed, pushing him.

And Blake, too – he must have been measuring himself against the fastest sprinter in history on a daily basis. 'Nothing big, it was nothing big,' he says. 'I was training with Usain from 2009 when I went to the Racers. I waited and waited. Then I was in the big time.'

Even when they became rivals as well as training partners, there was no problem between them in their daily sessions, insists Blake. 'We have good chemistry. He likes to talk to me; he's not that stuck-up guy who don't talk.'

As Blake began to emerge, there were rumours that he and Bolt were training separately, that they weren't talking. The stories annoyed Glen Mills. Asked to compare his two star sprinters, he said: 'One is tall and one is short.' Reluctantly he added: 'I'm happy to speak about each but I don't do comparisons because I coach them and have to maintain balance.'

I asked Zharnel Hughes, the eighteen-year-old Anguillan who broke Blake's 100 metres record at Champs, about the atmosphere at

Racers training. Hughes was a relative newcomer; it was still a novelty to him to be training with the best in the world. 'Bolt is friendly but he doesn't talk much,' he said. 'Blake, you'll hear him talking the loudest. Sometimes when he crosses the finish line he shouts out something funny. He makes you laugh. He's like a clown. Bolt, you really won't find him saying much, but you hear him with Blake, joking, "Come on, man, finish the programme! Don't cheat the programme!"'

Blake says that in Daegu, at the 2011 world championships, when they both qualified for the 100 metres final, Bolt didn't seem any different; he was his usual self. If he was anxious about the race, or wary of the man expected to be his main rival – who also happened to be his clubmate and training partner – it didn't show. Then again, Blake knew that Bolt's schtick was to be relaxed, or to appear relaxed. And what, in the end, is the difference? 'He always creates this atmosphere of being relaxed, it is true,' Blake says. 'Then he goes out and does his tricks before the start. But in the call room he's alive, he's not too serious. When you're not too serious and you're relaxed, there is not a lot of tension in the body.' It echoes Dennis Johnson and Bud Winter and his 'relax and win' philosophy. 'That's good, you know,' Blake continues. 'Usain creates that atmosphere not only for himself but for other people.

'Some guys, you can see the tension. You can see their face tight, their body not loose. You think, All right, Yohan, you've got him covered.'

Daegu saw a decaffeinated final: no Asafa Powell, who had a groin injury, or Tyson Gay, also injured, and no Steve Mullings, the third fastest man of the year, after his second positive test.

At the start, it was business as usual. Salutes from Bolt to a large Jamaican contingent in the crowd – including his parents, sitting with Norman Peart. Bolt stretched his arms. He was in lane four, Blake in lane five; he grabbed his training partner's hand for a loose (relaxed) handshake as they passed. Nesta Carter, the third Jamaican and one of Stephen Francis's men, was in lane seven. As they lined up, Bolt pointed to his left and shook his head; pointed to his right and shook his head; pointed at himself and nodded. Then, just before he stepped towards the blocks, he let out a primal yell. The eight men settled, waiting for the gun, and the stadium fell into restless silence. One moved – Bolt. And then the gun went.

It wasn't a twitch, a reaction to a noise in the stadium or a reflex response to another athlete moving. It was one man breaking the line. It was an unequivocal false start, which meant automatic disqualification. And it was Bolt, there was no disguising that, though a couple of other finalists were sure the officials would find some way to exonerate the culprit. ('I actually thought they were going to blame it on me,' said Kim Collins. 'I really didn't think they was going to throw Usain out,' said Walter Dix, 'because, well, it was Usain.')

Bolt knew what he'd done. As he launched from the blocks, he opened his mouth in another yell, then carried on for a few strides down the straight. In one fluid movement he whipped off his vest and dumped it on the track. He slowed and turned round, walking back towards the blocks. Blake, wide-eyed, stared after him and slowly shook his head. In the stands, Jennifer Bolt's eyes were fixed on the track, her expression one of utter horror. Then she threw herself to the ground, as though trying to hide. 'He take off him clothes, he take off him clothes!' she cried when she got back up. Removing his shirt seemed to be a way for Bolt to spare himself the indignity of being disqualified – it saved the officials the bother of presenting a red card.

Topless, he marched past the blocks, shouting to himself, then slapped the wall beneath the stands and slumped to the ground, sitting there with his arms hooked around his knees, as dejected as he is usually so ebullient. The mask had slipped – here was the other Bolt: anguished and angry rather than relaxed and jovial. It betrayed what he tried to conceal: how much it meant to him.

The question was: why had he done it? To match the kind of time he ran in Berlin? Or because he feared defeat, and couldn't afford to concede even a centimetre to Blake? Bolt had qualified from his semi-

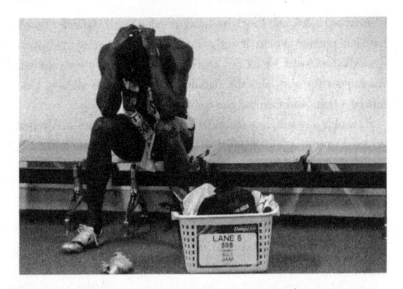

final in 10.05, Blake in 9.95. But in anticipating the gun, rather than reacting to it, Bolt broke Coach Mills's cardinal rule: 'My coach always explains that it's not about anticipation,' he said later.

The remaining finalists were called back to the start. The atmosphere in the stadium was now as deflated as a burst football. Blake settled in the blocks, the empty lane beside him as glaring as a missing front tooth. Thirty-five-year-old Collins got off to a flyer, but Blake, his head down for the first ten metres, powered smoothly along the track – gliding almost, his feet appearing to only dab the surface. He seemed to keep accelerating and crossed the line a comfortable winner, with a Bolt-esque margin over Dix of 0.16 seconds. The winning time: 9.92 seconds. Although it was into a stiff breeze, most believed Bolt would have beaten that even if he had waited for the 'G' rather than going before the 'B' of the bang (a little over two weeks later, in Brussels, he ran a season's best 9.76).

There were parallels with Shelly-Ann Fraser's win in Beijing in the mystery over the winner. Who was this guy Blake? Victor Conte was among those who wondered. 'OK, so initially you hear that Usain Bolt is a genetic freak, that he's very tall, with this stride length which means he takes fewer strides than everybody else. Then here's Yohan Blake – he's not tall!' Yet Conte could, begrudgingly, admire his run. 'Oh, Bolt and Blake are very talented, genetically gifted athletes. They have great technique. They are very well trained.'

Blake was a 'meanwhile' at the foot of news reports: 'Meanwhile, the race was won by . . .' Few were interested in him as the winner, even as the youngest ever 100 metres world champion. 'I've been working hard for this moment,' he said after a lap of honour draped in a Jamaican flag given to him by Bolt's mother. 'I've been dreaming of this moment.' It had cost him restless nights. 'I haven't been able to sleep; I've been up at night praying.'

When his training partner was disqualified, 'For a split second I was breaking down inside,' said Blake, 'but I said to myself, No, you have to get focused, you have to get the job done.' His only sadness was that he and Bolt couldn't go home with the gold and silver medals, as planned. 'The key', he added, 'is Coach Mills and God.'

Bolt, meanwhile, had bolted. He was shadowed throughout 2011 by a French film crew, and they couldn't find him. Neither could Ricky Simms, his agent, who appeared after the race looking bewildered. He gave an interview on Bolt's behalf, then admitted he hadn't spoken to him, nor had he any idea where he was.

When Bolt reappeared, reporters and TV crews stalked him as he strode across a dark car park outside the stadium. He was surly, in a foul mood. 'No comment,' he said. 'Looking for tears? Not going to happen.'

Bolt was sharing an apartment with Blake and Asafa Powell. His first post-race exchange with Blake was captured by the documentary crew. He is slumped on the sofa when Blake appears, and he adopts an announcer's voice: 'The new world champion, Yohan Blake!' Blake smiles. 'It's not a team sport, but if I didn't get it, I'm happy he did,' says Bolt. 'I've seen him train, man. I've seen the work he put in.'

At 1.50 a.m., Bolt is still slumped on the sofa, computer on his lap, phone in his hand. He seems to be the only one up – other than the light from his gadgets, the apartment is dark and quiet – and he looks in reflective mood. 'I was just pissed with myself, man. I just couldn't believe it. You see people on TV false-starting and you say, that's bad luck. Then you feel how bad it is. It's awful to false-start.

'I was in great shape, I was running fast, I was good. I was sure I was going to get the gold medal. So to know it's going to happen and then you lose. Or not even lose, you don't make it to the finishing line . . . Very hard, very hard. I was just frustrated, man.

'You can't dwell on the past, man, you learn that. I grew up in the church. You learn that God has a plan for everyone. I have one more race to go.'

You can see him trying to look forward and put the disappointment behind him. But he can't let go. 'I'm kind of pissed at myself coz I've been working hard on my start especially.' He looks up, addressing the film's director, Gaël Leiblang. 'You've been along the way, you've seen the work I've put in. You've seen what I've gone through. It finally came together at the right time, and I pretty much squandered it, I would say. I don't know what happened. Can't believe it happened; I kept saying to myself, "Why did you false-start, why did you false-start, why did you false-start?" It's never happened. Major championships: that's what I live for.

'All I could hear was something said "Go" in my head and I just went. Then . . . what the hell happened? I guess tonight I was my worst enemy.

'But you can't dwell on the past, mate,' he adds, lurching into cockney. 'Moving on.'

Six days later came the 200 metres, and as Bolt and the other finalists settled in the blocks, an anxious silence descended. There was a look of dread on the face of Jennifer Bolt. When the eight runners rose in unison after the gun, the noise in the stadium was that of relief. Bolt won easily in 19.40 seconds, three-tenths of a second ahead of Dix and Christophe Lemaitre.

'Who's the champion now, uh-uh?' he sang, performing a jig inside the stadium.

Shelly-Ann Fraser-Pryce could only manage fourth in the 100 metres, though she teamed up with Veronica Campbell, the 200 metres gold medallist, to win the 4x100 (the men also won their sprint relay, with two of Mills's athletes, Bolt and Blake, and two of Francis's, Carter and Michael Frater, in a new world record).

It was a minor setback, reckoned Fraser-Pryce. She had problems with injuries after returning from her doping ban. She had other commitments, too: she had got married, and then there were her studies and her family. She had bought her mother a house in a safer part of Kingston and tried to do the same for her grandmother. 'She didn't want to leave,' Fraser-Pryce says. 'It's hard to convince somebody who is that old to move.' Then a solution presented itself. 'My uncle died and that left a big space at the front, so I built her a house there. She's OK there: nobody's going to harm her.

'Helping my family,' she says, 'I think is the most enjoyable and sometimes the most stressful part of everything. You try to see how you can assist with everything, but there are limits.'

It was difficult to keep the same focus on training and competing. There were so many demands on her time. She set up a charity, the Pocket Rocket Foundation, paying for seven youngsters to attend school: buying uniforms, books and food. Each was, like Shelly-Ann, from the inner city. They had been chosen by her, and had targets to reach at their schools; a report was sent to the foundation every month with an update on their progress. 'This is not for publicity, for the TV,' she says. 'I am concerned with them and what they do next. Their parents are poor. If they can understand that I care, outside of the foundation . . . and if they make it, they have a chance of helping someone else. Then it becomes a cycle, it spreads.' The foundation was, she explains, 'born out of what Jeanne Coke did for me. It's about education and sport and linking them to try and

transform individuals' lives, and [have] these people transforming Jamaica.'

Asafa Powell has his foundation, Usain Bolt has his, and after his success, Yohan Blake got in on the act. His is called YBAfraid (Why Be Afraid?) and helps vulnerable young people. He supports the Mount Olivet boys' home: a centre for homeless and abused boys, which includes 'Expressions Through Creativity' workshops in art, music and drama.

Bolt's is focused on helping young people through 'education and cultural development'. I was told that Bolt also helps individuals. While visiting the University of the West Indies one day, I asked for directions from a groundsman, who insisted on jumping in the car to guide me. 'Bolt help a lot of kids,' he said. 'He pay for a lot of kids to go to school in Kingston.'

Bolt can afford it, but the others' ability to keep pumping money into their foundations is entirely dependent on their continuing success on the track. So they end up not only running for themselves and their families, but for lots of other people too: for the poor of their country; for Jamaica. It is another cycle, in addition to Fraser-

Pryce's virtuous one, that puts a lot of expectation, and pressure, on the athletes. Fraser-Pryce's setback in Daegu didn't just affect her profile as an athlete; it affected her earning power, which affected her foundation and, in turn, the seven youngsters whose education depends on it.

She also has her hair salon, of course, where we are sitting in the plush pink-and-black reception area discussing how she recovered from the disappointment of Daegu and the previous season, with her positive test. Her appetite didn't diminish, she tells me, despite the demands on her time and attention. She says that after Daegu, her motivation was even higher. She was determined to defend her Olympic title in London. It was the same as being back at school: feeling that she had been written off. 'People always thought because I was short, and I wasn't very good in high school, I couldn't make it. For them to see me perform as I do . . . when people say, "When I see you running it makes me happy because you're so short but so fast."

'I still go to training as if I've won nothing. My husband said this to me last week when we were driving. I was saying, "People don't get me, they don't get why I always train, why I'm so focused", and he says to me that I train almost as if I am hungry. He told me, "You train as if you've never won anything. You train and if you can't train you sit there and cry – but you're the Olympic champion."'

While the world's best sprinters were preparing themselves for the London Olympics, their country's anti-doping agency was floundering. In July 2012, less than a month before the Games began, JADCO appointed a new executive director.

Renée Anne Shirley had done everything: she was a financial consultant before reinventing herself as a radio and TV presenter and newspaper columnist in the late 1990s; she then became a government adviser and sat on the boards of various task forces. She was chief executive of the Jamaica Rugby Football Union. She had a BA in economics and was the first black woman to graduate with an MBA from the University of Virginia; then there was the PhD in public administration from the University of Kentucky.

It was her work as a government adviser that took Shirley into the field of anti-doping. From 2003–7 she was senior adviser to Jamaica's first female prime minister, Portia Simpson Miller, leading and coordinating the development of Jamaica's Anti-Doping in Sport Programme. She headed the Jamaican delegation at the International Convention Against Doping in Sport in Paris in 2005, attended the International Convention on Doping in Sport at the UNESCO Headquarters, also in Paris, then the World Anti-Doping Code Review in Amsterdam, in February 2007. In November of the same year she was official observer to the Third World Conference on Doping in Sport in Madrid.

She knew her stuff, then. And when she took over at JADCO, she was determined to do the right thing, not necessarily the most popular. She was well aware that the organisation had problems, not least since the order from WADA to appoint a new board. She knew she'd have to roll her sleeves up. 'I am not a believer in patting ourselves on the back and saying, "We believe our athletes are not cheating." '

When she took over at JADCO, 'There were quite a few things I had to sort out and fix up,' she tells me over lunch at Ziggy's, a cafe at Twin Gates Plaza in mid-Kingston that she says offers traditional Jamaican food. It is also a place where the other customers are not likely to be interested in what she has to say: things that have previously got her in trouble.

Shirley's few things to sort out and fix up turns out to be an unusual case of her glossing over the actuality. You don't need to spend too long in her company to appreciate that she is to straight talking what Shelly-Ann Fraser-Pryce is to running quickly. 'JADCO was badly set up,' she sighs. 'The legislation was badly written. There was a lack of staffing, but my main concern was the lack of testing.' The absence of out-of-competition testing particularly worried her. 'Once you're successful – the kind of success that Jamaica had since

Beijing – it called for us to have really strong and rigorous and robust anti-doping.'

She saw immediately that JADCO couldn't do that. There was only one full-time doping control officer, no one in charge of running the 'whereabouts' programme, and the TUE committee (which decided when athletes could legitimately use banned products by issuing a Therapeutic Use Exemption) was without a chairman and had never met. The accounting department was non-existent, and no monthly financial statements had been produced in five years; bills were outstanding.

The situation had been infuriating JADCO's most senior drug-tester, Paul Wright. Yet some of the problems stemmed, Wright told me, from the WADA intervention in late 2010. 'The entire board was dismissed, right? Then the general election came up and the country voted out that government, and a new government was in. The election was in December [2011].' In all that time, JADCO was rudderless. 'I was testing all along,' Wright says. 'Then there was nothing in January [2012]. Nothing in February. We had no board, so there's no testing!'

The statistics for the period confirm this. When it came to out-of-competition tests, in February 2012 there were twelve, in April just one – and that was it. None in March, May, June or July. The Olympic Games in London were fast approaching. 'I was making phone calls,' says Wright, 'I drive to Jamaica House' – the office of the prime minister, who also looks after the sport portfolio. 'I said, "This is Olympic year. We are the biggest sprinters in the world and we can't just stop testing the year of the Olympics. People are going to believe we're hiding something. You've got to get this board in place and restart testing."'

Wright knew the names who were being considered for the new board. He also knew that the same problem would arise – that WADA would object on the grounds that there were too many potential conflicts of interest (perhaps an inevitable problem in a country with such a small middle class: these being the people who volunteer for such positions). When the board was announced, he was dismayed to see who was on it. He called the prime minister to complain and was told: 'Dr Wright, these are our friends, they have spent their life contributing to sports, you must stop maligning people of integrity.'

Still there was no testing. It was only when Renée Anne Shirley was appointed, one month before the Games, that things started to happen. 'I joined after the national trials and started the out-of-competition testing,' she says. 'But they had not tested for six months prior to the London Games. One of the reasons was that their test kits were out-of-date.

'It was a fight from the beginning. Every excuse was that we didn't have the money. But with the money we had, we could have done more.'

Even before she started at JADCO, Shirley had the feeling that more effort could be made to look into some of the darker recesses of sport. She was aware of the threads connecting Jamaican athletes and coaches to doping scandals, and of testimony during the Balco case alleging that Raymond Stewart gave drugs to his wife, Beverly McDonald, on the eve of the Athens Olympics. 'I went to the prime minister,' says Shirley, 'and said that as a signatory to the World Anti-Doping Code, we should at least investigate it. We should call [McDonald] in. What are we going to do: wait for them to take the gold medal away from us? I said, "You should at least be seen to be doing something."

'I can tell you that I got no traction from that at all.

'But listen, my friend,' Shirley adds. 'Jamaica is not unique. Kenya is not unique, China is not unique, Great Britain is not unique. It is the same everywhere. When any country is winning gold medals, they don't want to look too closely. Every country wants to hear their anthem, to see the gold medal around their athletes' necks.'

For Olympic year, ahead of the defence of her title, Shelly-Ann Fraser-Pryce made a renewed commitment to God. Winston Jackson, senior pastor at the Penwood Church of Christ, said that she had always been a 'church girl', and that the church had helped her and her family through 'some early struggles'. Now, said Jackson of Fraser-Pryce's running ability, 'she realises it's not her, it's really God. You can see the change in her.'

She also renewed her commitment to MVP, after reports of discord and several defections over the winter. Ristananna Tracey, Kimmari Roach, Peter Matthews and Darion Bent all left for Glen Mills' Racers Track Club, and there were rumours that Fraser-Pryce might follow them. It saw a deepening of the rift between MVP and Racers, especially when Bruce James, the MVP president, claimed that 'the other club' paid their new recruits. 'Unlike another track club in Jamaica, MVP does not pay our developmental athletes cash,' said James. Former MVP athletes had informed him, he added, 'that the other club pays them cash monthly, in addition to providing them with accommodation in apartments off campus, among other enticements'.

Racers responded with a statement: 'A clear distinction must be made between athlete recruitment and athlete support. Racers Track Club maintains a restrained policy of recruitment and an active policy of support.' It continued: 'Do we seek to support our athletes financially? The answer is, unequivocally, yes. We do try to assist our athlete members to keep body and soul together in the hard times before they become celebrities and before they excite the attention of potential sponsors.'

Fraser-Pryce had a quiet start to 2012. As well as preparing for her Olympic defence, she was finishing her studies; she graduated with a BSc in child and adolescent development and says her degree was as important as her athletics – in many ways it meant more. 'For me it wasn't sport or education, it was both. Both were my way out. It's possible. I lived it. I got my degree while being a professional athlete.' It was her 'greatest accomplishment', she says. Graduation day felt like another Olympic final. 'Everyone came to my graduation, because I grew up in the inner city and some things happen that you don't expect. Young girls getting pregnant, dropping out of school, not going to school . . . that happened to a lot of my friends, too many. Not being part of that statistic feels . . .'

Good? 'Yeah,' she nods.

As the clock ticked towards London, she gained ground. At the Diamond League meeting in New York in early June, she blazed to a win in 10.92 seconds. She was on track. She underlined it two weeks later, at the Jamaican trials, flying to victory in 10.70, a personal best, 0.12 seconds in front of Veronica Campbell-Brown. No arguments over selection this time.

In London, she was bidding to become the third woman to retain the Olympic 100 metres title, after Wyomia Tyus in 1968 and Gail Devers in 1996. When Devers won her first gold medal, in 1992, the woman she narrowly beat was a Jamaican, Juliet Cuthbert. Cuthbert now owns the gym in Kingston where Fraser-Pryce regularly trains. In 1996, when Devers retained her title, it was another photo finish: this time she just got the verdict over Merlene Ottey.

With the Games in full swing, the women's 100 metres, heats and final, are on the first two days of the athletics programme. Fraser-Pryce progresses smoothly, winning her semi-final in 10.85 to make it to the final, twenty-four hours before the men's. It's the night the home crowd are calling 'Golden Saturday', as Mo Farah, Jessica Ennis and Greg Rutherford win gold medals.

Fraser-Pryce is not everybody's favourite: Carmelita Jeter deposed her as world champion in Daegu and is in sparkling form. The American is a thirty-two-year-old enigma, a woman of few words who seems reluctant to engage with the media. She made a sudden improvement relatively late in her career, going from a best of 11.48 in 2006 to 10.97 in 2008. She is coached by Maurice Greene's old coach, John Smith, and her late blooming invites suspicion. 'I'm 32 and clean,' she told *Sports Illustrated*. When people doubt her, 'I pretty much accept it. But it's hurtful, and I'd like to get credit for what I've done.'

They line up for the final and the camera pans along the line.

Muscular and powerful, Jeter looks formidable and serious, frowning and chewing her lower lip. Whereas for Bolt, when the camera reaches him the view is of his chest, when it reaches the diminutive Fraser-Pryce, the view is of fresh air. It has to dip down to find her. She seems as relaxed as Bolt – genuinely, naturally relaxed. When the camera finds her, she flashes a megawatt smile and gives a vigorous wave, but there are no tricks, no showboating. Her only gimmick is a golden ribbon in her hair. She is introduced as the defending champion, an idea that seems to amuse her; her eyes sparkle, her smile broadens and becomes a laugh.

Fraser-Pryce lingers back as they are called to the blocks. Her expression is serious now. She breathes deeply, puffing out her cheeks, narrowing her eyes; she says she has tunnel vision before a race: 'Once I get in my blocks there is nothing in my mind.' The athletes settle and are called to 'set'; she is last to rise but first out of the blocks, though only just – it isn't her best start, which annoys and worries Stephen Francis, watching as critically as ever – 'very messy' is his verdict. At fifty metres, she and Jeter emerge at the front, one lane apart and impossible to separate. Just like in Beijing, Fraser-Pryce's head is tilted back, eyes locked on the big screen: watching the race? If she is, then she is oblivious as she crosses the line. She stops, hands on hips, sucking in oxygen, and stares at the screen again, watching the replay. Her brow is creased; she looks worried.

The time, 10.75, appears first, then the finishing positions. 1. Fraser-Pryce (Jam), 2. Jeter (USA), 3. Campbell-Brown (Jam). When she realises, she throws herself to the track, shouting, 'Thank you, Jesus!'

Back home in Waterhouse, they watch Fraser-Pryce's run in the house she built for her mother. More than ten members of her family squeeze into the living room, watching a small television, cries of 'Go, Shelly!' accompanying her all the way until she dips for the line. That is followed by a brief, stunned silence, and then an eruption of screams and yells and they spill out to join the street party. There are vuvuzelas,

Jamaican flags, one youth dressed as the Grim Reaper in black suit and mask, hanging on to a car, on roller blades. There are shouts of 'That's our Shelly! That's our Shelly!' Children using the lids of pans as cymbals, crashing them against each other. 'Big up to mi sister Shelly,' says Andrew Fraser, her brother, in a red NYC baseball cap, earrings sparkling in his ears, tears welling in his eyes. 'She train hard for this, mi see now, it pay off. Mi sister right now are mi icon. Right now mi don't even know, mi just feel overwhelmed right now, yeah.'

Inevitably in her press conference, with the men's final twenty-four hours away, Fraser-Pryce is asked about Bolt. Is she fed up with being in his shadow? 'I'm not one who loves the limelight,' she says, 'but sometimes I go to the supermarket they ask me questions about Usain. They ask me, "Where's Usain? Where's Usain?" '

Wherever she goes she is asked whether she trains with Bolt. 'I don't.'

As Bolt prepared for his final, the threat, as in Daegu, seemed to be Blake. At the national championships in Kingston at the end of June, their first meeting since the world championships, he had been blown away by the Beast. It was as though the memory of Daegu, and the fear of false-starting, weighed on Bolt's mind. He got a sluggish start and was never in the race. Blake won in 9.75, a personal best and stadium record. Bolt, a desperate look on his face as he chased his clubmate's shadow, trailed in 0.11 behind for second. Powell, back after his injury, was third: the top three qualified for London.

It didn't have the prestige, but winning the Jamaican title was harder than winning the world title. Blake, who after Daegu ran the second-fastest 200 metres of all time, 19.26 seconds in Brussels, also beat Bolt in his stronger event, with Weir third. Defeat in his beloved 200 metres cut Bolt deep. 'I was very sad with my turn,' he said. 'It was awful, but I've been working more on the 100 metres. I can't blame it on that, though. I just have to get my things together and get it done.'

Glen Mills wasn't worried. 'Usain, he has the experience, the ability. He has been there already. He might be a little off at the moment but I'm sure when the time of delivery comes around, he'll be on top of his game.' There were four weeks to go until London. 'We're right where we want to be, going into London,' Mills said. 'We just want to keep them healthy. That's the key.'

It was almost as if Bolt had been playing with people, cultivating a bit of mystery and suspense with the questions over his fitness and form. Keeping everyone on their toes, including himself. Ever since Berlin, when he had a quiet season in 2010, and then the Daegu debacle in 2011, rumours and gossip about Bolt have had a tendency to swirl around Jamaica. When I was there in April 2014, the story was that he had a debilitating foot injury, and that the minor op that had been reported was actually major surgery. 'I wouldn't be surprised if we don't see Bolt run again,' said one athlete's agent. A few weeks later, he returned to competition.

In July 2012, a couple of weeks before the London Games, Bolt did admit, 'For the first time I'm slightly a little bit nervous.' Because Blake was faster? 'I should think I'm definitely faster than Yohan Blake,' he clarified. Always, with Bolt, beneath the facade there lurks a steely competitor.

In fact, Bolt said later, Blake did him a favour at the national trials. 'It was like he knocked on my door and said, "Usain, this is an Olympic year. Wake up."'

When the 100 metres finalists enter the stadium and wait behind the blocks, to be introduced like prizefighters, all eyes are on one man; one man who couldn't have been more comfortable on this stage, with this kind of pressure. 'All right, this is it,' he says. 'It's game time.' He enjoys the crowd's response, the fact that 80,000 pairs of eyes are watching him, expecting another miracle.

Then a brief flicker of fear – a shadow flitting across his face – before he settles into the blocks. It's like the blood drains briefly from

Bolt's face. Daegu isn't on his mind. Or not much. 'First of all, my coach explained to me, it was all about reacting and executing. I got to fifty metres; the last fifty metres are my race.'

Justin Gatlin insisted that he started the race believing he could win. Earlier in the season, in Zagreb, Bolt talked about his American rival's macho posturing at the start: 'I just think that's what he's used to. He's pretty much an old-school athlete and, back in the day, it was all about intimidation.'

Gatlin gets an incredible start and has clear track in front of him. Then he senses Bolt. 'I mean, he's six-five, you can't miss him,' he tells us later. 'When his legs lift, you can see it, you can feel it.'

As Gatlin and Tyson Gay fade, Blake and Bolt emerge, then there is just Bolt. 'The last fifty metres,' says Blake. 'That's when he decided to pull up beside me, and I said, "Wow."'

Bolt wins in 9.63 seconds, beating his own Olympic record, second only to his time in Berlin. Blake's time in finishing second (9.75) and Gatlin's in coming third (9.79) would have won the gold medal in every other Olympic final in history – apart from Beijing. Gay misses a medal and breaks down in tears: 'Ain't nothing else I could do. I don't have excuses, man, I gave it my all. I feel like I let a lot of people down.'

The press conference begins just after 11 p.m., over an hour after the race. This is backstage, shorn of the Olympic sheen: a no-frills, brightly lit conference room, a table at one end, with bottles of (official) drinks, and seats arranged in front with space for about eighty reporters. The three medallists shuffle in together. Bolt smiles and jokes with Blake, who looks nervous, while Gatlin seems out of sorts, as though he wonders what he is doing here. He has a point: few are here to hear from the bronze medallist. Gatlin looks his age – thirty. And as they whisper and giggle to each other, Bolt and Blake look theirs, or younger.

Blake explains, 'Usain Bolt told me to keep calm. This is my first Olympics, so he encouraged me . . . It was just fun out there.

Bolt has a way of keeping me calm. I'm grateful of course, I'm happy.'

Gatlin: 'It feels good to be back here, being part of history. It means a lot to me. I'm really glad to be here.' The elephant in the room: his 'previous' for doping. Or, as Gatlin euphemistically refers to it: 'ups and downs'. He adds: 'You know, watching Bolt, watching Blake, and what they've done, has been the inspiration for me to work harder, to work the angles, to be a better runner.'

Bolt talked on the eve of the Games about attaining the status of 'legend'. 'It's a first step,' he says now. The 200 metres will be another step. He acknowledges one journalist's reference to the only other sprinter to successfully defend the Olympic 100 metres title, Carl Lewis (after Ben Johnson was disqualified). But Bolt is not rising to the Lewis bait. Not yet.

Towards the end of the press conference, a curve ball: 'A question from Germany, Usain. Dr Müller-Wohlfahrt is your doc: how did he help you? And how German is your success?'

'Dr Müller-Wohlfahrt is a major part of my success, a major part of my career,' Bolt replies, suddenly more animated. 'I have been going to him since I was probably nineteen, eighteen, since I first had an injury. He's really done a number, done great work on me. After trials I went to him, he looked at my muscles, he did his treatment, and said, "Usain, you're going to do great, go back, train." He gave my coach the go-ahead. So he plays a very important role.

'He's more than a doctor. He takes us to dinner, he really looks after me. He comes in on weekends to treat me. I thank him and the girls in the office.'

Later, Bolt celebrates his win in his room in the athletes' village with three members of Sweden's female handball team: a moment he captures with his phone and posts on Twitter. The Swedes bumped into Glen Mills in the dining room and asked if they could meet Bolt. He led them to Bolt's room, where they stayed until 3 a.m. 'It was awesome, he wasn't cocky or anything,' said Isabelle Gullden. 'He wasn't drunk, either, he'd just got back from the race.'

If the one-two in the 100 metres was extraordinary, then what was the 200 metres, four days later? Warren Weir had been a decent hurdler at school, spotted by Herb McKenley, and transformed into a 200 metres sprinter by Glen Mills. At Racers Track Club, training with Bolt and Blake, he couldn't cope with the workload initially; he wasn't strong enough, and kept breaking down, partly because of knee problems related – thought Mills – to the strain of hurdling. Weir is slightly built and wiry; in fact, he, Blake and Bolt are all very different shapes. Mills encouraged him to take things slowly. The secret to his eventual breakthrough? 'Patience,' he says. 'I was supposed to go to Daegu, but Coach said, "You're not fit enough; we're going to wait."'

In London, having qualified for the final, Weir was anxious. 'Before all the cameras and before the running was nerve-racking,' he tells me when we meet in a hotel in New Kingston. 'It was my first championship. The first day, I wasn't nervous. I had nothing to lose, but getting into the final, it was a bit nervous.' Yet, having run 19.99 to finish behind Blake and Bolt at the Jamaican trials in June, he believed he should be capable of a medal in his first Olympic final. 'Yes, because when I looked at the times going into the Olympics and the final, I was right in the medals. So I was expecting to get a medal, but at the same time I was saying to myself, "If I don't, it's OK, it's my first Games."'

In the call room before the final, he tried to ease the tension. 'I was laughing and running jokes. I was saying to [Wallace] Spearmon and Bolt and Churandy [Martina]: "In 2008, I was in high school watching y'all guys at Beijing on the couch. And now we're in the same final."'

Weir's game plan was to ignore Bolt and Blake and run his own race. Easier said than done, since he was in lane eight while in lane seven was Bolt. 'I was very realistic out there. I said to myself, I'm nowhere in the range of Bolt and Blake; they are running some extremely fast times. But third place was up for grabs. Everybody with a shout of third place was running pretty much the same time as I was.'

Bolt drew level with Weir in thirteen steps. He and Blake, in lane four, were already out front, running their own race, but Weir led the others coming off the bend. He was aware of Spearmon challenging and lunged for the line – dipping too early, so that his head was down. He didn't see whether he got it. 'I could not judge if I had come third. I had to wait for the replay and the scoreboard. You see people celebrate too early – I didn't want to do that. Then I saw the places and I ran over to Bolt and Blake, who were celebrating up the track. "Yo, I came third."

'It was joy,' says Weir, 'joy all over. To get a one-two-three from the same club, from the same country, from the same coach, and to know that we'd been training for like three years before the Olympic Games was wonderful.'

Is Mills someone who celebrates moments like this? 'I saw Coach after the race because I was in [anti-]doping. So Coach was very excited and he said to me, "Patience." He said to me then, "Patience pays off." Because it was all about building up gradually.'

Weir didn't make the team for the 4x100 metres relay, when Bolt and Blake were joined by Nesta Carter and Michael Frater: once again, two from Racers, two from MVP. Their winning time, 36.84, was a world record. Bolt confirmed afterwards that he was a legend now. But he'd got something else off his chest after the 200 metres, something he had been building up to saying. Flanked by Blake and Weir, he leant forward, into the microphone: 'I am going to say something controversial right now. Carl Lewis, I have no respect for him. The things he says about the track athletes is really downgrading, for another athlete to be saying something like that about other athletes.' Since 2008, Lewis had been voicing his suspicions about the Jamaicans.

Bolt had hinted after the 100 metres that he had something to say, but bit his tongue: 'Patience,' as Mills might say. In footage filmed by Weir in their living quarters in the athletes' village, Bolt can be seen lying on a massage table, muttering about Lewis. But once he finally started, he didn't seem able to stop. 'I think he's just looking for attention, because nobody really talks much about him so he's just looking for attention. So that was really sad for me when I heard the other day what he was saying. For me it was upsetting. I have lost all respect for him. It was all about drugs, talking about drugs, a lot of drug stuff. For an athlete out of the sport to be saying that is really upsetting for me . . .'

Lewis wasn't the only one in his cross hairs – Victor Conte had been in the news claiming that doping remained rampant. 'It is really annoying when people on the sidelines say stupid stuff,' Bolt continued. 'Without a doubt we are drug-free. We train hard. I see us all train together, we throw up every day, we take ice baths, we end up flat out on the track. When people taint us it is really hard but we are trying our best to show the world that we are running clean.'

Beside Bolt throughout the London Olympics, including at his press conferences, Blake smiled, but he wasn't overly happy. He reckoned his 100 metres had been one of his worst – a badly executed race (he would prove his form a couple of weeks later, running 9.69 seconds in Lausanne to make him, with Tyson Gay, the joint-second-fastest man of all time). 'That was my best race,' Blake says of Lausanne. 'At the Olympics I tightened up a bit.' It was a missed opportunity. He believes he could and should have won the Olympic 100 metres final. 'I was leading and I said, Yes, Yohan, you got this in the bag – as soon as I thought that, I tightened up.'

His time would come, Glen Mills was sure of that. Midway through the London Games, Mills confided in another member of the Jamaican entourage. Bolt had been hinting that he might finally give the 400 metres a go, and could do the 200 and 400 at the Rio Olympics in 2016, when he will be thirty. It seemed unclear; up in the air. His coach wasn't sure whether he would try the longer distance.

He seemed certain only about one thing, and it concerned the blue riband event, the 100 metres: 'There's no way', said Mills, 'that any thirty-year-old will beat Yohan Blake in 2016.'

18

AFTER THE HURRICANE

*A systematic and knowing failure . . . that is deplorable and gives rise to
the most serious concerns about the overall integrity of the JAAA's
anti-doping processes.*
The Court of Arbitration for Sport

The shadows darkened in the twelve months after the London
Olympics. Every doping case intensified the pressure on Jamaica
and on Usain Bolt in particular. It wasn't just his reputation at stake,
it was the whole sport's. After all, they were synonymous. Bolt *was*
athletics.

Not that he displayed any signs of being under pressure. In late
July 2013 he appeared in a small meeting room at the Grange Tower
Hotel in London, the day before he competed in (and won) the
anniversary games at the Olympic stadium. With the cases involving
the Jamaicans, in particular Asafa Powell, and also one of Bolt's main
rivals, the American Tyson Gay, there was only one topic in his pre-
race press conference. I sat in the front row, keen to hear what he had
to say and to study him as he said it.

A female journalist asks the first question: 'Usain, following the
recent doping scandals, only one out of the five fastest men in the

world now hasn't failed a drugs test. Lots of people, fans of the sport, will lose confidence – can they trust you?'

'Ah, I was hoping that question would come later,' Bolt laughs. He leans forward and looks in the direction of the reporter. 'I was planning to explain to people. How long have you been following Usain Bolt?'

'A good few years,' replies the reporter.

'2008 maybe?' Bolt continues. 'If you've been following me since 2002, you would know I've been doing phenomenal things since I was fifteen. I was the youngest person to win the world juniors, at fifteen. I ran the world junior record, 19.93, at eighteen. World youth record at seventeen. I've broken every record there is to break in every event that I've ever done. For me, I've proven myself since I was fifteen. I'm just living out my dream now and I've underperformed this season, as my agent would say, and I need to step it up.' He shrugs. 'I was always going to be great.'

There is another reason why the subject of doping seems bigger than ever, and why Bolt is under such scrutiny. Sport is reeling from Lance Armstrong's downfall in the autumn of 2012, which culminated in his confessional interview with Oprah Winfrey in January 2013. There are similarities between Armstrong and Bolt in that both transcend their sport; cycling became reliant upon Armstrong and his remarkable story, just as athletics now seems to depend on Bolt. That bastion of intelligence and measured discussion, *The New Yorker*, in a piece about Tyson Gay, makes the comparison: 'Bolt is in something of the same position that Lance Armstrong was in about 2003: a man dominating a dirty sport as his rivals and teammates fall. It wouldn't be a surprise if one day this summer Bolt starts talking about misreading the label on an herbal supplement – or if, a decade from now, he ends up talking to Oprah.'

Because so many of his rivals have cheated, Bolt is in the firing line. He insists he is different. In London he tells us: 'I was made to inspire people and to run. I was given a gift and that's what I do. I'm confident in myself, my team, the people I work with. I know I'm clean, so I'm just going to continue running and using my talent and trying to improve the sport and help the sport.'

You can see him scanning the horizon for landmines or tripwires. He has prepared for this, clearly – his response to the female reporter's question wasn't spontaneous. He is careful. He doesn't lambast the athletes who have tested positive. Should there be tougher penalties? Up to the authorities, he says, not him. Is the banned list too complicated? 'If it's banned, just don't take it.' When he lines up for a race, he is not thinking that his rivals may be cheating. He trusts his entourage to check that nothing he takes contains a banned substance. 'You have to be careful as an athlete, about what you do, the food you ingest, but I'm not worried because I have a great team around me.' He doesn't take supplements, only vitamins. 'Every athlete takes vitamins. I don't really take supplements.'

Finally he is asked a question that doesn't appear to be about doping, until the kicker, which is. Bolt laughs: 'You almost got there, you almost asked a normal question.'

Then Simon Hart of the *Telegraph*, who has written extensively about doping in athletics, puts his hand up. 'I've got a "normal" question,' he says.

'*You* are asking me a normal question?' Bolt responds. 'All these drug questions and you are asking me a normal question?'

Bolt laughs; everyone laughs. The tone, the mood and the atmosphere are in marked contrast to Armstrong's press conferences. Those were dominated by similar questions but had an edge: an air of hostility and confrontation. With Bolt it's all bonhomie. He seems as relaxed as when he lines up for an Olympic 100 metres final. Is that reassuring, or suspicious? That question is as complicated as asking how anyone can prove that they have *not* done something. You cannot prove a negative: that's what Armstrong used to say. (And therein lies one problem. Armstrong stole all the best lines.)

There is at least one difference between Bolt and Armstrong, however. Bolt says, 'I am clean.' Armstrong used to say: 'I've never tested positive.'

It's December 2014, and Stephen Francis is overseeing an MVP training session at UTech that includes Shelly-Ann Fraser-Pryce and Nesta Carter, but not Asafa Powell or Sherone Simpson.

Fraser-Pryce finishes training, strolls to her gleaming white Mercedes SUV, face glued to her mobile phone. Carter, who arrived late and is still dragging weights as Francis sits in a deckchair and watches him, has a black Honda sports car. It's strange to see the kind of vehicles that wouldn't look out of place in a Mayfair showroom parked beside a dirt running track so worn that the lane markings are not lines, but deep grooves worn into the ground.

When he has finished dissecting the morning's training with one of his assistants, Francis, wearing a floppy sun hat, hoists himself out of the deckchair and makes his way slowly towards the adjacent building, which houses the gym. It's still only 8 a.m., the sun is climbing over the mountains into a perfect blue sky, and he finds shade beneath a tree.

A new dawn beckons after a tempestuous twelve months for MVP. Powell, the man who pioneered the stay-at-home approach for Jamaican athletes, is now training in Texas with his brother Donovan acting as coach. Simpson has also moved to the US. Francis's disappointment is due not so much to the fact that they are no longer here, but to the circumstances of their departures. Their positive tests, he says, were symptomatic of other changes. With Powell, in particular, 'the discipline had started to go'.

He changed? 'Mm hmm, oh yeah,' says Francis, who adds that he told Powell: 'I don't want you to be somebody who you look at and tell the youngsters, "Here is an example of what not to be." '

Francis blames himself, to some extent. 'But if I tell you something five times, if you're not going to listen the fifth time, you're never going to listen. I should have said, "OK, you're on your own." ' He says he didn't know Powell was taking up to twenty supplements – he recalls the difficulty in persuading him to take vitamins or creatine. But more than that, it was his attitude. 'I mean,' says Francis, 'you expect some of it because he's had success, he's thirty years old, he feels he's a man.' The problems came when the younger athletes began copying him. 'I said to our youngsters, "OK, stop, stop, stop, stop. When Asafa was your age, he didn't behave like this. What made him good was that he used to conform. I have no problem if you win ten gold medals and decide that you're going to do your own thing, but do not make the mistake of thinking that at nineteen you can behave that way."

'I point out to my kids all the while, even as lackadaisical and idle as somebody like Usain Bolt appears to be, in the year between 2007 and 2008 he was a transformed person. He buckled down, got disciplined, stopped going out, stopped the drinking and so on, and focused on getting himself as good as he was in 2008. So I say to them, "Now, if that applies to someone who has talent oozing out of his ears, then it certainly applies to everyone else."'

Powell's departure means the club can reboot; re-establish some ground rules, 'with an emphasis on punctuality, emphasis on doing everything on the programme, participating fully in assessments and so on', Francis explains. 'A high level of ill discipline had crept into the whole system. The fact that Asafa chose not to be here this year meant that you can apply everything evenly across the board now without people saying: "But look at how Asafa is doing it."'

As for the club's anti-doping policy, it has been tightened up. Francis wants to know 'everything you put in your mouth'.

Yet despite all that, he says he would take Powell back. 'Oh yeah. I mean, as long as I still believe he has more to offer under the right disciplinary situation. But I don't think he . . . he has never understood his role in his demise. If he understands it and wants to come back, I have no problem. Asafa is a very nice guy, very kind, a very lovely person, but too easily influenced. Too eager to be influenced by the last person he speaks to.'

*

I was in Paul Wright's office as a verdict was reached in Sherone Simpson's case, ten months after she tested positive. Powell's would be decided two days later.

The phone rang: Simpson had been given an eighteen-month ban. 'Nobody can take joy out of somebody losing their job,' Wright says after putting the phone down. He takes a zero-tolerance approach: a banned drug is a banned drug and the athlete is responsible for what's in their body. End of story. 'What irks me', he says, 'is that you have prominent, powerful Jamaicans who go on national television and radio and say: "Why are we going about these people who have taken a little supplement: it's no big thing." Completely bamboozling the public.'

By the time of my visit, Wright appeared to have lost *his* job as JADCO's lead drugs-tester after giving an interview to the BBC in November 2013 in which he said the spate of positive tests 'could be the tip of the iceberg'. His main concern was that they were all in-competition positives. He backed up his old boss, Renée Anne Shirley, who argued that out-of-competition testing needed to be stepped up. With in-competition tests, he said, 'Months before, you know the date of the test and the approximate time of the test. You need to be stupid to fail.'

When Shirley wrote in *Sports Illustrated* about the drugs cases being like a 'force five hurricane', 'it went ballistic', says Wright. 'Then the BBC came here and spoke to me, I corroborate everything Anne said, so I was, according to public radio, an enemy of the state. I was vilified in the press. One newspaper had it that I was fired.'

He wasn't fired? 'I was never fired, because to fire somebody you have them on contract. I was just used as needed.'

Since speaking to the BBC, he hasn't been used at all.

Two days later, I go to Powell's hearing. Which is more than Powell does.

In room number five of the Jamaica Conference Centre, on the

Kingston waterfront, are fifteen reporters and four lawyers. Kwame Gordon and Danielle Chai are there to represent Powell. At 10.04 a.m., the three members of the anti-doping disciplinary panel appear. The chairman, Lennox Gayle, opens proceedings: 'I notice Mr Powell is absent, Mr Gordon?'

'I apologise,' says Gordon. 'I hope that will not be a problem.'

The wonderfully officious Gayle shuffles his notes and carries on. 'The defence team of Mr Powell did some real hard work,' he begins, the implication being that the ten months it has taken to reach a verdict owes much to the volume of material submitted in Powell's defence. Gayle speaks slowly for seven minutes, with lots of ominous pauses. 'We reached a unanimous decision,' he says finally, 'and . . . and . . . and it was our decision that . . . we are saying that Mr Powell was found to be . . . negligent.' As with Simpson, an eighteen-month suspension is the verdict.

Powell is devastated. His team had sent one of his supplements, Epiphany D1, to be tested by the US Anti-Doping Agency, who confirmed that it contained oxilofrine. The substance was not listed in the ingredients either on the bottle or on the company's website.[35] The man blamed by Powell and his agent, Paul Doyle, was Chris Xuereb, a Canadian masseur and nutritionist who began working with Powell and Simpson a month before both tested positive. Doyle told the Associated Press: 'Asafa and Sherone have been tested more than 100 times each through their career . . . and never turned in a positive test. Now they change their supplements and the first time they get tested, they have a positive test? It has to be something in those new supplements that has caused it. Chris is the one that provided those.' Xuereb responded: 'It is time the athletes took responsibility for their doping instead of looking around for a scapegoat, whether that person is their therapist, bartender or anyone else.' (The products seized

35 In February 2015, it was reported that Powell and Simpson's management company was suing the manufacturers of Epiphany D1 for $8m.

by Italian police when they searched Powell's hotel room included vitamins, Aleve and Actovegin – the calf-blood extract used by Dr Müller-Wohlfahrt. But nothing illegal.)

The hearing in Kingston is not the end. Three months later, Powell and Simpson, having appealed to the Court of Arbitration for Sport, have their suspensions reduced to six months. They are free to return to competition. The CAS takes the view that both were guilty of a minor offence, testing positive for a stimulant with negligible performance-enhancing effects. 'Thank u to the Court of Arbitration for Sport,' Powell writes on Twitter. 'Finally this weight has been lifted off my shoulders. Justice has been served. Now let's run!'

'A complete fiasco,' says Doyle. 'What took CAS ten minutes took ten months in Jamaica.'

There were other blows to the country's anti-doping movement, ranging from the embarrassing to the farcical. While I was in Jamaica in April 2014, the deputy chairman of the anti-doping disciplinary panel, an attorney-at-law, was arrested and charged in connection with a prostitution ring in Montego Bay – a charge he denies. Then the *Wall Street Journal* published a story alleging that JADCO's chairman, Herb Elliott, had fabricated his CV. The paper claimed there was no record of his master's degree in chemistry from Columbia University or his medical degree and PhD in biochemistry from the Université libre de Bruxelles in Belgium. It was an American vendetta against Jamaica, said Elliott, who insisted he did have the qualifications, even if he had mislaid some paperwork after his wife's death in 2010. But after discussing the matter with the prime minister, he stepped down as JADCO chairman. (I was told that Dr Elliott was in poor health and advised not to contact him on my visits to Jamaica.)

Far more serious was the other appeal to the Court of Arbitration for Sport, by Veronica Campbell-Brown. She had initially been given a two-year ban by the JAAA, which was ratified by the IAAF. However, she was cleared by the Jamaican disciplinary panel, who found the results from a polygraph (lie detector) test 'most compelling' and suggested a 'reprimand' would be more appropriate than a ban. But the IAAF Doping Review Board – which adjudicates in the cases of international-level athletes – was not happy, and reinstated the two-year ban. Finally she was cleared again by the Court of Arbitration.

It took several weeks for the CAS to publish the reasons for clearing Campbell-Brown. When they did, the fifty-eight-page report read like a charge sheet against the Jamaican athletics and anti-doping authorities. It detailed a catalogue of abject failings, which began the moment Campbell-Brown was asked for a urine sample at the Jamaican International Invitational meeting in Kingston on 4 May 2013.

She had won the women's 100 metres, which meant a drug test. A JADCO chaperone escorted her to the doping control area, where she met the assistant doping control officer, Danya Williams. It was 8.56 p.m. Campbell-Brown wasn't ready to give a urine sample, so she drank bottles of water and Powerade from a cool box in the doping control area. When she felt able to urinate, she was accompanied to the toilet by Williams. They passed a table with containers in sealed bags; Williams instructed Campbell-Brown to select one. Campbell-Brown washed and dried her hands before passing urine into the container under the supervision of the doping control officer.

She could only produce a partial sample (defined as less than 90 ml). Because of the risks of contamination, there are strict rules about how a partial sample should be stored. It should be transferred to a special container; it should be sealed; it should be kept by either the athlete or the doping control officer; a new container should be provided for any other sample.

None of these things happened. Campbell-Brown returned to the waiting room with her partial sample in a covered but unsealed container, which she left on the floor as she collected more drinks, did stretching exercises and ran her hands under water. Meanwhile, the assistant doping control officer had other athletes to attend to. It was an hour later when Campbell-Brown was able to produce an additional urine sample, and she did so not in a fresh container, but in the one she'd used earlier.

Now that the assistant doping control officer had 160 ml, she was happy. Campbell-Brown selected a storage kit, poured half the urine into one bottle (A sample) and half into the other (B sample). The paperwork was completed, but the box entitled 'partial sample' was left unchecked. It was 10.19 p.m. when the process was finished.

The next day, the sample was sent in a batch of thirteen to the Laboratoire de controle du dopage in Montreal. It arrived on 7 May. On 24 May, the laboratory confirmed it had detected hydrochlorothiazide (HCT), a diuretic commonly used to treat high blood pressure, but also thought to be used by athletes as a masking agent. On 3 June, the JAAA was informed of the finding; Campbell-Brown was told on the same day. Ten days later, she travelled to Montreal to witness the testing of the B sample, which confirmed the positive. She protested her innocence but accepted a voluntary provisional suspension. (In the same month, two other Jamaican athletes, the discus throwers Alison Randall and Travers Smikle, both tested positive for HCT; Smikle's adverse reading also followed a partial sample collected in violation of the anti-doping rules.)

On 3 July, Campbell-Brown underwent a lie detector test in Orlando, conducted by polygraph expert Donald Harper. 'It is the opinion of the examiner that the subject did not knowingly use hydrochlorothiazide, and further has never used performance-enhancing drugs,' concluded Harper. Campbell-Brown also sent her nutritional supplements to the Aegis Science Corporation in Nashville. They all tested negative for HCT.

Could her urine sample have been contaminated in the waiting area? Could the water in the taps where Campbell-Brown washed her hands be the source? At the CAS hearing in London, this possibility was discussed at some length. Experts were called by Campbell-Brown and the IAAF. They offered contradictory testimony. Campbell-Brown's expert said it was likely that contaminated water was to blame. The

IAAF's expert conceded that this 'cannot be ruled out in theory', but added that it was 'so unlikely that I discount it entirely'.

In the end, it didn't matter who was right. All that mattered was that the correct procedure hadn't been followed by JADCO. Ordinarily, under the strict liability rule, the athlete has to prove how and why a banned substance is in their system. In this case, CAS declared that the burden 'shifts back to the IAAF to persuade the Panel to the requisite standard of proof that the Athlete did consume the prohibited substance'. It was no longer up to Campbell-Brown to prove that a doping violation had not occurred: it was up to the IAAF to establish that it had.

And of course the IAAF could not do that. The CAS, whose panel was made up of Philippe Sands QC, Jeffrey Benz and Michael Beloff QC, had no choice other than to exonerate Campbell-Brown. They also gave JADCO a severe dressing-down. By ignoring the rules on collection and storage, they had 'engaged in a knowing, systematic and persistent failure to comply with a mandatory IST [international standard for testing] that is directed at the integrity of the sample collection and testing process . . . That systematic and knowing failure, for which no reasonable explanation has been advanced, is deplorable and gives rise to the most serious concerns about the overall integrity of the JAAA's anti-doping processes, as exemplified in this case by the flaws in JADCO's sample collection and its documentation.'

The CAS panel was convinced by Campbell-Brown's testimony, too, noting that she had 'given a detailed and materially consistent account of the relevant facts throughout the disciplinary process'. Dr Paul Wright was not involved on the night in question, but in Campbell-Brown's hearing he did concede that the rules were not always strictly adhered to – though he insisted that he had WADA's blessing in his alternative method of partial sample collection, for example.

Wright, for me, had some typical and endearing Jamaican traits. He was a maverick who recognised that solutions to problems were sometimes found by using his imagination and initiative – witness his use of dry ice to store samples for EPO testing, or, going a few decades back, his acquisition of testing kits for marijuana for the football team. What I did not doubt was his sincerity in trying to do the right thing. 'Just do the job' was his mantra, in his daily work as a surgeon as well as in drug-testing athletes. In Jamaica, 'just do the job' can mean trying to get things done despite the problems, challenges, obstacles, as well as the corruption that can seem endemic: circumventing the system, otherwise, nothing would get done.

P. J. Patterson, who helped Campbell-Brown prepare her defence – 'The only person I've represented since I left the bar and entered politics [in 1969]' – felt vindicated by the CAS verdict. 'The fact is, there has to be professionalism at all levels. The consequences for an athlete found to be engaged in those activities is so damning that the rules have to be very strictly applied. And they weren't, they weren't. And the Court of Arbitration confirmed that.'

Renée Anne Shirley resisted saying 'I told you so', but the Campbell-Brown case confirmed her worst fears. It was the reason she had spoken out in the first place. 'I didn't want someone to get off because JADCO did things wrong.'

Sweeping changes followed at JADCO: a new chairman, Danny Williams, a businessman with no ties to sport; and a new executive director, Carey Brown, formerly a financial analyst at the Ministry of Finance. After a couple of visits from WADA, they were also being mentored by the Canadian Centre for Ethics in Sport. 'They are holding our hands, and that is proving very helpful,' is how Williams put it.

The negative headlines were too much for Shelly-Ann Fraser-Pryce. She was fed up with the foreign media – American and British in particular – running their stories fuelled on sensationalism and innuendo, and failing to make any distinction between, say, Tyson Gay's positive test for a steroid and the Jamaican cases. This was like equating a petty thief with a murderer, in her view.[36] She was even angrier with the authorities in Jamaica, the JAAA. 'We are the ones out there competing and yet we read articles and listen to people making accusations about Jamaica, and there's nobody there to take a microphone, be a big person and say, "What you're saying is wrong and it's a lie." ' If the situation didn't improve, she warned, she and her fellow athletes would go on strike – they would refuse to compete for Jamaica.

Glen Mills also felt that the suspicion was part of a vendetta against Jamaica, motivated by jealousy. 'They target Jamaica because of its success. There is no doubt about it,' he told the *Gleaner*. 'Nobody wants to see Jamaica continue its dominance of sprinting at the world level. And the international media – again, one has to question the balance of their reporting. I have read some terrible articles written about Jamaica. I have read some terrible articles trying to insinuate that Usain Bolt's success is false because of all of this.

'We have had some adverse analytical findings for stimulants and those other things,' Mills continued, 'but there are so many cases of steroid use in other countries in the past couple of months, yet there is no sensationalising around those countries or athletes. Yet everyone is banging on the Jamaicans because of our success, and the truth of the matter is that our success has come through hard work, excellent coaches, and making the best use of our facilities that are below world-class standards.'

Fraser-Pryce and Mills had a point in one sense. While Shirley's article in *Sports Illustrated* rightly highlighted the failings of JADCO, it contributed to a misconception that the Jamaicans were not tested at all in the run-up to the 2012 Olympic Games. That wasn't the case.

---

36 In April 2015 Bolt said he thought Tyson Gay should have been 'kicked out of the sport' for his positive test. He told *Runner's World*: 'I was really upset about that. He got a year just because he talked to the authorities about how it was done and who helped him. That sends the wrong message ... it's the stupidest thing I've ever heard. The message should be: "If you cheat you're going to be kicked out of the sport." '

As part of the IAAF's anti-doping programme, forty-seven Jamaican athletes were tested a total of 208 times in 2012. Bolt was the most tested (25 times) then Blake (18), Powell and Fraser-Pryce (both 13).[37] A spokesman for the IAAF anti-doping department told me in an email: 'Please be clear that even if there was not the right level of out-of-competition testing by a national agency (and this is understandable when you consider the limitations of resources and technologies in countries around the world where top athletes originate from), this does not mean that there is a sort of testing "gap" for the very simple reason that the IAAF guarantees a top-level out-of-competition testing system – of INTELLIGENT testing of top-class athletes. Simply put, the top three ranked countries in terms of tested athletes for the IAAF are: Russia, Kenya and Jamaica!

37 Of Bolt's 25 tests, 12 were in-competition, 13 out-of competition: of the former, 3 were blood, 9 urine; of the latter, 6 were blood, 7 urine. The blood tests were a combination of drugs tests and samples for the IAAF biological passport, which monitors an athlete's blood values over the long term and can reveal the effects of doping.

'So all references to deficiencies in the national anti-doping programme of Jamaica should remain in context – in 2012, it was very early days in terms of said agency – perhaps mistakes were made, resources were inadequate, etc., but there was always a powerful IAAF system in the background to cover any deficiency. By 2013, of course, the situation was radically different and the high-profile testing and sanctioning of Asafa Powell was as a result of work done by JADCO.'

I felt there was a guardedness, a wariness and a testiness about some of the Jamaicans when they competed in Europe. It was most evident in Fraser-Pryce, who could seem frosty and unapproachable. She is quite different when I meet her in Kingston. Why is that? I ask her. Is it because she is fed up with fielding questions about doping? 'Ah, sometimes. It depends how many times I get asked.'

She echoes Mills: she argues that there is no serious doping problem in Jamaica, and that people's suspicion is due to jealousy at their success, or a failure to accept that it is possible. It is possible, she says, thanks to the virtuous circle effect. Young Jamaicans see the senior athletes winning at the highest level, 'and they want that success. And we train together. It's not segregated. The fact you have persons doing so well, training with them, it gives the other athletes motivation. The young athletes are so motivated.'

But surely she cannot blame outsiders for thinking there's a problem when there have been so many positive tests? 'I've been in that situation, and you hear what persons are saying,' she says. 'It's heartbreaking. I haven't spoken to Sherone in a long time because she's in the States now, but I speak to Asafa a lot. He was devastated.

'But a lot of our athletes are naive, I think. I think they should read more, research more, try to get more educated in what's out there. Because it is hard. When persons sit and go, "I'm taking this supplement but it's fine because there's nothing in it," you go: "OK." But they think because they're not taking steroids, they're fine. They're not doing the deep research they need to do to protect themselves.

They think, I'm not doping, I'm just taking this vitamin they have on the shelf and it says it's OK. That's the downfall for a lot of Jamaican athletes.' Like Bolt, she says she doesn't take any supplements, only vitamins.

How did her call for a strike go down? Was she called in front of the JAAA? 'No, I wasn't called in.' She remains bitter, particularly over Wright's 'tip of the iceberg' comment. 'When persons make accusations about us, a lot of these persons need to visit Champs. They need to come and see the structure. They need to see how we train. They need to visit our tracks. The fact that a lot of these athletes come from poor communities, that the only way out is track, so the desire and the motivation is high. It's not somewhere where they're used to first-class facilities. Look at the rooms they stay in, the shoes they train in. That's exactly why they are so motivated to do well.'

Much of this chimed with what Yannis Pitsiladis had told me.

It is early 2015, and I am sitting with Pitsiladis in his office in Eastbourne, listening to him enthusing about his marathon project – the quest to break two hours with a clean runner in the next five years. It is a mission that consumes him. But on some distant horizon he sees another project: the first 9.55-second 100 metres. 'It's the logical next step,' he says. 'The sub-two-hour marathon is only the beginning.

'We will get a sprinter below 9.55 seconds. You've heard it first. You're the first person I've told it to.'

He would approach it the same way: identifying athletes who might be candidates, selecting the optimum course or track (more of a challenge with the 100 metres than with the marathon), then surrounding them with experts, analysing their training to the nth degree. He doesn't think much is known about training really – hence his observation that the training in Jamaica is not sophisticated, and that the approaches of Mills and Francis are 'both wrong . . . and both right'. What he means is that training, and adaptations to it, are highly individual. Studies have been done about the effects of exercise on different people, 'where everyone did the same and some got better, some remained the same, and some got worse. Which shows you that everyone responds differently.'

When it comes to elite performance, though, the doping question hangs over everything, casting its long, dark shadow. Pitsiladis has been stung by some of the reaction to his new project, with some claiming that a sub-two-hour marathon could only be achieved with drugs (he makes it clear that he sees the project as a collaboration with the anti-doping authorities; he works closely with WADA). Some have also been dismissive of his work in Kenya because of recent revelations about the extent of the doping problem there.

He is a little bruised, but undeterred. Fundamentally, he doesn't think the drugs issue is very relevant. Although it is difficult to quantify the effects of doping ('I can't at this stage,' he admits, though he is looking at how it might be possible), he believes it is of only minor significance. 'Having done this research for fifteen, twenty years in East Africa, there are so many factors,' he says. 'The drug issue is a tiny component of it that in itself could not have produced this success.'

He points out that 'Other countries have serious drug problems but don't have the success. So that's not the issue.'

Interestingly, he adds that, despite the claims that Jamaica also has a serious doping issue, he doesn't believe it is on the same scale as Kenya. 'Imagine a Kenyan family,' he says. 'No food, suffering, but quite good at running. Running on a track in Eldoret. Trying to find a manager. Someone comes up to them, says, "You're running quite well but I'll give you some EPO." The kid doesn't know what EPO is. The manager says, "I want 20 per cent when you start earning."

'Is that a difficult decision to make?' Pitsiladis asks. 'No, of course not. It's an easy decision.'

So why does he not think the same could happen – or does happen – in Jamaica? 'That's a very good question.' He thinks a long time. 'I'm not talking about Jamaican athletes who leave the island, but locally, in Jamaica, I don't see the same issues.' There are several reasons: there

isn't the money in sprinting that there is in road running, with lucrative
events throughout the world to support Kenya's 3,000 professional
road runners. And he isn't sure what drugs would be involved. 'That
would be one of my arguments,' he says. 'The only reason I don't put
it at the top is because up until now I haven't had the opportunity to
study those drugs. What's the EPO of sprinting? It's not very clear.'

In the end, Pitsiladis explains that his view is informed mainly
by his own experiences in and of Jamaica. 'I would argue', he says,
'that the level of sophistication needed to oversee a systematic doping
programme is almost beyond what the island could do.

'They'd be caught on day one.'

19

THE IN-BETWEEN

Look out, greatness is coming.
Jaheel Hyde

On my first day back in Jamaica, I ask Dennis Johnson why he thinks his country produces so many top sprinters. He turns the tables. 'You have been travelling around, speaking to people. Why do *you* think we have these sprinters in Jamaica?'

'I think there are lots of factors,' I reply.

'Like what?'

'History, culture, environment . . .'

'All very generic,' says Johnson. 'What empirical evidence is there for these things – history, culture, environment – being important?'

'How about genes, then?'

'A hypothesis. No evidence.'

'All the sub-10-second sprinters bar one originally come from West Africa,' I say. 'Surely that's not a coincidence?'

'So tell me, where are all the West African sprinters? The Ghanaians? No, why are there so many here, in Jamaica? There must be a reason, man! All these sprinters from this island of three million people: from these two groups under Glen Mills and Stephen Francis.

It's total dominance. There must be a reason why that has happened in the last ten years.'

'Well, some would say that it must be drugs,' I venture.

'Bah! The Jamaican cases have been minor transgressions – stimulants, supplements – apart from the ones who train in America. No steroids, not like the Americans. Come on, one reason. It's like Ebola: it's in three countries but no others – why? There must be a reason.'

'You think there's one specific reason?'

'Yes, man.'

Was I any closer to knowing? Before going to Jamaica, I was as sceptical as anyone. Well, maybe not as sceptical as Victor Conte or Carl Lewis. Then along came the positives in 2013, which reaffirmed my scepticism. And yet where were the Jamaicans who made sudden improvements in their mid-to-late twenties? Where was the heavy-duty stuff – the steroids, the blood doping? Most of the cases implicating home-based Jamaicans involved supplements produced by an unregulated industry that preys on athletes desperate for an edge. (Two Welsh athletes tested positive after taking a poorly labelled supplement in 2014; nobody accused Wales of running a systematic doping programme.)

Most of the people I met in Jamaica made a convincing case. Even those who had suspicions, like Renée Anne Shirley and Paul Wright, had no firm evidence of wrongdoing. Yannis Pitsiladis, an outsider, held the view that drugs are not the secret ingredient in the Jamaican sprint factory. 'Don't make it about drugs,' he urged when I told him about this book.

If only it were that simple. You cannot ignore the fact that so many of the fastest sprinters in the world have tested positive. Nor can you overlook the fact that drugs are easily acquired and tests – apparently – easily passed. You are alarmed to hear that a Jamaican schoolboy tested positive for a steroid – and more alarmed that the school didn't appear to investigate. As the journalist David Walsh puts it, when it comes to drugs in sport, there are two choices: to manage it or confront it. Both approaches have been in evidence in Jamaica. Some seem content to manage the problem (and keener still to deny one). Shirley was eager to aggressively confront it. She didn't last long.

So, drugs might be part of the Jamaican success. But they might not be. There could be sophisticated doping programmes in operation, masterminded by Glen Mills and Stephen Francis. But who is helping them? How are they paying for it? Perhaps I was looking in the wrong places, or speaking to the wrong people. Bert Cameron, until recently a member of the Racers Track Club coaching staff, told me that I didn't find the infrastructure because it doesn't exist. But if he was part of it, he would say that.

Pitsiladis's argument is that it is a cultural phenomenon, like Brazilian football, Dutch speed-skating or Austrian skiing. Sprinting is in the Jamaican DNA. In Britain, the country's most promising sprinter, Adam Gemili, is a failed footballer (he was on Chelsea's books). In Jamaica, it's the other way round: Jaheel Hyde walked out on the national football team to be a hurdler.

But the success of Jamaica says something about the state of athletics, too. Its blue riband status at the Olympic Games gives it a veneer that is misleading. For two weeks every four years, athletics has a mass audience; the rest of the time it is the Grand Budapest Hotel of international sport – with its magnificent facade, it looks impressive and imposing, but inside are creaking floorboards, threadbare furniture and a sense of faded grandeur. It belongs to a different time.

It means that Usain Bolt occupies a curious and paradoxical position: a global star whose fame comes from a sport that is beset by scandal and faces a desperate struggle for sponsors, support and relevance.

Apart from in one place: a Caribbean island of fewer than three million people.

*

From the Norman Manley International Airport, perched on the end of a long peninsula, I drove across the narrow strip of tarmac to the mainland, then around the wide bay towards the twinkling lights of Kingston. It was dark, and the Blue Mountains reared up like ghostly shadows behind the city. Along the front, towards downtown, swerving to avoid enormous potholes and people wobbling on bikes, or walking along the unlit road, I passed the huge, imposing prison – high walls, watchtowers, barbed wire – then turned right up South Camp Road. The alternative, Mountain View Road, is more direct, but had also been the scene in recent months of gunfights.

Leaving behind downtown Kingston, with the ghettos of Trench Town, Tivoli Gardens and Waterhouse shrouded in almost total darkness, I reached the bright lights of New Kingston and recognised some of the beggars, windscreen cleaners, banana salesmen and higglers who spend all day (and night) at the junctions. One began cleaning my (already clean) windscreen as I indicated that I had no money. 'Next time, boss,' he said, flashing a gap-toothed smile and finishing the job he'd started. The experience summed the place up: you hear the stories, read the reports about the violence and the murder rate, heed the warnings, feel the edginess and sense the danger, check and double-check that your car doors are locked when you stop at traffic lights, and then find friendliness and good humour in the most unexpected places.

'Think you're in heaven, but ya living in hell,' as Bob Marley sang in 'Time Will Tell'. This was Jamaica: beguiling and maddening; friendly and violent; laid-back and restless; where 'the boiling point is always quite near', as one of their greatest athletes, Arthur Wint, put it. A place where life seems to move slowly while at the same time being home to the fastest humans on the planet. Of course, Jamaicans tire of depictions of the island as a place of extremes. 'You visitors are always getting it wrong,' one local told Ian Thomson for his book *The Dead Yard*. 'Either it's golden beaches or guns, guns, guns, guns. Is there nothing in between?'

I felt the same about the doping question, which is so often presented as one of polar opposites and extremes: as binary, black or white, with only two possible verdicts, hero or cheat. As in many things, perhaps the truth more often resides somewhere in between. There is a vast grey area of supplements, painkillers, prescription drugs, therapeutic use exemptions, creatine, cortisone, caffeine, calf-blood extract, crushed cockerel crest. A 'clean' athlete could be pumped full of all this stuff but be one mislabelled supplement away from 'dirty'. To reduce it to 'clean' or 'dirty' is too simple. It misses the in-between.

Apart from wrestling with this question, I found it impossible not to become fascinated and intrigued by the place itself. Remarkable things do happen here, and not only on a running track. I was struck, as many people have been, by the comparison between Bolt and Marley as totemic figures but not one-offs. Rather they are the towering symbols of a much wider, deeper phenomenon. Between the mid-1950s and 2000, proportionally more recorded music came out of Jamaica than anywhere else: one new recording a year for every thousand people. About eight recognised genres have their roots in Jamaica, including rap, which came through reggae and dancehall. This must be the musical equivalent of placing first, third, fourth and fifth in a global athletics final, as Jamaica did in the men's 100 metres in Moscow in 2013.

I hadn't fully appreciated that the excellence on the track came first. 'You must understand,' P. J. Patterson told me, 'that our appearance on the world stage in sports preceded our appearance on the world stage in music.' He was talking about Herb McKenley, Arthur Wint; 1948 and 1952. But now Bolt, like Marley, has transcended his field. 'Bolt has become a new word in the dictionary,' Patterson said. 'It's a noun, it's a verb, it's an adjective.'

I mentioned the parallels between athletics and music to Yannis Pitsiladis. 'Exactly,' he said. 'But nobody talks about a music gene, do they?'

*

In August 2014, at the end of the quietest season of his career, Bolt made a cameo appearance at the Commonwealth Games in Glasgow, helping Jamaica to gold in the 4x100 metres. He competed for nine seconds, then took over an hour to do a lap of honour. Two weeks later, he called time on his season. It was, Ricky Simms says, a 'regeneration year for him, not beating his body up too badly'. On 8 October 2014, he began training for the 2015 season. During the Olympic Games in Rio, he will turn thirty. Can he win his third straight 100 metres title? 'Yes,' says Simms. 'He's just so much better than anybody else.'

His father, Wellesley, told me that Bolt found his life 'too hectic sometimes. Everything he does, the camera finds him. He says it's hectic, he worries sometimes, because he cannot live a normal life. He just cannot live the way he wants to live.'

When I asked those who know Bolt what they thought he would do when he retires, most said he would leave Kingston and move to the countryside to live in a large house surrounded by friends (and his future family), passing his time playing dominoes. It seems entirely believable.

Yohan Blake was in Glasgow, but not at the Commonwealth Games. He competed in the Diamond League meeting at Hampden a couple of weeks earlier but didn't even last the full 100 metres, crumpling to the track clutching his hamstring. He left the arena in a wheelchair. His next stop: Munich, to see Dr Hans-Wilhelm Müller-Wohlfahrt. He would visit him again in November, and again in January 2015. 'It was really tough,' Blake told me. 'I'm not a patient guy. But you know, everything happens for a reason. I think it was my body saying: "Look, Yohan, you need a rest. You're going to have three hard years."

'That's nature,' he added.

Shelly-Ann Fraser-Pryce was below par too. Her best 100 metres was 11.01 in Monaco – the first time since 2007 she'd failed to break 11 seconds. Her coach, ever the ruthless taskmaster and dispenser of tough love, wondered aloud whether she would go on to win a third Olympic gold medal in Rio – something he thought her capable of, and which would surely confirm her as the greatest female sprinter of all time, irrespective of the 'impossible' world record. 'At the end of 2013 I would have said definitely she was going to get better,' Francis reflected.

Now he was not so sure. 'I am a realist, and understand that there's a reason why people don't keep going up, up, up, up. Sometimes your motivation falters, sometimes there are other areas of your life that take precedence. But what I will say is that if she is like she was in 2013 in terms of the hunger, and other things are not more important, then yeah, she will get better. But at her age it is hard to predict that is going to be the case. Because especially with women, many things start to go through your mind – is it time for this, is it time for that? What is my husband saying, blah blah blah blah blah. So you're realistic. It's all going to depend how she handles that kind of stuff.'

On my return to Jamaica, I wanted to try and identify the next superstar – a successor to Bolt. It meant catching up with three of the stars of Champs eight months on from that extraordinary gathering of people and talent: athletes who could be on the cusp of greatness, or not. These in-betweeners are on a knife edge: the margins between success and failure seem minuscule.

Since Champs, there had been the world junior championships in Eugene and the Youth Olympics in Nanjing. The 2014 Champs programme had proudly proclaimed that every global male 100 metres champion was Jamaican. By the end of the year, that was no longer the case. But something interesting seemed to be happening: a new phenomenon – or an old one, recycled – the return of the 400 metres specialists, reprising the previous golden generation almost seventy years after Helsinki and London.

But first, a 100 metres specialist. At the IAAF High Performance Training Centre I meet Zharnel Hughes, the nineteen-year-old from Anguilla. Glen Mills is the head coach here, but Leo Brown is in day-to-day charge. The nine athletes occupy the ground floor of a blue dormitory block on the edge of the University of the West Indies campus, close to the perimeter fence. It is a shabby building with peeling paint. Inside there is a kitchen, dining area, a list of rules for the athletes, and a living room with threadbare sofas and a small portable TV.

Bolt is a graduate of the centre and Hughes is in a similar mould. At six-three-and-a-half, he is tall, engaging and charming. Brown is convinced he has what it takes, whispering, 'This kid, I'm telling you, he can be the next Bolt.'

He is whispering because Hughes is in his room at the end of a small corridor, but he overhears, appearing and smiling: 'I *can* be the next Bolt.' Brown carries on regardless: 'I told his mother: "You must have done something. Because he is perfect: he doesn't curse, he doesn't do anything bad." Trust me, I have had lots of athletes. This one is special.'

Hughes grew up in the neighbouring island of Anguilla with his Jamaican mother, Zarnalyn (his name is an amalgamation of hers and his father Howell's: she is a housekeeper; he is a taxi driver). When I first met him after Champs, he spoke about his two passions, flying – he would like to be a pilot eventually – and athletics. He pulled out his phone, opened his YouTube favourites and showed me his 100 metres from Champs. It had been watched 40,000 times in a couple of weeks, with Hughes himself accounting for a fair few of the views. 'Look,' he said, as he pressed play and relived the race, 'I think I could have improved a little bit more on my start. It wasn't bad; I got out pretty good this time. But then I dipped a little too early. If I pause the video before the finish, I can see that I reached too soon. That cost me.' Yet his time, 10.11, was a full tenth of a second quicker than Yohan Blake's Champs record.

'Aaaarrrgggghhhh!' was how Blake greeted Hughes at training a few days later. 'He yelled like a beast,' Hughes says, 'but then said:

"Congrats, man. I'm proud of you. You're gonna run 19 and 9 this year." '

It didn't happen. Injuries interrupted his year. At the world junior championships, having reached the 200 final, he felt a twinge in his hamstring as he came off the bend and limped across the line. He didn't make it to the Commonwealth Games. 'I have to be patient,' he says. 'Coach Mills tell me that. He encourages me. "Zee, these things happen. Look at Yohan."

'I wanted to do well this year, but sometimes you shouldn't have your expectations too high. I have a long way ahead of me, I know these things happen. I do believe I can become something great.' He seems remarkably sanguine. But in an unguarded moment he adds: 'Man, I hope I'm not going to be one of them athletes who is always injured.'

Hughes started off thinking he would be a 200 and 400 metres specialist. Now he is a 100/200 sprinter. In the past, an athlete of his height wouldn't have been considered for the 100. But after Bolt, they are looking for tall sprinters: youngsters who are 'unusually coordinated'. Brown explains: 'All you need is for the tall one to get the same rhythm as the shorty and he's going to win by miles. If he can run with the same frequency, he'll kill these guys with the tiny steps.

'I told Zharnel,' he continues, ' "God made you, and a coach can help you develop that to the maximum, but this" ' – he points to his head – ' "is what determines it." '

At Wolmer's Boys' School, in the noisy, congested centre of Kingston, I meet Jaheel Hyde. Just seventeen, he's serious, self-contained, surly and shy, yet also sure of himself. At the start of the season he posted a picture on Instagram with the message: 'Look out, greatness is coming.'

He was right, as it happens. Yet in some ways he seems to be the anti-Bolt. In July, at the world junior championships in Eugene, he was introduced to the crowd before the 400 metres hurdles. He stood and scowled, his hands resting casually on his hips. The look on his face said that he really couldn't be bothered with the preliminaries; it said: 'Let's get on with it.' And when they did, he was in a class of his own. As at Champs, where he dominated the 400 and 110 metres hurdles, he was so smooth, so casual. As he moved into the lead on the final bend, he kept glancing to his right, to his left, but nobody was close. It looked easy. He barely celebrated.

At the Youth Olympics in Nanjing a month later, Hyde elected to do his other event, the 110 metres hurdles. The two are completely different: the 400 is all about pacing and rhythm, the 110 requires rhythm but also pure speed, power and explosivity. Nobody has ever been a global champion in both.

In Nanjing, Hyde burst out of the blocks, stealing a march on the others, then increased his lead as he appeared to glide, or float, over the hurdles. This was even more impressive than Eugene. All around him were the slumped and dejected bodies of his rivals, but he didn't stop to commiserate – didn't even seem aware of them – as he set off around the track for a lap of honour. His time, 12.96 seconds, was a world youth record by 0.16. That is Bolt-esque.

Hyde's father, Lenworth, is a Jamaican footballing legend, whose international career spanned thirteen years. 'Lenny' has five children: four boys and a girl. Predictably, Jaheel is the youngest. He began kicking a ball with his father when he was four. He was encouraged to play football, but he walked out on the national under-17 team to concentrate on athletics. 'It's my decision,' he tells me. Was his father happy? 'My parents on the whole will just have to support me whatever I do. My father knows I love track and field.'

How did he decide? 'You sit down, analyse which one you'll be best at.'

He is uncompromising. He wanted to go to Kingston College, but his brother Jamie, also a talented footballer, was already there. 'I said to myself, I didn't want to be living in his name. I wanted to make a name for myself.'

Stephen Francis would like Hyde to join MVP when he leaves Wolmer's, not least because he attends his old school. But it would have to be on Francis's terms. 'I've never spoken to him about coming here,' Francis told me. 'Whenever I speak to him, it's as one Wolmerian to another. I would hope he will come over here but I am not going to get into the war of recruiting him.'

Hyde loves hurdles, loves the technical side to it, the fact that 'you have to be very focused, you can't take your eye off no hurdle at any time'. He is a curious mix: a steely confidence runs through him, yet he is modest, almost bashful. He says he doesn't particularly enjoy the attention that comes with being a world champion – especially at school. 'People come up to you at school just to touch you, to spend five minutes with you. I tell them they can be themselves around me; talk about what they want, doesn't have to be track and field, could be life as a whole.'

I ask him what it's like to be surrounded by so many superstars in Jamaica. 'I must correct you there,' Hyde says. 'I'm not really in contact with the big athletes. I look up to Usain Bolt, the way he goes about things, but I haven't met him or spoken to him. He's a winner, just like myself. But I'm a very humble child, very quiet.'

*

Jaheel Hyde is the special one now, rivalled only, perhaps, by an even younger athlete, yet another 400 metres runner: Christopher Taylor of Calabar. In early 2015, he broke the age group world record in Kingston, running 45.69 seconds. He was fifteen: just like Bolt when he made his breakthrough. 'The quarter-milers are coming,' said Bert Cameron as he surveyed a burgeoning crop of 400 metres runners.

Twelve months earlier, the special one was another 400 metres runner and another Calabar boy: Javon 'Donkey Man' Francis. In July 2014, he signed as a professional with Puma. Pascal Rolling, the marketing executive who signed Bolt, was behind the deal. He saw similarities. 'The guy is also very charismatic and open, maybe not as much as Usain, and not as gifted as Usain was.' Like Bolt, he is raw and 'needs work'. Puma were arranging English lessons for Francis, as they once tried to do for Bolt. 'If he gets it together and if he progresses the way he has in the last two years, he can be a very good ambassador for Puma,' said Rolling.

I meet Francis at Calabar, the bond with his old school as strong as ever. He has decided to stick with what he knows, which meant remaining with his high school coach, Michael Clarke, training at Calabar's rough, bumpy old track, and living with his guardian, Andrea Hardware. Hardware says it was an easy decision, despite 'lots of very good offers'. Sitting on a bench inside the school grounds, overlooking the track, she explains that 'Calabar is a family and Michael Clarke and us have got him so far and we want to keep that structure around him. I did not want to break that up. Let's just see where his team can get him over the next two years.'

After Champs, Francis struggled to overcome the hamstring injury he suffered in the 200 metres: the race that everybody said he shouldn't have run. It was decided that he shouldn't compete in the Penn Relays a few weeks later. But he went anyway, to Franklin Field in Philadelphia, to support Calabar. 'I sit in the stand at the Penn Relays,' Francis tells me now, 'and watch my team lose. I started crying. I said to myself, If I was there, they would win.'

'He bawled,' Hardware confirms. 'He bawled in the stands when they lost the 4x400.'

Then he missed the IAAF world relays in the Bahamas in May. One night Hardware returned to find him crying in his room. She asked what was wrong. 'Mum, my picture's on the billboard in the Bahamas! It's my picture on the billboard and I'm not going to go!'

Francis kept trying to train and then having to stop and rest to give the injury more time to heal. It was a form of torture. And in the midst of all this he had to decide about his future. 'When the time come to leave Calabar, it was a sticky decision,' he says. 'Everywhere want me to come overseas, and I said to myself, Overseas, no. Jamaica, yes. I love Jamaica so much and if I go overseas I'm not going to see my mum, my dad, my relatives, my guardian. I'm going to stay here and work with my coach, Mr Michael Clarke. He do a lot for me, he's like a father to me.'

In the end, the only real bright spot in Francis's year, apart from his record at Champs, was signing with Puma. 'Yes, sir. Usain Bolt is a Puma lion, I'm a Puma lion too.' Bolt has encouraged him. 'Usain Bolt told me, "Track and field is an unfair game." He said, "Work hard, and make sure you have your education." He said, "Javon, you know that if you have education, no one can take that away from you. Track and field, God can take that away from you."'

A week later, I am back at Calabar talking to Michael Clarke, who is overseeing a training session involving twenty or so athletes. There is no sign of Francis. 'Javon is in Germany,' says Clarke. Germany? 'He's seeing a doctor. Something Puma has set up.'

The doctor . . . is it Dr Müller-Wohlfahrt? Clarke looks thoughtful. 'Dr Müller? That sound right, yes.'

It seems that Puma will have a big say in Francis's future. Rolling says they'll be watching carefully. Clarke is a proven coach at high school level. 'Any Jamaican coach thinks he can be as good as Mills and Frano [Stephen Francis],' Rolling says. 'Everyone thinks they can do it. It remains to be seen.'

Thinking about Javon Francis and how much is at stake for Clarke, for Calabar, but mostly for him, it can seem overwhelming. He is a man-child who dreams of greatness, of telling his grandchildren 'that when I was young I was the champion in high school, the greatest schoolboy in history, I can tell them that'. But he wants – needs – so much more. If he doesn't fulfil his great potential, he will become one of those athletes Raymond Stewart talked about who disappear, who remain only in people's memories as a candle that burned brightly but too briefly. Francis relates another conversation with Bolt, who told him that when he first went to a senior world championship, in Paris in 2003, he didn't even get to run, never mind win a medal, as Francis did in Moscow ten years later. 'But you come and get a medal at eighteen!' Bolt told him. 'Bwoy, the sky's the limit!'

'Yes, Usain, but the sky is not the limit – the sky doesn't have a limit. If you go to space, the sky goes on and on.'

'Well, Javon,' said Bolt, 'that's a good one.'

Hardware says she is confident Francis will be back: that we didn't see the best of him in Moscow, or at Champs. 'A couple of days ago I said, "Javon, how do you really feel?" "Mum, mi good, mi good. I'm popping the blocks, I'm getting out ahead of some of the sprinters in the club." He feels healed.'

After our conversation, Francis stands up, shakes my hand, says, 'Thank you, sir.' My eyes follow him as he jogs in the direction of the rutted track. Is he moving freely, without pain? It's hard to tell.

I am back in Dennis Johnson's house in the hills overlooking Kingston. On his porch, with DJ sitting in his usual seat, holding court in his shorts and flip-flops. He seems a little short of breath, a little older. But he is as combative and dogmatic as ever. And still questioning. 'Well, my friend? What do you think is the reason for this . . . this total dominance?' He emphasises the word to make sure I get it. Not success: *dom-in-ance*. Not that he gives me a chance to answer. 'Because this phenomenon is tantamount to a special disease, you understand?' he continues. 'A virus. Why does no one notice that?'

I have noticed. That's why I'm there. But I persist initially, arguing that it must be a combination of things. Surely there is no one single reason. Johnson isn't having it. 'Well,' I try, 'here's one interpretation: you came back to Jamaica in the 1960s, you brought Bud Winter's ideas about technique and relaxation, then you brought Bud Winter himself, and you began a culture of . . . teaching people how to sprint correctly, with form and technique, at a young age . . .'

'Now you're cooking on gas,' says Johnson.

'Because sprinting is a skill,' I say.

'Sprinting is a skill, yes. Very good. He's learnt something. So you've listened to Dennis Johnson. Why don't you write that?'

'I will.'

AFTERWORD: THE WEEBLE

If it was a hurricane that tore through Jamaican athletics in 2013, it was a tsunami that devastated world athletics in 2015. Systematic doping was exposed in Russia, with the country's anti-doping authorities complicit, as well as individuals at the world governing body itself. In February 2016 the IAAF, battling to restore credibility under its new president, Sebastian Coe, announced that in addition to Russia being barred from international competition, a number of Russian athletes were indefinitely suspended.

The number of suspended athletes was 4,027.

The sanctions against Russia followed revelations by the German journalist Hajo Seppelt and the Sunday Times, and an investigation commissioned by WADA and headed by its former head, Dick Pound. Pound's findings represented, he said, 'a complete betrayal of what the people in charge of the sport should be doing.' Among the allegations were that the former IAAF president

Lamine Diack had taken bribes to cover up positive tests, as had his son, Papa, who for years criss-crossed the globe as an IAAF marketing consultant. The governing body's former head of anti-doping, Gabriel Dollé, was also implicated.

Coe, who described Diack as the sport's 'spiritual leader' when he succeeded him as president, initially reacted angrily to claims of widespread doping and that the IAAF had been ineffective in tackling it. Although Pound backed Coe to clean up the mess, Coe had been too involved with the IAAF (as vice-president since 2007) for his reputation not to be damaged—especially when his key lieutenant, Nick Davies, stood down after an email to Papa Diack, in which Davies appeared to be recommending covering up Russian positives in 2013, on the eve of the Moscow world championships, was made public.

It was Davies who had emailed me answers to my questions about the IAAF's anti-doping programme, assuring me that 'the top three ranked countries in terms of tested athletes for the IAAF are: Russia, Kenya and Russia!' Where local agencies might be deficient, Davies added, 'there was always a powerful IAAF system in the background.' Under Diack's leadership it seems that there was indeed a powerful IAAF system—one that assisted rather than exposed cheats, in Russia at least. But I don't think this is quite what Davies had meant in his email.

Where did all this leave Jamaica? Of the three countries named by Davies, Russia was discredited and Kenya was also in the dock. This undermined the reassurances and claims that a robust international system acted as a safeguard against occasionally shambolic local anti-doping efforts. Yet as the drip-drip-drip of allegations by whistle blowers, journalists and Dick Pound and his team went from trickle to stream to waterfall, there was nothing to directly implicate Jamaica.

It meant that when the 2015 world championships got underway in the Bird's Nest stadium in Beijing and Bolt lined up in the final of the men's 100 metres against the twice-banned Justin Gatlin, who was undefeated in 27 races, it was billed as a confrontation of 'good versus evil.' Gatlin had a season's best of 9.74 to Bolt's 9.87. But Bolt's camp was talking a good game, predicting he would run 9.6 in Beijing. That looked optimistic when he stumbled in his semi-final and only just managed to qualify.

For the final he was in lane five, alongside Tyson Gay in lane six, with Gatlin in seven. Bolt brushed the bushy tufts of beard on his chin but his usual antics were missing; he was as serious as Bolt can be, managing only a smile that could be mistaken for a grimace. Gay tripped out of the blocks, making Bolt's start look better than it was. But Gatlin was flying. And Bolt was chasing, and closing, then drawing level, but, for once, not pulling away. He didn't seem able to engage that sixth gear: he was flat-lining, and Gatlin was still fighting. But Gatlin's desperation got the better of him. They were level in the final 10 metres when Gatlin's arms began flailing, his dipped for the line too early, and, as Bolt nodded and just edged it, it cost the American the race. Bolt had, in the words of the commentator Steve Cram, 'saved his sport.' 'Good' had prevailed over evil.

The result put a false gloss on the performance. It was the closest Bolt had ever come to losing a major 100m final (if we exclude Daegu in 2011, when he false-started). Look at his trajectory in major finals throughout his eight years as the world's fastest man: 9.69, 9.58, 9.63, 9.77, 9.79. Gatlin ended 2015 with the five fastest times of the year, but he would be 34 in Rio; in Beijing there were two younger sprinters snapping at the older pair's heels and tying for third place in 9.92, and they were not Jamaicans but Trayvon Bromell of the USA and Andre De Grasse of Canada. Asafa Powell was the only other Jamaican in the final. As for Yohan Blake, 2015 was another injury-ravaged season with a best of 10.12 at a low key meeting in Dublin. He hadn't broken 10 seconds since 2012.

There was a similar story in the women's final, where a resurgent Shelly-Ann Fraser-Pryce defended her title in 10.76, but it was close. Dafne Schippers, the Dutch woman who in 2015 switched from pentathlon to sprinting, was closing so fast that it looked as though she would get it. Fraser-Pryce, with her explosive start, stuck her hand up in celebration five metres before the line: an act she almost had cause to regret. Schippers went on to win the 200m ahead of two Jamaicans, Elaine Thompson and Veronica Campbell-Brown.

In the atmosphere of scepticism that prevailed at the Beijing championships, Schippers' transformation from pentathlete to sprinter seemed so spectacular that it gave rise to suspicion. Nothing was off-limits; she was asked about her acne, a condition that can be a consequence of steroid use. It ran in her family, she explained. Then there was the colour of her skin. 'I understand the question,' said her coach, Bart Bennema, 'because she's white. But it's not a factor for me. She just has the right genes.'

Speaking of genes, Schippers' success brought to mind a conversation with Yannis Pitsiladis, in which he told me about his ambition of replicating the Jamaican system elsewhere: somewhere he believed there to be an abundance of sprinting talent that could be nurtured and developed. Curiously, the place he named as a possible candidate was the Netherlands, where Schippers is from.

After winning his fourth consecutive world 200m title, Bolt was completing his lap of honour in the Bird's Nest when a segway-mounted cameraman working for the host broadcaster approached from the rear. The segway crept up on Bolt but collided with a rail, throwing it off balance and altering its trajectory. It charged towards Bolt, slamming into the back of his long legs. He went down as if he'd been taken out by a sniper, falling but somehow managing to execute a backward roll and jumping back to his feet in one fluid movement. He then jogged away, rubbing his calf. Remarkably he was unhurt and anchored the Jamaicans to gold in the 4x100m two days later.

It was a moment of farce—a segway, of all things—that acted as a metaphor for the beleaguered state of athletics and, conversely, Bolt's robustness. It was tempting to think of Bolt as bullet-proof. No matter what is thrown at him, he seems to stand tall, resolute, answering the questions he is repeatedly asked both on and off the track—like a Weeble, one of those children's toys that wobbles, but is impossible to knock over.

Watching him in Beijing in 2015, it seemed there might only be only one trick that could prove beyond Bolt and it is the hardest one of all. Like all champions, he dreamt of the perfect ending: to exit on his own terms and still be standing in triumph, not bruised and defeated and carried from the ring. So few achieve it because knowing when to end is impossible. Bolt said before Beijing that he intended to carry on after the Rio Olympics and bow out at the world championships in London in 2017. But after winning three more gold medals in Beijing he admitted that this idea came from his sponsors. Glen Mills seemed to know better. 'My coach said, "Listen, if you're not going to be serious about going to the world championships in London then you shouldn't do it,"' said Bolt. 'It's all about how I feel after Rio. If I feel I can put my body through one more season, if I can be focused and determined, that will determine if I compete after Rio.'

Bolt always says that he lives for major competition, that training is the means to this end, and that it is this, his appetite for training and his willingness to put his body on the line day after day, that will ultimately determine when he retires. But it will also determine how he retires: in triumph or defeat. He might echo Muhammad Ali: 'I hated every minute of training, but I said, "Don't quit. Suffer now and live the rest of your life as a champion."'

ACKNOWLEDGEMENTS

Several people in Jamaica provided a great deal of help, but two stand out. Renée Anne Shirley was a source of knowledge, encouragement and inspiration. She is now setting up projects in education and sport which, if they come off, should be of enormous benefit to Jamaica. I also owe special thanks to Michelle Neita, who runs Kingston's best guest house, Neita's Nest, on one of the hills overlooking the city. I loved it there. As well as being a wonderful host and a good friend, Michelle helped with introductions and interviews. Thanks also to Charmaine Smith for her sensational Jamaican cooking.

To Virginie, my wife, thank you. In the days after the London Olympics, when I was boring on about the contrast between the saccharine atmosphere of the Games and the quagmire of suspicion and innuendo that was the Tour de France, she suggested this book, possibly as a way of shutting me up, maybe also because she fancied a trip to the Caribbean. By good luck, another visit to Jamaica coincided with an assignment for my brother Robin, a brilliant photographer whose images feature on these pages—thank you, Robin (www.robindmoore.com).

I've known Matt Phillips, the editor at Yellow Jersey, for a few years, but this is the first time we have worked together. Matt's great enthusiasm and ideas helped make the book much better—as well as a far more enjoyable and rewarding process—than it would otherwise have been. Thanks too to Fiona Murphy, publicist extraordinaire, and to Mari Yamazaki and Kate Bland, who took up the publicity reins when Fiona was lured away. To Jack Skelton, thanks for help with transcribing interviews.

I am grateful as ever to my agent, David Luxton, for moral support and for never panicking. Or never appearing to panic. And heartfelt thanks to colleagues who helped in di erent and significant ways: Alan Pattullo, David Epstein, Mike Costello, John Leicester, Vikki Orvice, Rick Broadbent, Ian Chadband, Laura Williamson, Martha Kelner, Donald McRae, Shaun Assael, Sean Ingle, Simon Turnbull, Matt Slater, Lionel Birnie, Daniel Friebe and Susan Egelsta. In Jamaica, thanks to Andre Lowe of the *Gleaner*, who always responded to my countless requests for phone numbers. Thank you Charlotte Elton for sneaking me in to Usain Bolt's party in Brussels. Thanks to Matt Rabin for helping me find out more about Dr Müller-Wohlfahrt. For his insights on Jamaica, and for writing a fascinating book, *The Dead Yard*, I am grateful to Ian Thomson. And big thanks to Ned Boulting, who provided invaluable feedback on a flabby first draft.

To the following I am especially grateful: Dennis Johnson, Stephen Francis, Glen Mills, Shelly-Ann Fraser-Pryce, Yohan Blake, Warren Weir, Paul Wright, Javon Francis and Zharnel Hughes. I am also indebted to Bruce James, Timothy Spencer and Omar Hawes for their help. Thanks to the other people I interviewed in the course of my research, most of whom appear in roughly the following order: Keith Barnier, Mark Ricketts, Michael Fennell, Donald Quarrie, Albert Corcho, Wellesley Bolt, Devere Nugent, Lorna Thorpe, Gloria Grant, the Most Honourable P. J. Patterson, Andrea Hardware, Noel Facey,

Michael Clarke, Gregory Daley, Vilma Charlton, Maurice Wilson, Edward Shakes, Pat Lightburn, Rachael Irving, Jermaine Gonzalez, Norman Peart, Ricky Simms, Steven Ming, Pascal Rolling, Simon Lewis, Mike Davison, Daniel Drepper, Stephen Roche, Mike Fish, Victor Conte, Dick Pound, Steve Mullings, Raymond Stewart, Jimson Lee, Errol Morrison, Yannis Pitsiladis, Jaheel Hyde, Bert Cameron, Carey Brown, Danny Williams, Leo Brown, Lascelve Graham, Orville Byfield, Martin Manley, Delano Williams, Daniel England and David Gillick. And thanks to Usain Bolt, who inspired the quest at the heart of this book (not to mention the title).

The following books were useful in helping me understand more about Jamaica and athletics, or Jamaican athletics:

Black Superman: A Cultural and Biological History of the People Who Became the World's Greatest Athletes, Patrick Cooper (Silent Partners, 2004)

The Dead Yard: A Story of Modern Jamaica, Ian Thomson (Faber & Faber, 2009)

Born Fi' Dead: A Journey Through the Yardie Underworld, Laurie Gunst (Canongate, 2003)

Drumblair: Memories of a Jamaican Childhood, Rachel Manley (A. A. Knopf Canada, 1996)

Slipstream: A Daughter Remembers, Rachel Manley (A. A. Knopf Canada, 2000)

The Longer Run: A Daughter's Story of Arthur Wint, Valerie Wint (Ian Randle Publishers, 2011)

The Voice of the Jamaican Ghetto: Incarcerated but not Silenced, Adidja Palmer (Vybz Kartel) (BookBaby, 2012)

Jamaican Athletics, A Model for 2012 and the World, Patrick Robinson (Black Amber, 2009)

The Making of a Sprinting Superpower: Jamaica on the Track, Arnold Bertram (2013)

Usain Bolt: Faster than Lightning, Usain Bolt with Matt Allen (HarperSport, 2013)

Champs 100: A Century of Jamaican High School Athletics, 1910–2010, Hubert Lawrence, ed. Michael A. Grant (Great House, 2010)

Jamaican Gold, eds. Rachael Irving and Vilma Charlton (University of the West Indies Press, 2010)

Jamaica Gold: Brilliance & Excellence, Mark Ricketts (2012)

The Gold Mine E ect: Crack the Secrets of High Performance, Rasmus Ankersen (Icon Books, 2012)

Sprinting Into History: Jamaica and the 2008 Olympic Games, Delano Franklyn (Wilson Franklyn Barnes, 2009)

Game of Shadows: Barry Bonds, Balco, and the Steroids Scandal That Rocked Professional Sports, Mark Fainaru-Wada and Lance Williams (Gotham Books, 2007)

The Sports Gene: Talent, Practice and the Truth about Success, David Epstein (Yellow Jersey, 2013)

Beyond a Boundary, C. L. R. James (Yellow Jersey, 2005)

Beyond C. L. R. James: Shifting Boundaries of Race and Ethnicity in Sports, eds. John Nauright, Alan Cobley and David Wiggins (University of Arkansas Press, 2014)

The Talent Code: Greatness Isn't Born. It's Grown, Daniel Coyle (Arrow, 2010)

Outliers: The Story of Success, Malcolm Gladwell (Penguin, 2009)

Pulphead: Notes from the Other Side of America, John Jeremiah Sullivan (Vintage, 2012)

Bass Culture: When Reggae Was King, Lloyd Bradley (Penguin, 2011)

Usain Bolt: Fast as Lightning, Mike Rowbottam (BlackAmber Inspirations, 2011)

Usain Bolt: The Story of the World's Fastest Man, Steven Downes (SportsBooks Ltd, 2011)

So You Want to Be a Sprinter, Bud Winter (Bud Winter Enterprises, 2010)

Friday Night Lights, H. G. Bissinger (Yellow Jersey, 2005)